Electric Children

Electric Children

ROOTS AND BRANCHES OF MODERN FOLKROCK

Jacques Vassal

Translated and adapted by
Paul Barnett

Taplinger Publishing Company | New York

First Edition

Published in the United States in 1976 by
TAPLINGER PUBLISHING CO., INC.
New York, New York
by arrangement with Editions Albin Michel,
22 rue Huyghens, Paris, France

Originally published in French as
Folksong: Une histoire de la musique popularie aux Etats-Unis
Copyright © Editions Albin Michel, 1971
English translation and adaptation
Copyright © 1976 by Paul Barnett
All rights reserved. Printed in the U.S.A.

Published simultaneously in the Dominion of Canada by
Burns & MacEachern, Ltd., Ontario

Photographs credited to Diana Davies are
Copyright © Diana Davies / *Insight*

Library of Congress Cataloging in Publication Data

Vassal, Jacques, 1947–
Electric children.

Translation of Folksong.
Bibliography: p.
Discography: p.
Includes index.
1. Folk-songs, American—History and criticism. 2. Music, Popular
(Songs, etc.)—United States—History and criticism. 3. Rock music—United
States—History and criticism. I. Barnett, Paul. II. Title.
ML3551.V3813 1976   784   75-8198

ISBN 0-8008-2382-6

Designed by Mollie M. Torras

contents

illustrations

translator's preface

On the face of it, it may seem odd to go to the trouble of translating and publishing a book by a Frenchman on what is, after all, principally an English-language phenomenon. And it *would* be odd, were it not for a couple of factors that are not immediately obvious.

The first is that it would be unfair to class Jacques Vassal as solely a Frenchman. He is very much a citizen of the world, and has done much, by his travels abroad and by his activities in bringing to France a consciousness of the folk music that has come into being beyond its shores, to hasten the coming of the kind of internationalism he so eloquently pleads for in this book. His activities as editor of Albin-Michel's Rock & Folk series are further steps along this road.

The second is that Jacques Vassal *is* a Frenchman. He is therefore much more able than a British or American observer to evaluate trends and to ignore the fickleness of fashion. This is perhaps best typified by the extent to which he examines in this book the work of Phil Ochs, a name forgotten or never learned by most of today's pop music audience.

It is now five years since *Folksong*, as the original edition is titled, was published in France. In that time, of course, there have been many important changes in what is at the best of times a rather fluid musical field (had it been pop music proper, of course, the picture would have changed entirely) and so there has been a considerable amount of updating to do, as well as the revision necessary to cover British musicians in greater detail than in the original French version. I have attempted to do this in the way that M. Vassal would have done himself, and I hope that I have been successful. At the same time, it is only fair to indicate the areas where there have been changes.

The whole of the first part of the book is straight from the French with the exception of one or two notes, which can be differentiated by my initials following them. Part Two contains only a few additions to take account of Bob Dylan's later activities, as those of the various other modern artists dealt with. In Part Three, the chapter on British "electric children" is about 75 percent my responsibility, as is a small proportion of the chapter on the Americans.

The translation has taken very much longer than originally expected—for various reasons beyond my control—and I would like briefly to thank those who have given me help of various kinds over the last fifteen months. First of all, thanks must go to Jacques Vassal himself, who has assisted me in cases where I have had difficulty, and who has kindly provided the texts of English originals that I have been unable to find. I would also like to thank the staff of Frederick Muller for tolerating my tardiness and for remaining encouraging throughout. If I listed the army of friends, colleagues, and relations who have given spiritual help I would be bound to offend by inadvertent omission: gratitude to all of them is nevertheless much felt. But most of all I would like to express my thanks to the one whose comfort and companionship in times of need have created the conditions necessary for this English version ever to be completed.

Paul Barnett

part 1
Roots

blacks

Though blacks represent only about 10 percent of the total population of the United States, their music occupies a prominent position in American folklore. Not only is it a rich vein in itself, but it also has and has had a considerable influence on the rest of American music, whether it be the commercial pop song—for example, the close relation between rock and roll and rhythm and blues—or white symphonic music, which may, like that of George Gershwin, contain strong jazz influences; and, of course, folkrock is in many areas heavily influenced by black music.

This broad range of musical types in which the influence of black music is overt serves to emphasize its importance. It is worthwhile, therefore, to trace briefly the history of blacks in America and thereby the origins and evolution of their music.

Since the arrival in North America of the first shipload of slaves, the black population has been dominated by the white, which has assumed, as of right, the role of master. It is only natural, then, that blacks have had of necessity to find consolation in various ways, such as—depending on the times and the situation—alcohol, dancing, religion, and love. But whether in the bar or at the dance, whether in the church or in the home, music is omnipresent in the black American world. Blacks have traditionally found their most reliable and efficient means of escape through the media of music and song: this help has been necessary to complete life, to complete the man; and, for the American black, these can be used to express religious feeling, laughter, protest, tears, love, hate, resignation, prayer, and even—if we look into history—a call to arms.[1]

[1] It would be beyond the bounds of this book to deal here with jazz. Our prime consideration here is song alone. The reader who wishes to learn of jazz should look elsewhere.

There are two principal trends in black American music, both of which have had their effect on the mainstream American folk tradition: the first, religious in nature, is typified by the spiritual and, to a lesser extent, by the gospel song; the second, secular, is typified by the blues and its derivatives. The work song represents a midway stage between these two types.

There is an African proverb which somehow sums up the principle lying behind the negro spiritual: "Without song there is no hope." The history of the American blacks starts at roughly the same time as that of the white colonists. The black slaves did not enjoy the same rights as their white masters, either materially or spiritually. In most cases the slaveowner would work deliberately to eliminate the negro culture from his black possessions, and in so doing he methodically smothered the "Africanness" of his slaves: their beliefs, their arts, and their mores. To do this it was also necessary to kill the negro gods.

As numerous writings from the seventeenth and eighteenth centuries testify, the African religions in the United States died with increasing rapidity as the birth came about of the "American negroes," black Americans, a new type of persons who had little in common with their African roots, nor with white Americans. But the slaves could not live without any religion at all, and little by little they embraced the faith of their masters.

Historically, the conversions to Christianity were concentrated into two particular eras.

Around the end of the eighteenth century, in most cases, the slaves themselves had converted themselves of their own accord, as in general their white master had not taken the trouble to effect their religious education. The white considered his slaves to be inferior beings, animals—or even lower. So the logical question was: how can an animal have a spiritual life? The answer, in the eyes of the whites, was equally obvious: it couldn't. Yet, all the same, blacks became Christians to satisfy their need for religion—any religion—since Christianity offered them at the same time a spiritual refuge and (or so it appeared to them) similar rights to those of the whites. Indeed, in Africa (as in many other parts of the world) the tribes have traditionally adopted the gods of their conquerors as supreme over their own.

The first conversions in the Southern states took place among those slaves employed in domestic tasks, who by the nature of their position had more contact with the white family, and hence more opportunity to see the white customs at work.

The process of conversion, urged by the early missionaries among the slave states, accelerated during the early years of the nineteenth century. However, having adopted the religion of the whites wholesale, the blacks created a form of worship that derived little if anything from the Protestant hymn: the negro spiritual. The essential simplicity of the negro, which the whites had attempted almost successfully to banish, promptly reasserted itself in the form of this new music. The spiritual, a collective creation augmented by numerous improvisations, was all the more rich and living because, until the latter half of the nineteenth century, secular music was forbidden to blacks.[2]

Thus was born one of the most emotive expressions of religious feeling in human history, one of the most honest and sincere, particularly when one realizes the constant suffering that these people underwent. It is when comparing the everyday life of a Mississippi slave with the lyrics of certain of the spirituals (including some of the best known) that the poignant reality behind the spiritual is brought fully home to us:

> *Swing low, sweet chariot*
> *coming for to carry me home . . .*
> *Sometimes I'm high, sometimes I'm low*
> *sometimes I'm lying on the ground . . .*
> *If you get up there before me*
> *tell all my friends I'm coming too . . .*

One is forced to make the remarkable observation that, in many spirituals, the lyrics, their theme being essentially religious, are in fact rather more cleverly constructed than one would expect when considering the hand-to-mouth existence and daily suffering of the slaves. Most noticeable in this respect is the frequent theme of spiritual liberation and admission into the kingdom of God, a goal that is

---

[2] In his remarkable volume, *Blues People,* LeRoi Jones (Imamu A. Baraka) tells how, during the era of slavery, the Church classified as blasphemous the playing of the violin, irreligious (secular) songs, and dance tunes: certain of the Church fathers considered even the corn songs diabolic. Moreover, certain musical instruments like the violin and the banjo were said to be the servants of the devil.

above all Christian, but moreover symbolic of liberty (or, at least as a start, the end of slavery). One could quote the striking example of "Follow the Drinking Gourd." This song gave to the slaves of the Mississippi, with considerable realism, a recipe for escape, describing the route whereby they could, they hoped, reach the land of liberty. The "drinking gourd" which must be kept in sight is in fact the constellation taking that form (known as the Plough and the Big Dipper in Great Britain and the United States respectively, part of the constellation Ursa Major), and situated in the northern sky. The listener is instructed to follow the drinking gourd, using the stars to light his route. The riverbank traces a fiery highway, dead trees show the way to go, an old man waits on the other side to give directions toward freedom—so follow the drinking gourd. In this song the combination of the concepts of escape and redemption, of liberty and the heavenly kingdom, are overt. One is tempted to ask if this was deliberate and conscious. Almost certainly, since the development of the spiritual was a necessary forerunner to the birth of the blues; and also because the slaves, despite their undoubtedly genuine religious fervor, were unable to retain merely spiritual preoccupations—for the obvious reason that, contrary to the beliefs of their masters, the slaves were, indeed, men. It was not long before they proved it with the development of the work song and the blues.

A form of music complementing but not identical with the spiritual, the gospel song appears to us both as a logical corollary to the emergence of the middle-class negro, the black *petit bourgeois,* the "Uncle Tom" who thinks that freedom can be found by imitating the whites and accepting their values (a type that appeared after the emancipation of all American slaves after 1865), and as a replacement for the spiritual.

Why a replacement? Listening to records of a few gospel songs makes everything clear: here the wild improvisations are exchanged for an elaborate *planned* musical construction; the musical themes of the song, hardly changing, return regularly in each couplet; the lyrics, paraphrased faithfully from the Bible, seem to be prepackaged, leaving no room for personal interpretation on the part of the performers; the choruses are frequently polyphonic; the "beautiful" rule of the master—all dressed up in superficial lyrics easily understandable by the whites. The rhythms, moreover, are generally slower and simpler.

These are the technical differences, and there is a sociological and psychological explanation behind the transformation. After the Civil War, the negroes were legally freed. That is to say, a black had the right, if he were capable (according to the traditional principles of democracy), to be his own master. For example, he could farm, and the profits of his labors would come back to him—at first to pay his debts, later to increase his wealth, though this latter to a lesser extent than he had been led to believe by whites. However, this equality was more theoretical than practical as, though whites no longer blamed a black for being black (or, at any rate, their prejudice was to a certain extent curbed), they still blamed him for being a black man as opposed to a black white-man. From there to an admission of inequality in fact, if not in law, in the blacks' implicit acceptance of the whites' sociological and cultural values as being superior to their own was only a short step. Certain of the blacks accepted the franchise: from them was born the negro *petit bourgeoisie,* which represents in our day a complete social class of black America.

In this light, it is easier to understand the aseptic aspects of the gospel song, bourgeois religious music, little different as it is from the Protestant hymn, and its (perhaps deserved) vogue among the whites. A predictable combination that can be interesting is the inclusion by numerous white popular singers from the Southern United States, typified by Elvis Presley, of a gospel repertoire at one time or another in their acts.

The birth of the work song, as might be expected, is directly traceable to the labors of the slaves. In the same breath one can talk of work songs, "shouts," and "hollers."

They are built up of several kinds of rhythmic cry, with a variety of lyric themes, but with a form always of the utmost simplicity. The rhythms of the work songs are designed purely for utilitarian purposes, as a form of punctuation for the slaves' usually agricultural tasks. The archetypal example of the work song is the often-quoted "Take This Hammer":

> *Take this hammer, uh!*
> *Carry it to the Captain, uh!*

The "uh!" is no more than the punctuation accompanying each stroke of the hammer (or whatever other tool). For practical reasons that are evident the work song was almost always sung without musical accompaniment: one can see why it would be impossible for the slave to chop cotton, for example, while strumming the guitar.

At the end of the nineteenth century the work song gradually gave way to the blues, though during the twentieth century the work song has its place in prison farms, where detention is accompanied by compulsory labor, thus perpetuating the situation that existed most probably for all American blacks before the Civil War.

While the spiritual continued to express the religious life of blacks after the abolition of slavery, there appeared little by little a new form of secular music. Rooted in tradition and yet quite original, it would eventually influence a substantial portion of Anglo-Saxon twentieth-century popular music. It was, of course, the blues.

There has been a vast amount written and spoken about the blues, but it is nevertheless still far from easy to define the term itself. The word has been used by many artists of modern pop music, mainly white, but frequently such use is in fact abuse. It would be ridiculous to suppose that a single, exclusive, and undebatable definition of "blues" can be provided here; much better neither to explain nor analyze but to listen to the blues, play the blues, sing the blues, *live* the blues. After that, any form of analysis is unnecessary.

By considering first the four basic criteria, handed down orally from generation to generation, we can examine the differences between the two main types of blues, urban and rural; though this distinction of types may appear a little arbitrary, it does at least correspond to two sufficiently contrasting life-styles.

The first criterion is technique. Considered quasi-mathematically, the form of the songs is as simple as possible. Initially it is almost always based on a twelve-bar rhythm (though very occasionally eight-bar blues do turn up) maintained throughout each song, thereby creating a pulsing effect which, though regular, is nevertheless far from monotonous. The ideas contained within the lyric are developed along conventional lines, and almost always adhere to the following scheme: initial statement (A); its repetition (A); the development (B); and a return to the initial statement (A).

Some blues have superficially a more complex lyrical form, but this can be reduced to fit the same scheme:

I was standin' at the station when the woman I loved got on
  board (A)
You know I was standin' at the station when the woman I
  loved got on board (A)
I was just standin' there cryin': baby please don't go (B)
When that train were leavin', woman I love all inside (A')
When that train were leavin', woman I love all inside (A')
Well you know I could do nothin' but just hang my head and
  cry (B')

One of the characteristics essential to true blues, one of the best known and a heritage from the spiritual, is improvisation: the blues are essentially a spontaneous form of music, and structurally like a chant. In this we notice the influence of Africa.

To be capable of aesthetically understanding and appreciating the blues, it is essential for the Western European listener to make an elementary intellectual effort to abandon his or her habitual criteria of judgment. It must not be forgotten that these criteria are basically white and can in no case be applied to the evaluation of an art form that is basically black. As LeRoi Jones justly observed in *Blues People,* in the same way that a European might say that a Wagnerian opera singer has a better voice than that of an African or a blues singer, a non-African could equally decry Beethoven's Ninth Symphony on the grounds that it contains no improvisation.

So far as the vocal interpretation of the blues is concerned, it can best be described as rasping, a quality it owes to the fact that, in the tribal languages of West Africa, the ancestral home of the vast majority of black Americans, words are pronounced with varying timbres and tones to correspond with differences in meaning.[3] It has been shown that this came about through, or caused, the rhythmic and tonal variations in the sort of Morse code by which messages are communicated on the tom-tom: that is to say, there is a direct semantic link between the drumming and the spoken language, tone for tone, rhythm for rhythm. And of course it was natural for blacks, having adopted English as their everyday language, nevertheless to speak it in an African fashion and to sing it, in work songs and blues, in an African way. In this light it is easier to understand

---

[3] In a similar way, there are certain nuances and intonations shared by both the French and Arabic languages.

why the quality of a blues artist lies less in the words and music of the songs than in the way he or she sings them.

The blues are neither pretty nor polite: blues are the product of a *way of life* that is neither pretty nor polite. The beauty of the blues lies in their honesty, their authenticity.

We have already mentioned how the gospel song, in losing the authenticity of the spiritual, lost also its Africanness but gained the sympathetic audience of the whites, and the way in which the gospel song indicated the birth of the black bourgeoisie. The famous line of Alfred de Musset, *"Rien ne nous rend si grand qu'une grande douleur,"* [4] points toward the reason behind the origin and growth of the blues as a distinctively black form of music. It must never be forgotten that the blues are a mouthpiece for the suffering of a poverty-stricken people, oppressed and exploited by another race; an exhausted people for whom, at the end of the day, the only salvation was dreaming or perhaps the merciful oblivion that can be found in their own music. One is brought to ask: if, from the very start of colonization, the blacks of America had enjoyed equality in law and in fact with the whites, if they had always known the same rights, the same salaries, the same privileges, and the same participation in cultural activities, would the blues ever have come into being? One is driven to the conclusion that they would not. Almost certainly, black music would have been no more interesting than the gospel song, if that.

Should we then deplore the existence of the blues because it was so costly to the blacks? A racist might reply that to sing the blues is, on the part of the blacks, merely a form of masochism; an overly conscientious liberal might say that to listen to and love the blues is, on the part of the whites, merely a form of sadism (or, at least, an unjustifiable acceptance). For our part, we can just conclude that, in essence, the blues are a music of the poor and oppressed—and leave it at that.

We then come to a consideration of the moral of the blues—for they do have one, and that gives them their *raison d'être*. The blues have sometimes been defined as the expression of the revolt of the blacks against segregation, against racism, against the whites; as a plea for integration and a statement of black power, and so forth. This is definitely dubious since, as the lyrics so clearly point out, the

[4] Freely translated, "Nothing makes us so great as a great sorrow."

blues are an *individual*'s vehicle of expression. Whether the song be
about women, prisons, trains, police, unemployment, rain, sun, whiskey, or the eternal highway so close to the roots of all American folk
music, all these subjects are treated in the first person singular.
Proof is to be found either by listening to a few blues records or by
reading interviews with bluesmen: [5] "I," "me," and "my" abound,
while one looks in vain for "we," "us," or "our." [6] Songs like *"We
Shall Overcome"* cannot possibly be termed blues.

No, the blues do not directly express revolt, nor do they express
class consciousness or the desire to put an end to injustice: they *testify
to* injustice. Is this a result of the social and political ignorance in
which the whites, following their own best interests, kept the blacks
for so long? Or of the resignation common to oppressed races?
Probably both at the same time. As an example of resignation one
can do no better than quote a line from a blues of Lightnin' Hopkins, on the rain: "It stops me from going out to plow my field."

One has to look hard for any signs of revolt in the blues. The
songs of the movement for integration, like the masses inspired by
Martin Luther King, are far from being blues; [7] in contrast, the
music to which Stokely Carmichael's Black Power or Bobby Seale's
Black Panthers adhere is overwhelmingly jazz.[8] Though the blues
came about through prevailing social conditions, the end result has
no particular sociological point to make. The blues are a form of
musical expression both introspective and resigned.

[5] For example that with Fred McDowell in *Sing Out!* for July / August 1969, p. 16.
[6] Only the punctilious would consider a phrase like "me and my baby" equivalent to
"us."
[7] King, in his fine book *Where Do We Go from Here? Chaos or Community,* devotes a
chapter to black cultural values of which, he writes, the blacks must be proud. He
reviews black literature, citing numerous fine black writings, as well as the other arts.
On music he explains in great detail his love (quite understandable in view of the fact
that he was a churchman) for the negro spiritual, but says not a word regarding the
blues. In this he is typical of his followers. On the same subject, one could cite the case
of the great black interpreter, Odetta, who participated in the 1963 March on Washington, and who does sing, among other types of music, the blues. But this double
role in the integrationist movement is quite exceptional, as otherwise the songs of this
movement haven't the slightest rapport with blues.
[8] There again, one does find a single exception to the rule, that of Julius Lester, who
is, on the basis of certain of his songs and many newspaper articles, a keen supporter
of Black Power. But his effect (alas) is marginal and makes no impression on the general trend.

The differing life-styles of the black population, on the one hand rural, on the other hand urban, have created two different forms of the blues called "country blues" (or rural blues) and "city blues" (or urban blues) respectively. The latter form is chronologically rather later in origin than the former.

The instruments used in country blues give one an understanding of the nature of the music:

The six-string acoustic guitar is overwhelmingly the most frequently used instrument. It would seem that the guitar was originally introduced into South America by the Spaniards, and that the blacks adopted it little by little through contact with the whites. It must be kept in mind that stringed instruments, the ancestors of the guitar and the banjo, are to be found in Africa—moreover, the *rumberos* still use in our times instruments of guitar type but with only three or four strings. The traditional bluesmen of most of the Southern states use a guitar with a wooden sound box and steel strings (as for example Lightnin' Hopkins, originally from Texas, or Snooks Eaglin', one of the youngest traditional bluesmen, born in Louisiana in 1936). On the other hand, many of the artists from north of the Mississippi Delta (in particular Son House) more usually employ the accompaniment of a steel guitar, one which has a sound box of steel, and which has, obviously, a very different tone.

The Mississippi delta, often referred to as the cradle of the blues, has produced a special guitar style known as "bottleneck guitar." The musician makes from the neck of a bottle a tube which he places on his left index finger. He then plays chords by barring on an open-tuned guitar to produce an accompaniment with an extremely unusual tone, both rich and jangling. More recently, of course, the bottleneck has been replaced by a tube of steel which, being more precisely made, produces a rather different tone. (Fred McDowell, a devotee of bottleneck guitar, uses both glass and steel tubes according to whichever he prefers for a particular song.) This style came to the fore when the rural blues were brought into an urban environment (Chicago, around 1955) by Elmore James.

Before we leave the topic of guitars, remembering that very frequently they are made by the musicians themselves, it is worth noting that sometimes blues guitars are found with rather unusual characteristics: some are made with seven strings, or (after Big Joe Williams) with nine or even ten. The twelve-string guitar, well

known to whites as well as blacks, is also found among certain bluesmen: the climax of its use came with Leadbelly, a unique black artist
with whom we shall deal at greater length later.

The banjo is very rarely if ever used in performance of the blues:
its tone and technique clash with the true blues sound and sen-
timent. (The banjo formed an integral part of the black minstrel
shows to be seen around the end of the nineteenth century.)

Keyboard instruments and the double bass, for obvious reasons
of awkwardness and weight, were certainly not part of the equipment of strolling rural blues players. One did find them used occasionally in the small towns of the South which are in essence more
rural than urban, at the time of the popular shows that toured bar-
relhouses, taverns, bars, theaters, and halls.

So much for string instruments. Wind instruments are only very
rarely found in country blues, with the obvious exception of the harmonica, a prized possession of the bluesman. Its advantages are its
immensely expressive tone and its unapproached transportability:
even where a bluesman can't take his guitar he can at least slip a few
harmonicas into his pocket. There are numerous kinds of harmonica, capable of expressing the full gamut of every emotion and
producing all sorts of sound effects—notably the trains of the blind
Sonny Terry, probably the best living harmonica player of rural
blues. One also comes across the harmonica, amplified and modified, in urban blues, yet another example of that form's heritage
from inexhaustible tradition.

The accordion and its more primitive relation, the concertina,
were at one time very much in favor with Louisiana rural bluesmen
because of the cultural influence that the Creole and French population had for a long time exercised in that state. At the 1968 American Folk Blues Festival, Clifton Chénier gave a fine example of the
survival of the use of these instruments.

Percussion instruments are of limited importance and play a limited role in country blues, comparable to those of the piano and bass,
as discussed above.

The themes of rural blues are, as one might expect, closely
linked with the life and problems of the country and relate principally to the states from which rural blues emanated, of which the
archetype is Mississippi: trains and highways, vagabonds (particularly the hoboes), crops and cultivation, hunger and climate, to

which list one can add the universal themes of love, loneliness, death, alcohol, sickness, and so forth, but here stamped with a sort of local color, without the derogatory connotations of the phrase: rural bluesmen never used these themes as merely clichés; they had no choice but to sing of the life they knew.

Urban blues are definitely a more recent creation. Their evolution is a direct result of the growth of the great metropolises of the northern United States and the increasing black populations therein. The most obvious example in this respect is that of Chicago in the late 1940s, early 1950s, to the extent that the term "Chicago blues" has almost replaced that of "city blues."

Like rural blues, urban blues are a faithful reflection of the epoch and the social caste from which they emerged: it is enough to explain the considerable instrumental differences between the two forms, the postwar towns producing music influenced by the reign of electricity and its instrumental applications. The jazz big bands between the twenties and forties showed the way for blues artists who, trying to find a way to give a breath of fresh air to their medium, eventually found it in the fifties and thereby gave birth to blues groups, generally consisting of between three and six individuals, including a singer and several instrumentalists.

As the blues groups became more and more popular in the towns and cities of the northern United States, there developed along with them new guitar styles—as with artists such as T-Bone Walker, B. B. King, and Buddy Guy. They were new styles that were extensions of the old but only now made possible by electronic amplification. At the same time, amplification was used with the harmonica, the organ, the bass guitar, and the use of a rhythm section became indispensable. With new ways of life, new forms of music: a relationship quite logical, and one that proves yet again the living character of the blues.

City blues take us into the world of modern black Americans, their life and problems in the concrete throes of the huge modern cities: the ghetto, the police, unemployment, the housing shortage, and even war (as in J. B. Lenoir's "Vietnam Blues") all have their place. But it must be stressed again that these themes are not used as instruments of protest, not as a way of awakening political consciousness: they are *blues* and no more.

Leadbelly, an artist who is perhaps a little forgotten these days, cannot simply be described as "a bluesman plus" because his musical inventiveness and influence over an entire generation of American singers (many if not most of them working in media other than the blues) are paramount. To quote just one example, Bob Dylan associated the memory of Leadbelly with that of Woody Guthrie and their friends, both famous and unknown, in the well-known "Song to Woody"; in 1962 he paraphrased the great black artist in his celebrated song, "I Shall Be Free," a song which in its turn served as a model for countless songwriters all over the world.

As is often the case, the work of Leadbelly merges intimately and indistinguishably with his life. It was around 1885 (even the date is not certain) that he was born in Mooringsport, in the Lake Caddo district of Louisiana, as Huddie Ledbetter. The son of a worker on a cotton plantation, Leadbelly learned during childhood to pick cotton and to play music. He started off by playing the concertina, then the mandolin. One day he met by chance an old musician who proffered his instrument: "Do you know how to play this?"—"this" being a twelve-string guitar. The young Huddie Ledbetter had never seen one before. He tried it and, finding that he could play it well, adopted it for regular use. Much later, it was he who more than anybody popularized the twelve-string.

In 1910 Leadbelly joined in Dallas a ragtime group from New Orleans, and from this experience learned a great deal. In 1917 he met up with the legendary bluesman Blind Lemon Jefferson. Friends immediately because of the nature of their music, they formed a duet and traveled all over Texas. But, on June 7, 1918, fate separated the two men: arrested during a vicious brawl and accused of murder (no one knows quite the truth of this), Leadbelly was incarcerated in the prison farm of Shaw State. Brutally condemned to thirty years' forced labor he was eventually freed in 1925 through the benevolent friendship of the governor, Pat Neff, a lover of the blues who couldn't resist Leadbelly's music.

Leadbelly dropped out of sight until February 28, 1930, when he was once again arrested, this time after a scuffle with two unknowns who tried to steal his whiskey. He was condemned to ten years in solitary confinement and taken to the Angola Prison in Louisiana, the home of many other detained musicians—a recent example being Robert Pete Williams—and well known for the brutality of its well-armed guards. The record of Leadbelly's punishments there is revealing: in 1931, ten strokes of the lash for "laziness" (a little surprising, for Leadbelly, built on the same scale as a wardrobe, was according to legend capable of picking five hundred pounds of cotton in a single day, singing the while!); and, in 1932, fifteen strokes of the lash for "impudence."

Around this time one of the great pioneers in American folklore research, John Lomax, was in the process of compiling a comprehensive collection of American traditional music, and for this work he was visiting all the penitentiaries of the South. On a primitive tape recorder, heavy and cumbersome, Lomax made a recording of Leadbelly singing, among others, a supplication to Governor O. K. Allen pleading for his freedom. The wonders of music! Unfortunately, the miracle of Texas was not to be repeated in Louisiana. Leadbelly continued in Angola Prison until his release in 1934, his term having been luckily reduced for good conduct. Lomax engaged Leadbelly as his chauffeur while traveling to do research or visit conferences, introducing him at several universities.

Accompanied by his fiancée Martha Promise and using Lomax's car, Leadbelly arrived in New York in December 1934. The following month he married Martha at Wilton, Connecticut. Between January and March 1935 he made many recordings for the American Recording Company (forty-five titles in all, of which only six were commercially released during his life) without significant success. In 1936, while his protégé and chauffeur was with Martha working his way along the Louisiana highway, John Lomax, with his son Alan as coeditor, published with Macmillan a collection of songs entitled *Negro Folk Songs as Sung by Lead Belly*.

The next time one hears about Leadbelly is April 1, 1939, recording in a New York studio for Musicraft: during this session he laid down one of his great classics, "The Bourgeois Blues." This can be seen from the vantage point of posterity to have been the first protest song ever written by a black. On May 20, 1939, the police descended on Leadbelly yet again, and this time he was sentenced to a year in New York's Riker's Island jail. After his liberation on June 15, 1940, he recorded with RCA Victor.

Paradoxically, the dates became much more vague toward the end of his life, but at least we know that he made a fruitless sojourn to Hollywood and a voyage to London and Paris, but his home remained New York. While in New York in 1946 he was visited by various artists that we will come across again (Woody Guthrie, Aunt Molly Jackson, and Jim Garland). Leadbelly sang frequently in Greenwich Village clubs like the Village Vanguard, sometimes accompanied by Sonny Terry. Around this time Leadbelly also recorded for Moses Asch, director and founder of a firm that was to do much to further the cause of American folklore, Folkways.

In 1948 the first symptoms of the disease that was to kill Leadbelly appeared, a rare form of sclerosis which progressively paralyzes the muscles, and that is to this day considered incurable. Meeting Leadbelly close to the end, the beat writer Jack Kerouac dedicated to him a text entitled "Deadbelly." Eventually Leadbelly died in a New York hospital, never to know that his life's work would be made famous and almost worshiped by others to follow.

Leadbelly had found a way of communicating with the people that Woody Guthrie summed up well: "A single glance at their hands tells you the history of their feet." On records alone is left to us the powerful sound of his metallic voice and the songs bequeathed as public property: "Goodnight Irene," a charming love song made famous much later by The Weavers, and of course the pathetic "Midnight Special," symbolic of a freedom he had been expecting throughout the entire course of his life.

During the post-World War II years, the active struggle of the blacks against segregation and toward a fair recognition of their rights as men and women and citizens gave them a new opportunity to show the vitality, truth, and efficacy of their songs as a weapon of the entire movement toward social progress.

One finds music used this way for certain of the great prointegration marches, like that in 1963 in Washington, during which "We Shall Overcome" acted as a rallying song, almost a national hymn for black America. It is important once again to retrace our steps in time to examine briefly a few of the contributory factors that led to the emergence of the folk song as a means of protest, a battle cry.

Around November 1932 there was founded in Tennessee the Highlander Folk School, directed by Miles Horton and Don West, the latter a songwriter and interpreter of white traditional music.

The avowed aim of this school was to furnish a center where "citizens could deepen their knowledge through history and sociology in search of solutions to their social problems." The school contacted and set up permanent relations with all the major trade unions and integrationist movements in the country. Between 1935 and 1956 (the year of her death) Zilphia Horton was musical director of the school and collected more than thirteen hundred trade-unionist and socially oriented songs, of black or white origin, which through the years formed a fruitful source of musical learning essentially directed toward political and social action. As the collection continued to grow, the best songs were incorporated into anthologies that were sent to the directors and representatives of various organizations. On this topic, one could cite the example of "We Shall Overcome" which, under its original title of "We Will Overcome," Zilphia Horton included in a collection of material that dealt with the grievances of tobacco workers around 1940.

Zilphia Horton died at the time that the black antisegregation struggle started to gather momentum after its first positive results (with the first bus boycott in Montgomery, Alabama, in 1956), and the role of the Highlander Folk School in the fight increased in proportion. At the suggestion of the black Esau Jenkins who had started to teach the illiterate Southern blacks the arts of reading and writing, the Highlander created a similar, though permanent, course for black adults with a black teaching staff.

In 1959 Guy Carawan was named musical director of the school: the same year he had been one of the principal participants at the Nashville sit-ins. During these demonstrations the Nashville Quartet, Guy Carawan, and other musicians directed communal singing among the throng and used this medium to draw attention to the most violent and dangerous activities of police and prison guards— who showed the truth of the charges by responding with numerous arrests, gunfire, and attacks with tear-gas grenades. According to the testimony of some of the most active participants (among whom was Julius Lester, the black composer and interpreter who played a considerable part in the movement by uniting the militants of North and South, and by uniting black artists with white), the recourse to traditional song (such as "Oh, Freedom!" "We Shall Overcome," "If You Miss Me at the Back of the Bus," and "Battle Hymn of the Republic") helped the demonstrators to lose neither their courage nor their patience. The songs had a definite stabilizing effect on their nerves and helped to present a common front in face of all the dangers, not only those cited above, but also hostile white mobs, sometimes in collaboration with the police, with which they were confronted.

New proof of the efficacy of popular song as a medium of protest came with the Albany movement. Created during the winter of 1961 / 62 by two secretaries of SNCC (Student Non-Violent Coordinating Committee), both singers, Charles Sherrod and Cordell Reagon, this was the first truly mature movement of its kind. It contributed strongly toward, for example, making possible the voter registration of blacks and also the nomination of a black candidate in Georgia. This was also the first time that all of the black community adhered to a social movement through the agency of its songs.

Apart from Julius Lester and Len Chandler, the principal black artists active in the struggle for full rights were the five members of the Freedom Singers. This quintet was founded by Cordell Reagon and his wife Bernice at the beginning of 1962, with slight financial aid from SNCC, for whom they became one of the most valuable mouthpieces with gigs around the country to collect funds. Unknown and very poorly paid to begin with, the Freedom Singers attained a certain measure of popularity and fame by the end of their first year, an ascent that culminated in the North among whites with their memorable participation in the 1963 Newport Folk Festival. They always had the integrity and sensibility to use the payments that they received through their relative commercial success (concerts, broadcasts, records) to help fund SNCC and a number of other prointegration organizations.

In 1964 Guy and Candie Carawan published under the imprimatur of the Highlander Folk School a collection of songs entitled *We Shall Overcome*. The majority of the song lyrics were adapted to go with traditional melodies that were already well known, in particular negro spirituals, so that the songs could rapidly be learned by all.

Later, the song-as-ally-of-social-protest was demonstrated by the Poor People's Campaign in Washington in 1968, where white singers like the indefatigable Pete Seeger joined forces with their black colleagues, such as Bernice Reagon and the Reverend F. D. Kirkpatrick, and where the blacks showed once again that their songs provide for them a genuine, living battle weapon.

Unfortunately, you can't sit down at a desk and, following a prees-tablished program, say to yourself: "Well, today I'm going to write me a protest song about freedom and . . ." This kind of artificial method is a hundred miles from the way in which the black militants of the South wrote their songs. For example, during one of their trips through Alabama, the Freedom Singers came across the town of Tuscaloosa where, by the side of the road, they saw a placard bearing a picture of a Ku Klux Klansman riding on a horse, below which were the words "Welcome to Tuscaloosa, the friendly town." Immediately and spontaneously Chuck Neblett composed the "Bal-lad of the KKK."

The spontaneous creativity and the direct impact of the typical black militant song from the South influenced in no small way a good number of Northern white composers. One of the major of these, Tom Paxton, after having participated at the "Sing for Free-dom" meeting in Atlanta in May 1964,[9] reported that the thing that most impressed him in the songs was their characteristic of action. They were songs to be sung in the fray, without the accompaniment of guitars or microphones, because as soon as the first bar was sounded, all the people joined in chorus.

Structurally, he found that the songs were designed for the masses and could be sung right beneath the noses of the police or even in prison. So the spontaneous black songs he found were much more useful in emergency than the ones produced by the white pro-test singers of the North, who could find through their songs a measure of fame and certainly a little money, but whose songs were hardly much use as battle cries.

Helped by the individual creative efforts of Guy Carawan or the Freedom Singers or the Nashville Quartet, by the hard work of the pioneers of black folklore, each marcher, each demonstrator can become in his or her turn a writer and a singer for freedom—and black music, in the most natural of ways, is returned to the people who gave it birth.

[9] At this festival, where a considerable crowd was gathered, the only representatives of the press, to judge from published reports of the meeting, were from four of the magazines that specialize in folk music, and a television network . . . from West Ger-many.

reds

Paraphrasing the well-known opening of the gospel according to Saint John, one could say: "In the beginning there was the Indian . . . and the Indian was America; he was in America, and America was in him; and America knew him not . . ." This more or less describes the way in which the Europeans, in conquering North America (we are not here concerned with South America), treated the numerous tribes who, by right of chronology and the natural laws of life, should have formed the ancestry of the population of the United States. Unfortunately, the action of various factors, some well known and others obscure, has had the effect over the centuries of draining the vitality of their culture.

Of these factors, we can note a few: internal wars, repeated massacres, and the proliferation of reservations, all of which, when added together, constitute virtually a genocide. On the other hand, some of the factors are more "natural," less deliberate: with increasing numbers and sizes of towns and cities, there was an increase in the amount of crossbreeding with other races, and, to top it all, the overwhelming domination of the white man, aided by the religious authorities, contributed largely to this cultural starvation. At the present time we seem to be witnessing (though it would be nice to deceive oneself) the last gasps of the almost moribund Indian popular culture. In the past this was remarkable for, among other things, its widespread diversity.

It would be an error to think that the music of all the diverse Indian tribes sounded alike. Even in our day there still exist music schools of the tribes, and in them the traditional songs are sung in a hundred different languages and dialects.

Traditional music of a religious and ceremonial type is the best preserved of the folklore. This music is the collective property of each tribe, and only minimal interpretation rests with the individual. Moreover, tribal tradition requires from the singer a rigorous adherence, note for note, word for word, in rhythm and in tone, to the original version of the sacred song. In practice there exists no such thing as a personal version of any religious song in the tribe.

There is an interesting proof of this. Around 1920 anthropologists made the first known recordings of ceremonial music in a number of Indian tribes. The same songs were rerecorded several decades later by other anthropologists. Now, even though performed by a completely new set of artists, the second set of recordings is almost identical with the first.

Can one then assume that the cultural genocide that has been the lot of the Indians of both the United States and Canada has had the effect of reducing them to a state of total artistic stagnation? Not exactly: for, if tradition has always played a dominant role in the life of these peoples, it nevertheless leaves room for a parallel development of more personal aesthetic creation, creation that is regenerable.

Personal songs, of which the themes are necessarily more secular than sacred, were and still are composed by individuals, known or anonymous, who put into the form of word and music their dreams, their preoccupations, and so forth. They thus contrast with the sacred songs, whose origins are communal.

There were also the songs designed to be sung at powwows. During these intertribal conferences Indians exchange their songs, their musical instruments, and their ideas. Theoretically, of course, this artistic interpenetration should help each tribe in its cultural evolution and in the development of its popular expression; however, during the twentieth century, not only Indians gather at the powwows, but also tourists. Accordingly, as powwows multiply and their popular success increases, there is a tendency in them toward commercialization, and inevitably they are absorbed by and submerged in the stewpot of American civilization.

We have already mentioned the diversity of the musical forms of each tribe, and this diversity is reflected no less in the musical instruments that they use. For a very long time the drum has been the most commonly employed instrument of all. It provides the unique and faithful accompaniment to a number of solo singers. The Cayuga or Seneca of the Canadian Iroquois tribe, for example, use a water drum which they hold between their knees.

Among rhythm instruments, apart from the drum and the tambourine, one also comes across rattles which are in effect batons made out of wood or bone and tintinnabulated together. These latter are typical of the Hopi, the Sioux, and various other tribes, all scattered at a fair distance from each other.

The bow is sometimes used as a type of one-string bass, variation in note being produced by bending the bow and thus varying the tension of the string.

The most common wind instrument is a distant relative of the flute. The material used for its construction varies from the wood of the red cedar to bone, though a popular piece of opportunism is the use of a gas pipe cut at length.

Today, the urgency of the struggle for survival of the Indians is a desperate one, perhaps even more so than that of the blacks, because the Indians tend to be forgotten. To illustrate the cause and justice of this struggle, rather than a long discourse, the few statistics that follow will serve. In 1970 the infant birth rate among the Indians was ten times higher than the average for the rest of the American population, but the rates of suicide and infant mortality were fifteen times higher. The life expectancy of the North American Indian is forty-three years. It is more dangerous to be an eighteen-year-old Indian than to have been a soldier in Vietnam. According to Buffy Sainte-Marie, in a five-year period during the Vietnam war, more Indian children died from illnesses for which there exist cures than there were men killed in the war. In the majority of the reservations there are neither doctors nor medicines. And the education that is sparingly given to the Indian children is white: history starts with the "discovery" of America by Christopher Columbus.

Over the last decade or so efforts to safeguard and, better, to renew the Indian population have formed an integral part of the folk revival of the sixties (the main elements of which are dealt with in Part 2).

This stirring in favor of the Indian way of life has its source in the coming together around 1960 in New York of a group of artists who created a humanitarian movement, with a political role far from negligible, known as the Federation for American Indian Rights: FAIR. The name of the movement is a clear explanation of its aims: in short, FAIR and its militants agitated against the physical, cul-

tural, and more generally political death of the North American Indian tribes—or at least to attempt to put off the final expiration. One
hardly needs to mention that folksingers have always played a
vanguard role in this organization, traveling and singing regularly at
community meetings, and going on gigs around the country to
spread the "good word" and collect funds for the Indians from the
rest of the American population. Of the militant artists who are involved with FAIR it is necessary to mention at least three names:
Buffy Sainte-Marie, Peter La Farge, and Patrick Sky.

Buffy Sainte-Marie was born in Canada of Cree stock. Notwith-
standing her blood, she received a typical white education. "I was
adopted," she recalls, "when I was very small. I don't know what
happened to my parents, whether I was an orphan or a bastard or
what—there's not much point in trying to find out. I was brought up
by a part Indian mother and a non-Indian father, in a non-Indian
town."

Although without the benefit of an education in musical theory,
Buffy Sainte-Marie has been playing music for a long time. Her
adoptive parents having one day bought a piano, she taught herself
to play—although she was only four years old. At seventeen, still
teaching herself, she began to learn the guitar, which she discovered
could be tuned in no less than thirty-two different ways. She also
made a specialty of the Jew's harp (or mouth bow), a curious instrument that makes use of a vibrating strip of material, amplified by
the mouth as sound box, and which is found here and there in the
folk music of the five continents.

It was during her studies at the University of Massachusetts,
where she was preparing for a degree in Oriental philosophy, that,
giving in to the persuasions and encouragements of her friends, she
consented to make her first public appearances in the cabarets and
clubs of Boston and Cambridge, Massachusetts.

Another time, now a teacher, she came to perform in New York
at the folk clubs of Greenwich Village, the temples of the urban folk
revival: "I sang at the Gaslight, the Bitter End, Gerde's Folk City—
Bob Dylan was there. I made my entrance at an open evening when
all the world could be found there; managers, people from record
companies. I came on with my guitar and my stiletto heels. I'd come
by coach from Maine and was living in the YWCA. People had told
me: in New York, you can sing for free. Really, I replied, you don't

have to pay? Tremendous—I'm going there!" And so began her time in New York.

After a little while, Buffy abandoned—though with the intention of taking it up again one day—her teaching career, and signed a contract with Vanguard, a label which, like Elektra, was a product of the folk movement and then on the way up, principally through the commercial success of Joan Baez. The first album that Buffy recorded for Vanguard, *It's My Way!*, made a great impression among other artists and critics, and also on the general public.

Very quickly the position of spokesman involuntarily acquired by the young artist contributed, with the help of the publicity campaigns of FAIR, to awaken a vast public to the Indian problem. Buffy's stern looks and her fabulous voice, alternating between a torrent of devastating passion and the deepest subtlety, would pierce the conscience of any white person.

In this respect, the opening track of Buffy's first record, "Now That the Buffalo's Gone," is at the same time revealing and symbolic. She sings to the average white man and woman, pointing out to them that they may have forgotten or tried to forget the plight of the Indians. They never bothered to try to save the buffalo, and it became nearly extinct; surely it's time to help the Indian before he goes the same way.

All that concerns the Indian also concerns Buffy Sainte-Marie, and vice versa. She stated it clearly in *It's My Way!* (apart from "Now That the Buffalo's Gone," there is on this record a song that tears at the emotions, sung in the language of her tribe: "Mayoo Sto Hoon"); in her third album, *Little Wheel, Spin and Spin,* she returned to the theme with "My Country 'Tis of Thy People You're Dying," which deals with the Indians of North America and their political situation. But at the same time she realizes the absolute necessity of ensuring that her music does not remain in some kind of Indian cultural ghetto. Because she is working in the field of the commercial disc, and because she hasn't completely forgotten that her childhood and youth were hardly that of a "normal" Indian confined to a reservation, it is only natural that she speaks and sings in English: it is her adopted tongue, and moreover the one that she must use to communicate with the whole of the American population. Perfectly natural, then, that on her second album, *Many a Mile,* she borrows also from the blues ("Fixin' to Die"), the negro spiritual ("Lazarus," to the sole accompaniment of handclapping), and the British ballad ("Johnny Be Fair").

With the exceptions of Judy Collins and Odetta, though in a different way, there is no other American singer who so constantly renews her style, while yet remaining essentially the same, distinctive artist, as Buffy. The fact that she composes the majority of the songs in her repertoire ("Usually," she said about this, "I write down the things which actually happen to me in the form of either songs or poems") doesn't stop her from either interpreting the compositions of other modern songwriters (Joni Mitchell's "The Circle Game" and "Song to a Seagull," Richie Havens' "Adam," are a few examples) or from producing faithful renditions of more traditional forms of popular music such as, apart from the examples already discussed, country and western in the album *I'm Gonna Be a Country Girl Again.* This album is one of the finest produced in the genre, and was released substantially in advance of the country-rock revival spearheaded by Dylan's *Nashville Skyline* (April 1968 as compared with April 1969).

Illuminations, released simultaneously in the United States with *I'm Gonna Be a Country Girl Again*—and the difference between two albums presumably recorded about the same time is incredible—is an excursion by Buffy into the realms of electronics. In *Illuminations* there are both electronic accompaniments and electronic distortions of her voice and guitar. And still she is able to give us further surprises: for example, an astonishing version of "The Partisan," the song made famous by Leonard Cohen (on his album *Songs from a Room*), of whom she has been an admiring fan for a long time.

More recently, Buffy Sainte-Marie was again the object of public attention with her remarkably successful single, "Soldier Blue," the theme song of the film of that name. Her voice at its harshest, she uses the full force of an urgent rhythm section to put over her lyrics. The film itself is one of several of that era to speak out in protest against the popular conception of the history of the American West. In its final sequence, which is horrifyingly and effectively violent (and hence slighted by critics who probably missed the point of the film), a troop of American cavalry descends on a defenseless Indian encampment, torturing, maiming, slaughtering, and dismembering the inhabitants. Afterward the men are told by their commanding

officer that this day they have struck a fine blow for American freedom.

Nobody more fitting than Buffy Sainte-Marie could have been
chosen to furnish the theme song of that film.

Peter La Farge was an author-composer-interpreter of Indian
ancestry who was considerably and genuinely concerned with the
problems of the Indians. He was the founder and one of the principal forces behind FAIR. The Indians provided a continual theme
in his work. One of the best examples in this respect is "The Ballad
of Ira Hayes." Hayes, a Pima Indian, was a U.S. Marine, one of the
six who raised the flag atop Mount Suribachi on Iwo Jima after the
battle there in 1945. Whether called an Indian drunkard or a
Marine hero, La Farge says, Hayes, who died in 1955, can't answer
you back.

Through the frequent use of a totemic symbolism borrowed
from the Indians, Peter La Farge gave to his lyrics a breath of highly
evocative poetry. Thus, in "Coyote, My Little Brother," he compares
the "little brother to the defenseless coyote, a species fast on the road
to extinction. It is probably due to the quality of imagery in his work
that Peter La Farge is remembered (he died of pneumonia on October 27, 1965) even among academics. His "Vision of a Past Warrior"
and Bob Dylan's "A Hard Rain's A-Gonna Fall" are the only two sets
of song lyrics to be included in the anthology of modern American
poetry, *Poets of Today,* edited by Walter Lowenfels.

Of Cree Indian heritage, Patrick Sky, a young author, composer,
and interpreter, is the third "musketeer" to be involved in the formation of FAIR. At one time he was well known among folk music
circles (particularly in Greenwich Village) as a highly talented blues
singer and guitarist. Later he made his mark as a songwriter, and in
his arrangements, both in performance and on record, his individual
guitar style has remained one of his finest attributes.

His frequent contacts with the Indian tribes have directly sup-
plied the material for a number of his songs. A particular example is
"Leave Us Alone," where the Indian declares that he prefers isolation to the misguided paternalism of the white authorities. Patrick
Sky relates how he wrote this song at the end of a long conversation
with an Indian aged more than a hundred.

This short chapter cannot be closed without a brief mention of the role played by folk festivals, in particular the annual one at Newport, initiated in 1959. At Newport and also at Philadelphia the organizers made it a point of honor always to present to their public some authentic Indian artists. Nobody who was at one or the other of these festivals can fail to have been impressed and moved by, for example, the dances of Henry Crowdog or the songs of Alanis Obomsawin.

At the beginning of this chapter one could have raised a perfectly fair objection along the following lines: Aren't all these efforts to preserve the Indian culture both too late and too powerless? How many crusades of this kind are betrayed by the naïveté of the artists involved, touching no doubt, but fairly useless as a means of solving the problem of the Indians . . . which, it must not be forgotten, is only one of the problems facing the American people?

Of course, one could hardly hope to reverse in ten years of crusading the consequences of more than 380 years of history. Buffy Sainte-Marie herself, not without pessimism, views the future of Indian music as short. In an article in *Sing Out!*, July / August 1967, she explained how comparatively few young Indians are nowadays interested in the conservation of their traditional music as a part of daily life. In a generation or two, she predicted, Indian music will probably be of no more than academic interest, even among the Indians.

Nevertheless, the alarm has been sounded, and folksingers have played a large role as educators, as spreaders of the truth. For a long time the Indians have been the pariahs of American society: victims of the same sort of tyranny as the blacks, they have suffered in silence. Few talked about their situation, even fewer about their music. As proof—the complete impossibility of obtaining in the shops records of original Indian music. An irrelevance? Perhaps, but a symbolic one: jazz and blues records are everywhere.

A final thought. The birth of the concept of "Red Power," the popularity of Dee Brown's book, *Bury My Heart at Wounded Knee*, and the revolt of the Indians that led to their representatives being met on equal terms by the highest officers of the American government: all these provoke one to wonder whether it should be posterity, not ourselves, that gives the final judgement on the activities of FAIR.

whites

Modern British folkrock owes its origins to the development of modern American folkrock, which was obviously based upon American traditional folk music. However, before we can begin to look at the American tradition, it is essential to look back a little further, to the British traditional music that gave it birth. Confusing, but true.

During the eighteenth century, the three types of Briton who composed the vast majority of the white population of the United States possessed a very rich folk heritage. Ireland in particular, by dint of its abundant Celtic tradition, had a veritable arsenal of songs that covered all circumstances of human life: drinking songs, love songs; tragic, comic, or heroic ballads; and, to a predominant extent, patriotic songs in support of the struggle for national independence and against the rule of London. From "The Rising of the Moon" or "Bold Fenian Men" (eighteenth century) to "Kevin Barry" (1920), these songs attest to the resistance of a belligerent people against oppression. And it is probable that the recent and bloody renaissance of this same struggle in Ulster has been the occasion for a parallel, logical renaissance in this type of song, though the media have remained quiet on the matter . . . to the extent of banning popular songs that discuss the subject.

Scotland also has a rich treasure-house of songs concerned with its history of rebellion against the English throne. The songs of the Scottish people, among other things, denounce vehemently the wars waged from London, and in which the Scots find themselves forcibly conscripted, even though they do not feel themselves finally allied to England. "Wars of Germany" is one of the most outstanding examples in this genre that I have come across.[1] But by far the biggest

[1] Here there is a parallel with the Breton songs against Napoleon: once again a factor totally ignored by the French history books.

category of Scottish rebellious songs deals with the corruptness of the imported English overloads. "MacPherson's Rant," a traditional song that Burns updated, tells the story of a fiddler sentenced to death. On the day of his execution his captors find that a reprieve is on its way, so they put the clock forward and hang him just as the messenger appears.

Island peoples like the Irish, the Scots, and the English possess in common a tradition of sea songs of a pronouncedly utilitarian character. Sea chanteys have very rhythmic, captivating tunes since they were designed to accompany pulling up nets, turning capstans, hoisting sails, and even, in some cases, the labors of the oarsmen. Essential is the presence of a key phrase which appears at frequent and regular intervals (in general twice a verse), of which the purpose is purely to assist respiration; for example, in "Bullgine Run," the alternating repetition of "Heave away, haul away!" and "Clear away the track and let the bullgine run!"

Here we have the simple practicalities of the chantey: one can understand in the same light that the rest of the lyrics are without any real importance, often appealing to the humor of the absurd that has always been a specialty of the English—as "Way, Haul Away, Joe!" And one can further postulate that the chantey was to the English sailor as the work song was to the black slave on the plantations.

On examination, it would appear that the ballad is a more specifically English genre, since almost without exception the traditional ballads that are sung nowadays are of English origin, though in fact there is a multitude of Scots ballads, very few of which are sung now, including the famous "Sir Patrick Spens." The average ballad tells the tale of a hero's love, though with numerous permutations. The favored subjects are a love that is usually hopeless or tragic between a noble and a peasant ("The Lass from the Low Country," "Pretty Saro," "Matty Groves"); farewells (dozens of them titled "Fare Thee Well") and reunions ("John Riley," "So Early in the Spring"); overbearing parents ("Cruel Mother"); the devil and his domains ("The Devil and the Farmer's Wife"); crime and punishment ("Geordie"); stories of sailors and doomed vessels (quite distinct from chanties, these are less sea songs than songs about the sea, like "Henry Martin"); and the tragedies of war ("The Cruel War").

Extending for eight, ten, twelve, or often more verses, the performance of a complete English ballad can often last more than fifteen minutes and is packed with realistic, picturesque, or impressionistic detail. Generally, the narrator introduces his tale by stating his own truthfulness: "Come gather ye round me lads / and I will tell you no lies." The almost maniacal pseudoaccuracy is distinguished by a newspaper-like obsession with facts. One gives the number of sheep in the shepherdess' flock, the current market value of the spoils captured by a ship, the number of shots fired by the cannon of the king's ship, the exact amount of a charming prince's fortune . . . and the whole thing is helped out by sudden turns of fortune, just like in the films.

This aspect of the ballad is worth stressing since, as we will find out in later chapters, this photographic realism, this eye for detail, have become essential constituents of American folk song, not only in those songs that are truly "ethnic," but also in those composed more recently by contemporary writers such as Bob Dylan or Phil Ochs.

The ballad is not content merely to "tell a story": almost always, bowing to public opinion, the final verse is reserved for the iteration of a moral, obviously edifying, drawn from the facts of the tale: if the hero/heroine has maintained his/her virtue, the narrator holds him/her up as a shining example to the young; if, on the contrary, he/she has stepped from the straight and narrow, there is a prompt condemnation. And so the ballad is a complete musical fable.

A word about the musical aspects of these ballads: the tune is in general a solemn one, with a ponderousness that lends itself to slow diction, designed to allow the listener plenty of time to digest all the details. The sound is often apparently monotonous, and only rarely is it alleviated by the addition of a musical accompaniment. Nevertheless, ballad music can be extremely beautiful (and it is interesting that very few contemporary star-status folkrock groups can handle a ballad adequately).

For each ballad there exist numerous versions, for all have traveled both in distance and in time. Every ballad has distinctive descendants in every English-speaking land, however remote; each village, each family, each ship has made it their own by embellishing and enriching it with details with which they are familiar. Long before the modern era, in all times and in all places, imagination has been a prerequisite of a developing folklore.

The themes cited above by no means comprise an exhaustive list, nor must they be regarded as mutually irreconcilable within the framework of a single ballad, for one of the dominant traits of this genre is the mixture of subject matter, killing at least two birds with one stone. Hence the universal theme of love is dealt with through lengthy separations, betrayals, and reunions between sailors and their shorebound ladyloves. This is the case with the famous "John Riley" (a good lesson in fidelity since he returns, after seven years on the high seas, to find that his lover has waited all this time for him, rebuffing all other advances!); with the woman in "House Carpenter" and the rich captain who has debauched her—after a shipwreck they both land up in hell; with "Jackaroe," for whom an accidental meeting at a port of call provides suitable occasion for marriage; with the young woman in "Sailor's Life" who hails the captain of every ship that enters port searching for her Willie who has disappeared . . . In short, the ballad for all its length is usually just an excuse to moralize almost like Aesop or La Fontaine.

On land, the same sort of thing goes on. After having told us about a young girl smitten with love for a high-ranking noble, and who receives in return nothing but scorn, "The Lass from the Low Country" in its last verse advises young female listeners not to love noblemen, for they are heartless and pitiless. To back up this moral it points out that the "heroine" of the tale has gone to a watery grave because of her love.

Barbara Allen, that exemplary woman who did not wish to survive her lover William, had herself buried by his side. From each of their graves emerged a plant—from hers a rose, from William's a thorn. The two plants intertwined and joined in an embrace that would last for eternity. An example to all young lovers.

But the most celebrated of all English love ballads, and probably also that which has lent itself most to Americanization, is without question the melancholy "The Water Is Wide" (sometimes known, more correctly, as "O Waly Waly"). Its last verse goes:

> *Love is gentle, love is kind*
> *bright as a jewel when first it's new*
> *but when love is old it waxeth cold*
> *and fades away like the morning dew*

The more despairing are these songs then the more beautiful. . . .

Having rapidly sketched out a skeleton history of Celto-British folk-lore, let us now try to explain how this folk music, exported to North America by the first boatloads of white colonists, adapted itself to the new continent and became something distinctly American, though all the while retaining traces of its island origin. It must be remembered when one uses the word "traces" that in fact many songs became an integral part of American folk music while yet remaining almost exactly in their original form. The comments we have already made about ballads like "Barbara Allen" and "The Water Is Wide" hold true also for hundreds of other ballads and songs—to name a couple, "The Devil and the Farmer's Wife" and "The Dove." Even more notable is the status of "Greensleeves," now become the common property of Anglo-Americans the world wide, but having its origins as an aristocratic song of the Elizabethan era.[2]

If, among the early colonies of America, newspapers and magazines with their stories, lampoons, articles, and caricatures were, as in Europe, omnipresent toward the end of the eighteenth century, one must remember that these media were reserved for that fraction of the population that was literate and, in addition, able to afford books and journals (in general, of course, literacy and wealth went hand in hand). On the other hand, folk music had (as it has always had) the immense advantage of not being produced as a primarily marketable commodity. A form of expression that cost nothing, understood by all to the profit of all, it was used as a transporter of the news to those who could not, for whatever reason, read or write.

The first historical occasion that provided opportunities for American folk music to chronicle the point of view of one side against the other presented itself with the war between the English

---

[2] Or even earlier. Legendarily, "Greensleeves" was written by Henry VIII about one of his wives, traditionally Anne Boleyn, though opinions vary. In fact there is no evidence whatsoever to substantiate this attribution. However, the attribution itself is information in that it demonstrates the way that sixteenth-century aristocrats up to and including the rank of the king were more or less expected to imitate the comparatively low-ranking troubadours by writing love songs about their various ladies. As with the troubadours, one sang songs about one woman (preferably married) while quite happily sleeping with and possibly marrying another: it was almost an essential that the woman in question never granted the favors requested of her in song. —P.B.

Royalist troops and the colonists struggling for independence, the war which resulted in 1776 with the Declaration of Independence and the foundation of the first thirteen states of the United States of America.

It was for this event that, for example, the tune of an old English ballad was adapted for new lyrics which told how the Parliament in London had voted to send special troops to quash the rebellion: hence "Derry Down" became "What a Court Hath Old England." Here, by the way, we can notice the emergence of the concept of "Old England," which naturally suffered by comparison with the new. Other songs, veritable pieces of musical journalism, retraced the various quirks of an independence dearly bought: "Sergeant Champé" is a story of betrayal; "Maryland Resolves" gives the results of the deliberations of that state; "The Whole World Turned Upside Down" shows the symbolic significance of the American Revolution for the future of all mankind; and there is a deluge of other similar examples.

As we have already observed, folk music is an evolutionary process. The particular case which I will discuss below, equally valid for hundreds of other songs, will give some indication of the mutation of an English song into an American song.

The original English song (and one comes across it quite frequently on record) is known equally under the two titles "Come All Ye Fair and Tender Ladies" and "Tiny Sparrow." It's the usual story warning the female listener to be on her guard against the perfidies of passion, in which the singer mourns her hopeless infatuation for a heartless man. At the end of it all she wishes that she were a tiny sparrow who could fly away from the demands of her ruthless lover. All the verses, in a slow and plaintive monologue, are in the first person singular.

A century later one finds the song again, very popular throughout the Appalachian area of the Southern states: the tempo has been much increased, and an ironic dialogue between the lass and her lover has been installed. The mother of the girl has entered the story, and there has appeared a symbolic accessory to the whole story: a silver dagger, which gives the song its new title. From the first verse, the style becomes distinctly more humorous than before:

Don't sing love songs, you'll wake my mother
She's sleeping here, right by my side
And in her right hand, holds a silver dagger
She says that I can't be your bride.

The following verse justifies this attitude:

All men are false, says my mother
They'll tell you wicked loving lies
The very next evening, they'll court another
Leave you alone to pine and sigh.

The moral of the last verse still affirms the desire for independence common to American women of all eras:

Go court another tender maiden
I hope that she can be your wife
For I have been wounded and I've decided
To sleep alone all of my life.

The case of "Silver Dagger" is archetypal and, through it, we can gain some realization of the birth of white American traditional folk music.

Throughout the nineteenth century and into the beginning of the twentieth, this process of Americanization was accelerated with the development of an extremely important style so far as the evolution of American folk music is concerned: hillbilly music. Typical of the Appalachian and similar regions—Kentucky, Virginia, Carolina, Tennessee, Oklahoma—hillbilly music is defined more or less as one would expect from its name.

Its most easily recognizable characteristics are, first of all, the voice: an extremely nasal tone in a constricted and high-pitched accent. The final syllables of each line are often stretched out and exaggerated to produce an effect which is partly comical, partly insistent. The addition to the lyric of various cries in the form of yodels, common to both hillbillies and to certain mountain peoples of Europe, as in the Tyrol, would suggest that these are designed to exploit the echo effects produced by the mountains.

The basic instruments of hillbilly music are the violin, the banjo, the mandolin, the harmonica, occasionally the accordion, and above all the three-string dulcimer and the Autoharp; these latter have earned some celebrity through the recordings of Jean Ritchie. The guitar was something of a latecomer. In contrast to country and western, to which it is unquestionably related, hillbilly, a much older musical form (it is sometimes called old-time music), does not make use of percussion or amplification.

The themes are similar to those of the English ballad, the predominant mountain (as in the ubiquitous Old Smokey) replacing the sea. The tendency to include as much in the "plot" as possible, noted during our discussion of the English ballad, is intensified here along with a relished sniff of horror: theft, rape, adultery, dissolute crimes ("Omie Wise"), the death sentence ("Tom Dooley," based on a true story), and other catastrophes proliferate. Spilled blood in all directions, as in "The Banks of the Ohio"—"I killed the only one I love / because she would not marry me."

Perhaps surprisingly, all the events we've mentioned are described in a tone of drollery, and even a party spirit. The singer laughs at the misfortunes of others and hasn't the hypocrisy to pretend otherwise.

To a journalist who asked her if she considered herself a "folksinger," Joan Baez once replied that, if she were, she would live on an old farm in the Appalachians, wear dated clothes, and sing with a nasal whine. Here she was referring to the archetypal hillbilly from whom emerged the traditional music of the rural white American. The perfect example and, quite fairly, the most famous authentic hillbilly group is the Carter Family, whose period of glory (local, alas) stretched from 1920 to 1940. June Carter, the wife of Johnny Cash, is a member of the Carter family.

Brief mention is necessary of a kind of music known as bluegrass. Of a slightly more recent (over a half a century) vintage than hillbilly music, it shares the characteristic nasal whine, part of the instrumentation (banjo, mandolin), and the mountain origins. Geographically, however, it owes its allegiance to an area extended not much beyond the boundaries of Kentucky. On a musical level, bluegrass is a sort of elaborated and "civilized" version of hillbilly music. Its accompaniments contain skillful improvisations or elegant instrumental runs, in which the virtuosity of the banjo player is given full rein. The criticism is made against bluegrass of a certain academicism in its makeup. Without trying to put bluegrass down too much, and de-

spite the pleasure with which it can sometimes be heard (the recordings of The Dillards, for example, or of Lester Flatt and Earl
Scruggs—such as "The Story of Bonnie and Clyde"), one must admit
that it lacks the warmth and spontaneity which are characteristic of
hillbilly music.

That legendary figure of the United States, the cowboy, also has his
folklore, which constitutes a rich and varied ensemble. However, in
the light of all that we have just discussed and all that will follow in
the next few pages, it is clear that cowboy songs in the end result
contribute hardly at all to the mainstream of American folk music.

The first thing that stands out, if one braces oneself to listen at-
tentively to these songs, is that they present a daily life very different
from that which we have become accustomed to seeing in Western
movies. To explain this dichotomy one has to recognize that the picture painted by the songs is considerably more accurate than that
painted by the films, for the songs were of course born on the plains
where the cowboys rode, and written by the cowboys themselves.
The Western, however much one may enjoy it, is a purely artificial
creation based on a number of symbols and conventions which have
very little to do with the genuine daily life of real cowboys.

One's view of the cowboy would hardly be complete if one did
not take into account his profession. He received a pittance in exchange for difficult, specialized work: he herded or restrained cattle
and helped to drive perhaps thousands to market. The life-style of
the cowboy was determined by the people *with* whom, not *for* whom,
he worked. Inured to either solitude or the forced and prolonged
company of the same people, deprived of feminine company, the
cowboy was naturally a taciturn man, accustomed to expressing himself with minimum wordage.

For a long time the majority of the areas where the cowboys were
was otherwise deserted, solitary, and uneasy. The common song of
Lucky Luke—"I am a poor lonesome cowboy / and a long way from
home"—captures the pervading spirit. If it is to the modern band
nothing more than a pleasant little song, it still does not altogether
lose the air of disquiet which it must originally have held.

The cowboy could reassure himself by dreaming of the town to
which he might return for a day of pleasure—the prettiest town in

the world with the prettiest girls in the world kind of thing. Sometimes humor could take over, for laughter is another form of escape . . . though even then the mirth was often a little strained.

What could be more efficient than a mouth organ, a guitar, a violin, and a song to forget loneliness, the Indians that one feared because one knew so little about them, the wolves that are perhaps waiting less than a mile away . . . or simply to allow one to listen to something else but silence? The melancholy of the cowboys, for this reason, can often be very poignant indeed.[3]

> *Oh bury me not on the lone prairie*
> *where the coyotes howl and the cold wind blows*
> *lay me to rest among my friends*

Laughter or loneliness, the cowboy—real and mythical—has become the hero of more literature and legend than any kind of American worker.

One mustn't confuse country and western with the music of the cowboys, though the name "western" might justify such an error. What is country and western, then? As one might expect from the double name, it is a bastardization (the charitable would say a combination) of two different kinds of music: country music (sister to hillbilly and bluegrass) and the vague remnants of cowboy music—vague remnants because, historically, this type of music first made itself popular among the whites of the Southern states, Tennessee in particular, between 1920 and 1930. At this period the great figure in country and western, as well as the author of a number of charming songs, was Jimmie Rodgers, nicknamed "America's blue yodeler." He was one of the first artists in the history of American popular song to benefit from the star system: at the moment of his appearance, modern electronic-acoustic effects were developed enough to make the star system possible, with the widespread distribution of records and the widespread influence of the radio stations.

The use of a traditional violin (giving a new lease on life to the jig and birth to the square dance) as well as various other saving graces allowed Jimmie Rodgers to stand out from, while yet being a part of, the stock from which he sprang.

One of the most brilliant country and western artists who fol-

---

[3] The peaceful, slow tunes derive also from a practical standpoint: that of calming the restless and nervous cattle and lulling them to sleep. —P.B.

lowed him was the legendary Hank Williams, Sr. More than twenty years after his death (he was killed in a car crash in 1953), Williams, by reason of his eventful life and a certain purity which he retained in his music, remains still an example both venerated and inimitable (though much imitated). In the meantime the radio and television networks, the record firms, publicity, and show biz had all developed considerably, and in particular Nashville, the capital of Tennessee, had become also the incontestable capital of country and western, to the extent that one talks of the "Nashville Sound." The numerous recording studios in Nashville have produced through the years an astronomical quantity of records by dozens of artists (Glen Campbell, Jim Reeves, Buck Owens, and so forth) that all have the unique trait of being virtually indistinguishable. For obvious commercial reasons, their music is strangled with the most dubious type of gimmicks—Hawaiian guitars, syrupy violins, choirs of women and children, insipid lyrics of plastic love. One aim only, and an openly admitted one: the hit parade, which assures the successful a comfortable income.

Nashville and its studios, by reason of their excellent production equipment and musicians, have in recent years attracted the attention of a good number of singers from the North, and by no means minor ones: Bob Dylan, Joan Baez, and Buffy Sainte-Marie are among their number. In terms of the genuine artistic value of certain of these records, there is a problem posed to which we shall return in the pages to come.

For Nashville and the commercial success of its music represent a social phenomenon that must be looked at objectively. The radios of Tennessee and of certain neighboring states broadcast country and western more than 80 percent of the time. The vast majority of the Nashville record production is purchased by the local whites—more accurately, the white Anglo-Saxon Protestants, or WASPS.

We've already mentioned that the states where country and western became and remained popular were those in which racism was dominant, and where the Ku Klux Klan and the John Birch Society still to a certain (sometimes large) extent hold sway. It is also commonly known, through the testimony of soldiers, deserters, visitors, and journalists, that the American-speaking radio stations in South Vietnam, notably those whose aim was to alienate the American and South Vietnamese troops, had broadcast practically nothing else but country and western from the start of the Vietnam War. (You would think it was enough to have to fight a war . . .)

Despite all criticisms, sarcasm, and other derogatory comment, several singers-songwriters-interpreters are actually worth listening to: one thinks of Marty Robbins with *Gunfighter Ballads and Trail Songs* and *The Drifter* or Johnny Cash with *Orange Blossom Special* and *Johnny Cash at San Quentin*. But listen with an ear elsewhere: Johnny Cash, the recognized big daddy of country and western, has shown a most equivocal attitude. On the one hand, his sympathies for the Indians (it's rumored that he has Indian blood in his veins) and his belief in the rights of prisoners (he has in fact been imprisoned several times himself) are well known, and perhaps he is sincere. On the other hand, he is a man perfectly integrated into the hideous American show-biz syndrome: his guitar (a splendid Martin decorated with his initials in mother-of-pearl) cost him more than two thousand dollars, and his annual income is tremendous. And then there's the tour in company with Billy Graham, the right-wing WASP "Christian," whose principal claim to fame might be his practical suggestion that the punishment for rape ought to be castration. And to finish it all off in style, at the beginning of 1970 Cash went to the White House, accompanied by his wife, to give a performance with his musicians in response to a personal and official invitation from President Richard M. Nixon to sing for his friends and himself. We know a number of singers who would have refused, but the vast majority would never have been invited. . . .

For a moment we must leave the examination of American traditional music in aesthetic terms and retrace our steps once again in time.

Throughout the growth of the United States, there is a close parallel between history and folk music. The Civil War offers a proof of this relationship, at the same time providing us with an excellent occasion to reflect on those songs known as "pacifist." For war and the reactions of the people who suffer from it have always been one of the great themes of American folk music.

Curiously, this aspect of folk music is one of the least known and least understood in Europe. In the first place it is often thought, particularly among the generations born since 1945 in France and in Britain, that their countries have never gone in in a big way for this type of song. And to a certain extent this is true. Certainly French folkrock poets are far less concerned with pacifism and the reaction against war than are their equivalents in the United States.

Pacifist and "protest"—a word that is now in disfavor—songs must not be considered as something new on the American scene. They are a continuation of a tradition that is as old as war itself. But the temptation is great to think that their birth and spread are linked necessarily to structured movements, to the actions of organized political parties or clearly formulated ideologies. The same sort of concept is justified in the case of the work of "intellectual" (for want of a better word) writers of the twentieth century, for whom the composing of songs represents some form of militant action. This has been true above all on the part of Joe Hill, and still more of Woody Guthrie and the revival of the sixties; which is why we will be coming back to this point again in the pages to come.

On the other hand: With the outbreak of the Civil War in 1861, what type of men were the soldiers? Combatants enrolled by force of circumstance, whose songs wept of frustration, sadness, or anger before the specters of ruin, starvation, and death, they were nothing but normal people, lacking in class consciousness or political education—or any other form of education for that matter. Many were totally illiterate and quite unable to understand what was happening to them. These young soldiers signed their conscription forms with a cross, ignorant of the real motives behind the war. Their lovers came to the station to kiss them good-bye. Very soon some of them would be receiving a small parcel containing the meager effects of their "soldier lad," accompanied by the inevitable little note of consolation signed by their officer: "His sacrifice was not in vain . . ."

Brother fought brother, father fought son, and often they did not know why they did:

> *Two brothers on their way*
> *One wore blue and one wore gray*
> *As they marched along their way*
> *Fifes and drums began to play*
> *On a beautiful morning*
>
> *One was gentle, one was kind*
> *One came home, one stayed behind*
> *Cannonballs don't pay no mind*

If you're gentle or if you're kind
Don't think of the folks behind
On a beautiful morning

Two girls waiting by the railroad track
For their darlings to come back
One wore blue and one wore black
Waiting by the railroad track
On a beautiful morning

The eighteenth century, with the victory of independence in 1776, had consecrated the official and administrative birth of the United States. The nineteenth was to allow the more adventurous colonists to make a conquest of the West and, during the second half of the century, to start the gold rush: the first important deposit had been discovered in California in 1849. However hard their epic journeys, the pioneers always took their songs with them. Even better, it was during these multiple migrations that the people, and hence its folklore, became distinctively American.

Gradually, as they settled down, progressively toward the west and south of the land, the new occupants of the American continent could no longer continue reerecting Europe wherever they went; it was no longer a case of grafting the old onto the new, but an absolutely original structure that they were creating. Inasmuch as these pioneers owed their birth to all sorts of different countries, it is logical that their songs bear the traces of their cosmopolitanism: French influences in Louisiana ("Cajun" music) and Nova Scotia (where the folklore is remarkably like that of Quebec), Dutch influences in Pennsylvania, to quote two classic examples.

The songs of the pioneers, as might be expected, reflect also the joys and sorrows of their day-to-day lives: road building, bridge building, canal digging; dangers of all sorts which beset the adventurous travelers in their legendary covered wagons: the rigors of climate, Indians, savage animals, all the difficulties that they had to work around . . . while singing. However much legend may have painted them, this is not just a myth but the genuine truth, and one hardly needs to repeat that their songs were born naturally, spontaneous cries from the heart in response to some urgent necessity.

The examples of pioneering songs that follow well illustrate this principle. First example: the penetration southward. At the end of the eighteenth century, surmounting the greatest of obstacles (the only roads at the time were Indian trails), the first colonists arrived and settled in Kentucky, near the Cumberland Gap. It is estimated that in 1784 there were thirty thousand there. In 1795 the state government had approved a project to construct a highway for vehicles to pass through the Cumberland Gap. As these highways were to be traced in part along the narrow trails of beaten earth already there, the first work to be done was to reinforce and enlarge these by laying logs across them, from which came the nickname of "corduroy roads." And from which came also the following song:

> Lay down, boys, take a little nap,
> Fo'teen miles to the Cumberland Gap.
> CHORUS:
> Cumberland Gap, Cumberland Gap,
> Mmm . . . 'way down yonder in Cumberland Gap.

The construction of the celebrated Erie Canal, which permitted water transport between New York and the Great Lakes region, gives us our second example. The canal was opened for use in 1825, and the official voyage of inauguration from Buffalo to New York was accomplished in nine days: an astounding performance. A symbol of the way progress cannot be held back and the first step toward Western mythology, the Erie Canal was quite naturally glorified in various songs, some of which are distinctly humorous:

> We were forty miles from Albany
> Forget it I never shall
> What a terrible storm we had one night
> On the Erie Canal

> An' the Erie was a-risin', and the whisky was a gettin' low
> I scarcely think we'll get a drink
> Till we get to Buffalo

> .   .   .   .

> The captain he got married
> The cook he went to jail
> And I'm the only damn drunkard
> That's left to sing the tale

It was during the second half of the nineteenth century that the pioneers, stimulated by hearing of the first fortunes that had been built up, set out in thousands for California looking for gold. The myth of the extraordinarily wealthy but merciless West built up rapidly. In the West, fortune was promised for all, even without having to work for it:

> *There's a lake of stew and whisky, too,*
> *You can paddle all around in a big canoe*
>
> . . . .
>
> *The barns are full of hay,*
> *I'm going to stay where you sleep all day,*
> *And the bars all serve free lunches*
>
> *O—the buzzing of the bees in the cigarette trees*
> *Round the soda-water fountain,*
> *Where the lemonade springs and the bluebird sings*
> *In the Big Rock Candy Mountain.*

For all, it was promised, there was gold in torrents:

> *Then ho boys, ho, to Californy-o*
> *There's plenty of gold, so I've been told*
> *On the banks of the Sacramento*

But naturally the numerous mines were very soon exhausted and boomtowns deserted by the hundred. From this era date the fortunes of several powerful California families and the astounding growth of cities like San Francisco. But it must instantly be made clear that there were far more seekers than finders, the riches were exploited and monopolized by a minority, and this constituted the first rude awakening from the Great American Dream, the start of disillusion. In this way, the alternative version of "Sacramento," with a new refrain, is revealing:

> *Then ho boys, ho, to Californy-o*
> *There's plenty of stones and dead men's bones*
> *On the banks of the Sacramento*

Before leaving the world of the prospectors, we must leave the last word for the disenchanted seeker of gold, who lives out the last days of his life modestly at the edge of the sea:

> *I've traveled all over this country*
> *Prospecting and digging for gold*
> *I've tunneled, hydraulicked and cradled*
> *And I've been frequently sold*

The following verses tell of his fruitless tribulations, and the last shows the wisdom of the old man who has finally become content with a little:

> *I think of my happy condition*
> *Surrounded by acres of clams*

Everyone knows that the railroads play an important role in the folklore of the United States. We've noted several times already the part played by distance and the communication across it—trails, horses, boats—but the roles of these precious ancillaries are totally eclipsed by that of the train. When one weighs all the evidence, the train is one of the essential themes (even *the* theme) of all American folklore. Omnipresent throughout the folk songs, in more than a century its importance has never declined.

It all started with the building of one of the very first lines and the legendary hero, John Henry, tunnel borer by trade, who died heroically after having attempted to beat the speed of a steam drill using only his own hand drill:

> *They buried John Henry in the White House*
> *Steam drill by his side*
> *And every locomotive comin' down the line*
> *Sings: here lies a steel-drivin' man!*

It is typical, of course, that John Henry is claimed simultaneously, with the same degree of vehemence, by both blacks and whites, who have raised him to the ranks of the heroes of America, in the better sense of the term.

Certainly, it was because of the vast dimensions of the country that the train, just like the highway, was able to play this title role. But the principal cause apparently of railroad folklore reaching its vogue is the way that the trains were (and still are) used by the vaga-bonds in a way that gave rise to the American word "hoboing," the hopper of trains being known as a "hobo."

Let us pause for a moment to describe this strange mode of transport, almost unknown in Europe. The hoboes constituted prac-tically a subproletariat of American society. Their state of constant traveling and the disfavor with which they were regarded by the police placed them in the situation of perpetual wanderers (see Woody Guthrie's famous "Hard Travelin' "). Their surest means of transport (it had to be free, of course, because they had neither money nor goods) consisted of secretly boarding freight trains—hopping the freights—toward the destination of their choice. With-out doubt the most astonishing thing about it all was that these men, for the most part illiterate, knew by heart the timetables of all the principal lines, as well as the time in days and hours that it took the freight trains to get from one place to another. They were ready at any moment to take off, or, on the other hand, if the train was approaching a station (without a watch, they somehow worked out the time), to leap off the moving cars. They had to dodge the sur-veillance of the police, the brakemen, and the guards. The hoboes would therefore go around a town on foot and wait for a train to come out the other side where, once again, they would leap on. In-side the cars (where it was easiest to remain hidden), the heat was in-fernal, the air asphyxiating. It was not unusual for as many as ninety or a hundred hoboes to congregate in the same boxcar, where some-times some of them would die of suffocation.

The hobo is a sort of perfect archetype of the American vaga-bond but there were all sorts of others as well.[4] "Rambling," "rov-ing," and "roaming" are among the commonest words in an in-calculable number of songs from the late nineteenth and twentieth centuries. And in recent years, one comes across frequent railroad references among the songs of, among others, Bob Dylan, Tom Pax-ton, and Eric Andersen.

Throughout there was the presence of the gambler, honest or otherwise. One happy consequence, among others, gave rise to the

[4] American literature also has often given within its pages an account of the lives of these tramps and hoboes, and in this respect one must recommend *On the Road* by Jack Kerouac.

emergence of the mythology of a legendary double character: the rambler gambler or the ramblin' gamblin' man.

The list of songs in which one comes across one of these terms or one of these characters in person is endless, and hence impossible to compile. It will suffice to stress yet again that a comparison of the content of these songs with whatever one knows of the history or geography of the United States is a supplementary proof of the value of human experience inherent in folk song.

Parallel with the development of the railroad, toward the end of the nineteenth century the industrial cities began to increase and enlarge at the expense of the rural areas. One can see already the advance signs of an emergent urban folklore whose influence was to become essential during the course of the twentieth century. The famous "The House of the Rising Sun," the story of a New Orleans brothel, announces this process of the urbanization of folklore. And, just as we mentioned a few pages ago when talking about "John Henry," it is symptomatic that, more than a century after the song entered the realms of folklore, the most eminent folklorists are still debating in all directions as to whether it was a black or a white creation. Both are probably true, as far as it's important.

The building of cities and factories and the exploitation of iron and coal mines brought in their trail quite new social problems, just as the Industrial Revolution in Britain had before them: unemployment primarily due to an exodus from the country areas and rapid advances in mechanization, the meagerness of salaries and the lack of security of employment, lack of lodgings—all became part of the day-to-day realities of life in various areas. Strikes were sometimes bitter and brutally repressed . . . at times by the intervention of the National Guard who did not always hesitate to open fire. And from this there was born a very active unionism that frequently turned its attention toward revolutionary political action.

The life of Joe Hill, one of the first American unionist singers, is tied up inseparably with the most active period of a revolutionary union that has become legendary, the Industrial Workers of the World, familiarly known as the "Wobblies." Joe Hill was in effect the lead singer of the Wobblies.

Originally named Joel Emmanuel Hagglund, Joe Hill was born in Gävle, a port on the east coast of Sweden. Very little is known about his childhood and youth, except that he had to leave school and start work at the age of ten after the death of his father. In 1901, tempted by the American Dream in which "everybody had equal opportunity," he emigrated, and landed in New York where he worked as a stevedore and a musician. In the evenings he played piano at a café in the Bowery. Much later, just like thousands of other immigrants from all the lands of Europe, he hit the road west, always looking for some sort of a job, working just as happily in the wheatfields as in the copper mines. At one time he was a stevedore on the Californian coast, at another time a sailor on the Honolulu line. He passed all his leisure hours writing songs.

It was in 1910 at San Pedro that Joel Hagglund, having taken at first the pseudonym of Joseph Hillstrom—which was eventually reduced to Joe Hill—became an active member of the Industrial Workers of the World. This union had been founded in Chicago in 1905. By contrast with the large central AFL (American Federation of Labor), whose activities were restricted to the defense of qualified specialists, the originality of the Wobblies lay in their attempt to organize *all* workers, whether specialized or manual, poor or rich, nomadic or sedentary, agricultural or industrial, under the umbrella of a single union.

The personality of Joe Hill and that of the union were destined to blend, and the musical talents of the Swedish immigrant found fertile ground in the social and political activities of the Wobblies. He wrote and sang to his comrades dozens of songs which served to stimulate the fight of the IWW with a vivacity and an efficacy that we find it hard nowadays to imagine. Very soon, the Wobblies issued their collection of songs in the form of a "little red book" entitled *Songs to Fan the Flames of Discontent*. This book, which ran into many revised and augmented editions, achieved colossal success among the workers, the unemployed, and the strikers. The majority of the songs in it were obviously products of the pen of Joe Hill. They were sung along the production lines, in the fields, on the ships, among the strike pickets, or even in the prisons where the strikers were frequently confined.

It would be an error to raise Joe Hill too much on a pedestal. He was simply one member of a movement founded to organize coordinated action on the part of the working classes. Through this and for this he and his comrades wrote and lived. They were certainly by no means the first to write on behalf of the working classes; we have already seen other examples. But the earlier songs did not in general attack themes other than those which were geographically and temporarily limited, with objectives that were purely local and short term. On the other hand, the originality and the merit of the Wobblie artists lay in their going beyond these limits and speaking to the working class throughout the land—even, when one remembers the word "world" in their title, with the aim of going beyond that limit in the long term. In this respect songs like "Casey Jones, the Union Scab," "Everybody's Joining It," or "The White Slave" are revealing. The first tells the tale of a habitual scab: after his death he is sent to Paradise. There Casey Jones is immediately reprehended by the union of angels, which sends him to spy in hell. "Everybody's Joining It" is of course a recruiting song to attract new members. It opened the way for a whole family of songs with the same basic idea that would appear much later, notably Woody Guthrie's "Union Maid" and The Almanac Singers' "Union Train."

"The White Slave" tells of the life of a poor young girl who, in order merely to survive, is reduced to prostitution. Where an older song would have concentrated on the individual lot of this girl, Joe Hill draws sociological conclusions and, in the last verse, denounces the exploiters of labor as responsible for her predicament:

> Girls in this way fall every day
> And have been falling for ages
> Who is to blame? You know his name
> It's the boss that pays starvation wages
> A homeless girl can always hear
> Temptations calling everywhere

The songs of Joe Hill, it must be remembered, have very little artistic value in many cases. It doesn't matter. They were efficacious for their purpose, and gave to the whole union movement an opportunity to expand on a grand scale; and their printing, before records were practicable, gave to song a much enlarged influence and a considerably more rapid diffusion than ever before.

Toward the end of his life, Joe Hill worked in the copper mines of Utah where he continued his militant activities. His name was of course inscribed on the blacklists of the local authorities, who hunted for a propitious occasion to arrest him, convict him, and put him out of harm's way. They found it on January 10, 1914, the day when a Salt Lake City businessman, Merlin Morrison, was attacked in his shop by two unidentified men who shot both him and his son dead with revolvers. Before dying, Morrison had the time to grab a firearm that he kept behind his counter and shoot one of his attackers. Both fled. A few days later, Joe Hill was arrested: by some unlucky chance he had recently received a superficial wound from a gun. He explained that a man had waylaid and shot him because he had won the heart of a woman, but he refused to divulge the identity of either on the grounds that he might compromise the woman involved. Of course, the police refused to believe his story and charged Joe Hill with the murder of Morrison, after which the whole procedure took a political turn: the classic procedure, which was to be used again many times in the future. . . .

Even President Woodrow Wilson, uneasy with good reason about the sentencing to death of Joe Hill as a provocative act toward the working classes, telegraphed Governor Spry to ask for the pardon of the accused. Thousands of letters, cables, and petitions inundated Spry's office, but to no avail. The governor telegraphed in return to the President, declaring that he couldn't go against the decision of the court. Joe Hill died by firing squad on November 19, 1915, after having addressed to his comrades a last will and testament that ended with the words: "Good luck to all of you."

In the twenties the Industrial Workers of the World suffered from internal squabbles and struggles with craft unions and the growing American Communist Party: all these factors contributed toward its rapid enfeeblement. In 1949 there were no more than fifteen hundred real Wobblies left. Nevertheless, Joe Hill is still set up as a good example among the American unions of today (though their right-wing dogmatism would probably have horrified him) as much as among the folksingers: Woody Guthrie wrote an extremely fine ballad about his condemnation; later, Phil Ochs wrote another (using, incidentally, the tune of "Tom Joad," another ballad of Guthrie's: a perfect example of the evolutionary processes of folklore); or one can see and hear Joan Baez sing "I Dreamed I Saw Joe Hill" in the movie *Woodstock*. In this way one could say that the author of "Casey Jones" is still very much alive.

At the end of the twenties and before the start of the great slump of 1929, the mining towns of Southeastern United States were populated by a subproletariat living in the most sordid misery. The miners and their families were at the mercy of company stores which demanded prohibitive prices for goods. They were stricken with the worst of illnesses, such as tuberculosis and silicosis, without the money to look after themselves properly and without any form of social or economic security. The consequence was inevitable: strikes took a sudden turn upward and, coming to a land where as we have seen the folk tradition (hillbilly in particular) was particularly strong, social themes began to be unfurled in their songs.

The beginning of the thirties was therefore rich in protest songs. Among the best known one could cite "Nobody Knows You When You're Down and Out" and "Beans, Bacon and Gravy," which gives a precise indication of the dietary predicament which the Depression had forced upon these people. In this era, even Bing Crosby, generally a crooner on radio, echoed the troubles of the time by singing the famous "Brother, Can You Spare a Dime?"

Definitely the protests were not on an individual scale. Wishing to transfer these sentiments to the realm of collective social action, three organizations distinguished themselves on this occasion by their use of songs: we have already spoken about the activities of the Highlander Folk School in the civil-rights movement of the 1960s. But we must recall here that this school had been created in a more primitive form in 1932 to lend assistance to the union activities of the local miners, with whom they effectively collaborated. It was not until after 1940 that the Highlander Folk School was recognized by the two major American unions, the AFL and the CIO.

The Commonwealth Labor College was founded before 1929 in Arkansas. The majority of its students were young militants from the towns of the North. Sis Cunningham, to whom we will return later, signed up there in 1932–33 and found that the songs in favor among these young people were not at all part of the customary folklore in the rest of the movement. One would hear there, for example, "L'Internationale," pro-Soviet songs of an evidently more recent origin, and certain classics of the Wobblies. For this reason, the contact with the local people was not as direct as one might have hoped. In the latter years of its existence, the school, thanks to the intervention of Lee Hays (later to be a member of The Almanac Singers and The Weavers) who brought to it a great traditional singer, Emma Dusenberry, the Commonwealth Labor College and the local population began at last to speak the same musical language.

The Kentucky Workers' Alliance, on the contrary, was an organization of the people in the Southern states, directing themselves and singing their own songs. Don West, the Georgia poet and cofounder of the Highlander Folk School, was charged to prepare a collection of these songs, *Songs for Southern Workers*. The spirit of the collection has much in common with that of the one published earlier by the Wobblies.

In November 1932 Franklin D. Roosevelt was elected President of the United States, succeeding Herbert Hoover and inheriting a social and economic situation that was rapidly deteriorating. In January 1933 the new President faced a considerable task: to stabilize the dollar, to salvage agriculture and industry, to reduce unemployment, to organize a vast plan of national improvement (highways, toll roads . . .); these were the principal points of his reconstruction program known as the New Deal. The country, according to eyewitnesses, was on the edge of revolution, and Roosevelt and his New Deal were acclaimed by the majority of Americans as the only reasonable hope for any kind of positive solution through the existing social structures.

His principal campaign toward economic reconstruction was the National Recovery Administration, the NRA, put into operation during June 1933. It consisted essentially of a program of price control with the cooperation of the business world of the United States. The NRA and its popular symbol, the Blue Eagle, soon became for millions of Americans synonymous with a return to prosperity for all and an end to the abuses of exploitation. Millions of stickers, imprinted with the eagle mascot and bearing the words "We do our part," were applied to the windshields of cars, the windows of shops, and the labels of articles within the shops. As might be expected, numerous songs celebrated the NRA, and among these Bill Cox's "NRA Blues" has remained the most famous:

> *I work down in the old sweat-shop*
> *I work like a mule and I never stop*

When we gonna join the NRA
I never have heard the big boss say

Unfortunately, the great illusion lasted less than two years. In principle the NRA restricted the practical monopoly of the large industrial concerns. It could only prevail temporarily and, as the abuses recommenced in even greater style than before, the Supreme Court in 1935 ruled that the NRA was unconstitutional. Its death was seen as the work of the devil. The song "Death of the Blue Eagle," by George Davis, sums it up:

> *The other day my paper came*
> *And here is what I read:*
> *The Blue Eagle it is ailing*
> *The little writer said*
> *But when he finished writing*
> *The Eagle he was dead*
> *They took him to the graveyard*
> *In the merry month of May*
> *Said who's gonna solve our problems*
> *Now there's no NRA? ***

Nevertheless the NRA permitted undoubted progress on the social plane, progress that one could compare with that brought about by the programs of the first postwar British Labour government. The principles of a minimum wage and a maximum working week were recognized on a national level. The employment of children was abolished, at least legally. More generally, it reinforced the position, the influence, and the means of action of the unions.

Among the most active singers in the union movement in the early thirties (apart from Woody Guthrie, who will be discussed shortly) the names of Aunt Molly Jackson and her son Jim Garland should be noted.

Originally local traditional singers from Harlan County in Kentucky, these two were among the first to turn the musical mouthpieces of the unions into a Communist form. Since the old UMW (the miners' union) collaborated to recruit new members to the ranks of the CIO, Aunt Molly Jackson changed one of her titles

* George Davis, "Death of the Blue Eagle." Copyright © 1968 by Stormking Music, Inc. All rights reserved. Used by permission.

"Join the UMW" to "Join the CIO." Around this epoch she and Jim Garland made numerous tours of the neighboring states, singing at village fetes or in taverns to collect funds to sustain the Harlan miners in their struggle. Many of their unionist/political songs were nothing but new lyrics set to traditional tunes so that they would be more easily learned by the audience. One of the most typical examples of this process is "Greenback Dollar," which Jim Garland composed to the tune of "East Virginia." Much later one would find Jim Garland singing at the 1963 Newport Folk Festival another version of "Greenback Dollar": "I Don't Want Your Millions, Mister."

Throughout this epoch of misery on the part of the industrial workers, one sees an obviously parallel phenomenon prevalent among the rural populations, with perhaps even more serious consequences, both at the time and later. But this period of extreme distress for both the farmers and the small landholders, and their desperate exodus toward California, played an important part in the life of the man who would become the singer whose influence on contemporary American folk music outstrips even that of Bob Dylan: Woody Guthrie.

part 2
Branches

guthrie

It is difficult, perhaps impossible, even to pretend to do justice to Woody Guthrie, as man and as artist, in a few pages. Not that he was in particular a complex character, nor that his work was likewise: we will show in fact that simplicity was one of his dominant traits. But nevertheless one can hardly do more than outline within the scope of this book a life rich in constant changes of fortune, to the extent that the hero of any novel would envy him; nor a man who, precisely because he *was* a man, had his fair share of quirks and self-contradictions.

Among the numerous homages that have been paid to him over the last two decades, one of the best was the album *Thinking of Woody Guthrie,* released in 1970 by Country Joe McDonald. In the spoken introduction to "This Land Is Your Land," the last track of the album, McDonald points out that

> I never really knew Woody Guthrie, but I can't help feeling that somehow I always knew Woody. This record is a collection of songs that I just naturally learned and loved in my early years of playing and singing. Woody said that he wanted to be known as "the man who told you something you already knew," and for me this is a clue into the beauty and the genius of Woody Guthrie. For he was just an ordinary man, he made all the mistakes, had all the vices, all the good and the bad things that every ordinary person has. He never gave you the feeling that he was better than you in any way, and he never gave you the feeling that he was worse than you; but that he loved you because you were just like him and he was just like you. Somehow, without

thinking, he tapped the reality and the dreams of what it meant to be an American.*

One of the worst errors which one might be tempted to make in regard to Woody Guthrie would be to admire him as a sort of genius or incomparable hero figure. On the contrary, he was interested not in heroes or geniuses but in each one of us, ordinary people who met him, discovered his abilities to live, to struggle, to create, to love.

It was on July 14, 1912 (the year of the election of Woodrow Wilson to the Presidency of the United States), that Woodrow Wilson Guthrie was born in the little town of Okemah, Oklahoma: soon he was known to everyone as simply "Woody." An agricultural town, Okemah underwent a period of rapid transformation, principally due to the copper mines and, even more, to the oil wells that were discovered in the area.

Despite the transformation, the land was nevertheless still full of popular tradition. Woody Guthrie remembered right from his earliest years having continually heard the blues of the blacks, the dance music of the reds, and the ballads of the whites. The legendary Pretty Boy Floyd, the softhearted bandit who stole from the rich to give to the poor, passed through Oklahoma at the beginning of the twentieth century. Much later, Woody was to transform this memory into the well-known ballad, "Pretty Boy Floyd."

In the Guthrie family, music was an all-important fact of life. Woody's mother, Nora Belle Guthrie, née Tanner, of Irish stock, played the piano. She and her husband, Charles Edward Guthrie, knew hundreds of songs. Woody's uncle and aunt had at their house one of the new technological marvels, one of the first phonographs in the county.

Woody Guthrie's father was fairly prosperous. Then sickness became a frequent visitor at his door—Woody's younger sister Clara was mortally burned in a coal oil stove explosion; not long after, their mother, heartbroken by this disaster and anyway inclined toward depression, had a nervous breakdown, aggravated by various complications (one of which was probably the genetically transmitted Huntington's chorea). She was taken to the hospital at Norman where she died a few months later—but the reversals of fortune

* Country Joe McDonald, *Thinking of Woody Guthrie*. Used by courtesy Vanguard Recording Soc., Inc., and Country Joe McDonald.

were not yet over for Charles Edward Guthrie: his house was burned down and his business was deteriorating. The new house that he built after the fire was itself burned down, and this time he was injured in the flames. Sent to a farm in Texas to recuperate, he never properly recovered.

It was thus that Woody Guthrie began his life as a "ramblin' man," wandering minstrel, transient laborer, permanent émigré, which would eventually lead him to sing of an America built on suffering and injustice, an America that the tourists never saw, and still less the President on his official visits. Setting off with nothing for luggage but his precious harmonica, Woody hit the highways of Texas, moving through Houston and Galveston and along the coast of the Gulf of Mexico. To earn enough to eat, Woody, who was only fourteen years old, got jobs of all kinds: giving out handbills, carrying wood, working for carpenters, builders, and miners. And also, of course, there was music. To earn money he would play and sing wherever it was possible to do so: in streets, at dances, fairs, marketplaces, cafés, and even beauty salons, with all sorts of partners, black or white, young or old, factory workers or farmhands. Naturally, while meeting up with all sorts of ordinary Americans, he picked up songs.

Woody eventually returned to the Texas farm where his father was ill. He worked a few times in Pampa, another oil boomtown, in a liquor store. His boss kept an old guitar behind the counter and Woody taught himself to play tunes on it in his time off. A little later his Uncle Jeff, himself a guitarist and violinist, taught him to play chords. Within a few months the two of them were playing at festivals in the area, accompanying square dances at dances or fairs.

We've already mentioned the year 1929 in connection with the great slump. Historically caused by panic selling on Wall Street which reached its height on "Black Thursday" in October 1929, it had in fact been building up since 1920. In the wake of the First World War the economic growth of the United States, activated by lack of foresight and the optimism of shareholders, was extremely rapid and haphazard. We have already spoken about the unemployment and the social problems which ran through industry at this time; we must here concentrate on the incredible difficulties which the farmers of the South and Southwest endured at the same time. Certainly the home state of Woody Guthrie, Oklahoma, suffered worse than any other during the thirties, for the social and economic stagnation that was the common lot was aggravated in this state by the natural calamities of dust storms. Three or four seasons of considerable rainfall caused a surplus of crops—that could not be marketed—at the price of extreme soil erosion. By sheer bad luck, the following years, which were also the years of the Great Depression, were incredibly dry. Arriving at a land already vulnerable to erosion, the dust storms blowing from the north annihilated with pitiless ferocity the meager crops that remained. Many farmers, already crushed by the dearth of crops and creditors of all sorts, had no chance of setting themselves up again. The only hope that remained to them was in the exodus to the magical West, toward a California that was described as prosperous and welcoming, where the disinherited of the earth would be able to get well-paid jobs, principally as pickers of fruit such as peaches and grapes. Taking the few belongings they still had, these families traveled along the famous Highway 66 at the end of which, assuming that they hadn't died of hunger, they would find the land of plenty where "the water tasted like wine" (an expression that was current among the refugees and that is reminiscent of numerous songs that were then current).

Admirably described by John Steinbeck in his novel *The Grapes of Wrath,* this exodus provided Woody Guthrie with one of his best and most important series of songs, and one that we will be examining at greater length a few pages on: the Dust Bowl Ballads.

Woody, having in the meantime married Mary Jennings, a pretty Irish girl who gave him two daughters, Sue and Teeny, also suffered troubled times. Leaving his family, he took to the road again in 1931, his only companions a guitar on his back (he didn't have a case for it) and a couple of paintbrushes in his pockets. These precious tools allowed him to be certain, for better or worse, that he could earn some sort of a living, by day offering his services to people who had signs that needed repainting, by evening singing and passing around the hat in cafés . . . unless he was kicked out. To travel from one place to another he hitchhiked along the highway; the rest of the time, like thousands of other vagabonds, he rode the freight trains. It was this life, full of danger and misery, but also possessed of a curious fascination, that Woody immortalized in one of his most famous songs, "Hard Travelin'."

Arriving in California, unfortunately, he was disenchanted:

Woody saw thousands of Okies', his fellow travelers, stopped at the state line, where the police checked identities and sent away everybody who didn't have an already assured job (with a full formal contract of employment, a rare document). They had to live in "jungle camps," shantytowns thrown together by the vagrants and unemployed. For these Okies', and even more for those who came after them, full of hopes and illusions, Woody wrote one of his first songs on a genuinely social theme: "Do-re-mi."

Woody himself, however, found his own "do-re-mi" in Los Angeles, where he luckily was able to earn money through his music. With a country girl who had emigrated from Missouri, and who like himself sang folk music, he formed a duo called "Woody and Lefty Lou." With her for the next two years he produced and presented a daily broadcast of popular music for the local radio station, KFVD. During this period, Woody and Lefty Lou received twenty thousand letters of encouragement from listeners. After a short trip to Mexico, Woody, who now shared a small apartment in Los Angeles with his brother George, had saved up enough money for Mary and his two daughters, who were still living in Oklahoma, to join him.

As well as his radio broadcasts, which he carried on without Lefty Lou, Woody was singing more and more often for the unemployed and the strikers, on picket lines, in the "jungle camps," or at union meetings. He carried out epic tours without cease, at the wheel of his Chevrolet (which he called affectionately his "Chevvery") and accompanied by his wife and one of their friends, the Hollywood comedian Will Geer. During one of these journeys Mary gave birth in the car to a son: Bill Rogers Guthrie.

In 1937 Woody received from the Federal authorities, who were in the process of constructing the colossal dams at Bonneville and Grand Coulee on the Columbia River, a telegram requesting him to go there, armed with his guitar. The aim was to encourage the laborers with his music and to write new ballads to the glory and the scale of this mighty project. It is one of the paradoxes of America that the job was taken on by the intrinsically revolutionary singer at the behest of a thoroughly capitalist government! It seems certain, however, that the paradox was born out of a mutual misunderstanding. The government sought to glorify its prestige by using the services of a poet who, contrarily, glorified the people who actually worked to build the dams: there is a difference. . . .

In 1939, on returning to Los Angeles, Woody by chance made the acquaintance of another legendary figure in American folk music: Cisco Houston. They met on the street, each carrying his guitar, and began to play together on the pavement; they were to become inseparable friends. In 1940 Woody, who by now had brought his family to New York, there met Pete Seeger, with whom he set out for the South and Southwest of his childhood. Sometimes as a duo, sometimes as members of The Almanac Singers, they increasingly made appearances at union meetings and strikers' demonstrations. Their favorite song at the time was "Union Maid."

Each day he published in the *Daily Worker* (the newspaper of the American Communist Party) a column entitled "Woody Sez." To those who always take things at surface level, this naturally meant that Woody was a Communist. We will return to this topic later in this chapter.

The year 1940 was also important so far as recording went, because it was during 1940 that Alan Lomax, eldest son of John Lomax who played such an important role in bringing Leadbelly to the public, invited Woody to come to Washington to record for the folklore archives of the Library of Congress several hours of conversation and songs in which he related his life story in an extremely picturesque fashion. In the opinion of many Guthrie connoisseurs, he never played and sang with such verve as he did on that day. One must be grateful not only to Lomax for finding and recording Woody Guthrie (remembering that at that time hardly anyone was in the slightest interested in this type of artist), but also to the firm of Elektra for having, with the approval of the Library of Congress, released this historic recording to the public in the form of a triple album.

In December 1941 the United States entered the Second World War and Woody (who had just divorced Mary), in company with Cisco Houston and an Italian *bel canto* singer, Jimmy Longhi, joined the merchant marine. But he hadn't waited for the United States to join the war before making his position in regard to Nazism abundantly clear: he customarily stuck to his guitar a little notice that read "This machine kills fascists."

Woody and his friends brought to the sailors all the support of their music, discovering in the course of their voyages North Africa, Sicily, and Great Britain . . . discovering not only the countries but their folk music. Meanwhile, he had the time to be torpedoed twice. And when he read about the wreck of the *Ruben James* in the newspapers, he was inspired to write another of his historic songs: "The Sinking of the *Ruben James.*"

Returning to New York, Woody married a second time, this time to Marjorie Mazia Greenblatt, dancer and teacher, with whom he had five children: Cathy Ann (who was to die in tragic circumstances reminiscent of the death of Clara Guthrie thirty years earlier), Gwendolyn, Joady, Nora, and Arlo, born in 1947.

In 1943 E. P. Dutton published his famous autobiography, *Bound for Glory,* often considered to be one of America's modern classics.

Once again he began to perform professionally. In New York he recorded with Cisco Houston and Sonny Terry more than 120 songs for Moses Asch's little Folkways label. Woody also met The Almanac Singers again, with Pete Seeger, Lee Hays, Millard Lampell, and occasionally Sis Cunningham. These were the pillars of a new union of artists, People's Songs. For several months Woody lived with Leadbelly and his wife. He describes this sojourn and the marvelous folk artists he met at the Leadbelly home in a most moving way in *American Folksong,* a collection of twenty-six songs interspersed with impassioned poetry and prose, published in 1946. He recorded several more times for Folkways, sometimes on his own, sometimes as part of a group: from this period date notably the *Ballads of Sacco and Vanzetti.*

During these years, Woody lived with his new family in a small house in Coney Island. His home was constantly full of friends and friends of friends, musicians and artists who came to visit him for an hour or a couple of weeks. All the same, Woody the "ramblin' man" had not lost his migratory predilections: one of his friends tells how he arrived at Woody's house to find him just leaving, saying that he was going to buy cigarettes and then wasn't back for two weeks. Sporadically, he took to the highways during his last three active years, in company with two singer-guitarists much younger than himself. One would like to avoid using the word "disciples" of Derroll Adams and Jack Elliott, but there hardly seems another suitable word to describe two men who modeled their music and their lives on Woody Guthrie.

One could still see Woody Guthrie, hirsute and weather-beaten, playing (for free, of course) with Jack Elliott in Washington Square in 1954. But all the time sickness was eating away at him and, at the end of this year, there started the first attacks of Huntington's chorea, and he had to be admitted to Brooklyn State Hospital. This incurable disease, which he had probably inherited from his mother, affects the nervous system and is symptomatized by frequent fits of convulsions, punctuating periods of progressive paralysis.

At the same time as Woody, several months after his admission to the hospital, sadly wrote one of his last songs, "I Ain't Dead Yet," he found that certain savants of America were hotly theorizing that his sickness confirmed the abnormal mental state that had possessed the author of "This Land Is Your Land" for a number of years, and that that "explained" a large part of his work. One mustn't forget that during that time Joseph McCarthy was organizing his paranoid Red witch-hunts.

Woody Guthrie died in the hospital on October 3, 1967, after twelve years of constant pain, aged only fifty-five, during which time the United States and even the world had had need of men like him. Pete Seeger remembers that the long-expected news came to him while he was on tour in Japan: his first thought was that Woody would never die so long as there were people who enjoyed singing his songs. In accord with what seems to have been a personal request, Woody had no funeral services. His close friends and relatives took his ashes to a Coney Island bridge and scattered them on the water beneath.

Rather than pretend to analyze and tabulate the multiple facets of Guthrie's work, we would prefer to spend the remainder of this chapter examining various traits that appear to us to be basic, as well as the way in which they link up with the life of the man as songwriter.

The Dust Bowl Ballads, with those written for the dams in 1937, constitute the major part of Guthrie's work before 1940. They form nearly all of the songs recorded with Alan Lomax in Washington. Later, in 1950, at the request of Moses Asch, Woody rerecorded the Dust Bowl Ballads in the Folkways studios in New York, and these latter are still available to the public in the United States and Great Britain in the form of a twelve-inch LP.

In his preface to the collection, the author recalled yet again that period of his life when he traversed the dust bowls, and described the difficulties of the people whom he met. For him, twenty years later, the problem was still a living one: as he explained, the dust bowls still exist and the wind still blows. The government hasn't repaired the damage and Congress can't stop the wind, and nobody has seriously tried to do anything about it. And he continued that this was the *raison d'être* for this new recording of the Dust Bowl Ballads, so that every listener could think of some way to help the refugees that the songs tell about.

The collection opens in a comic fashion with one of those talking blues that became a Guthrie hallmark: "Talking Dust Bowl Blues." After having told us how he swapped his scanty farm for a second-hand Ford to flee from the dust bowl, and how he crashed on the highway and found himself penniless in the Rocky Mountain area, he tells how his wife cooked a potato stew so thin you could have read a magazine through it.

"I'm Blowin' Down This Old Dusty Road" is the refusal of a man, poor yet proud, to be treated like an animal. As he walks down the road his two-dollar shoes are falling to pieces, but he swears that he isn't going to be treated this way forever.

We've already spoken about the famous "Do-re-mi," which reappears as "Dust Cain't Kill Me." The dust has killed everything else— the narrator's family, children, crops—but it won't get him. This song has recently had a new lease on life, having become a part of the repertoire of the short-lived group, Mungo Jerry.

The fifth ballad is probably the most important of all: "Tom Joad." In 1940 Guthrie had stayed with a friend in New York who had taken him to see *The Grapes of Wrath*. One can imagine how the author of "Do-re-mi" fell in love with the film: he went to see it several more times and learned its smallest details by heart. Finally, returning home late one night, after his friend had gone to sleep he seized a typewriter and worked until the morning composing "Tom Joad," a seventeen-verse ballad that adroitly and powerfully complements either the film or the book of *The Grapes of Wrath*. In his liner notes Woody mentions that he would like to thank the friend whose apartment he had shared while writing the song, if only he could remember his name. He later found that the friend in question was called Pete Seeger. . . .

The second side of the album opens with "The Great Dust Storm," which tells of the dust storms that never left the sky. From the first couplet it is obvious that the song is set on April 14, 1935. Nothing is spared us in this spectacle described at firsthand: the radio gives the news that throughout the region the dust blows angrily through the slightest cracks, beneath the doors, burying fences and tractors, until finally, in the early afternoon, the family contemplates the ruin of all that they have known before backing up their shabby baggage and making for Highway 66.

We can see in both "Tom Joad" and "The Great Dust Storm," by the construction and number of their verses, the dramatic tension, and their reference to the slightest details, three examples of the way in which the work of Woody Guthrie during this period resembled the traditional British ballad as we have defined it in chapter three.

The ever-popular "So Long, It's Been Good to Know You!" is also one of the Dust Bowl Ballads. In it one sees a preacher and his flock surprised during a service by the dust storm: the preacher couldn't read another word of his Bible.

The three songs that follow—"I Am a Dust-Bowl Refugee," "Dust Pneumonia Blues," and "I Ain't Got No Home in This World Anymore"—written in the first person, autobiographically if you prefer, are in the same vein as "I'm Blowin' Down This Old Dusty Road," but with more of an accent on the individual suffering of the refugee.

On the contrary, "Vigilante Man," the last track on the album, describes the character simultaneously feared and detested by every single American itinerant, the vigilante who could arrest you, denounce you, and eventually kill you. Each verse describes a piece of dramatic action and asks the question, "Was *this* the vigilante man?" The spirit of *The Grapes of Wrath* permeates this song also. Woody Guthrie, marked for the rest of his life by his experiences of the dust storms, once mentioned that he sometimes said to himself that he was nothing but an old package of walking dust!

Of the twenty-six songs written in 1937 to the glory of the men who built the dams at Grand Coulee and Bonneville, the three that are generally considered to be the most important are "Grand Coulee Dam," "Roll On, Columbia" (the power of the great river popularly symbolized progress and peace), and above all "Pastures of Plenty." Many consider that this last song is the finest piece of work that

Guthrie ever produced. It is true that the matching of the tune, rich and simple at the same time, and the expressive fullness of the lyric, is exceptional.

> *I worked in your orchards of peaches and prunes*
> *I slept on the ground in the light of the moon*
> *On the edge of the city you'll see us and then*
> *We come with the dust and we go with the wind* *

The inspiration of "Pastures of Plenty" clearly harks back to that of "Hard Travelin'."

In 1946 Moses Asch, who had decided to devote a Folkways album to the Sacco and Vanzetti affair, had the fortunate idea of entrusting the preparation and presentation of the album to Woody Guthrie. To this end, Woody went numerous times to Boston to consult the legal records and examine the testimony of several of the witnesses. The Sacco and Vanzetti affair (a sort of American equivalent to the Dreyfus affair, it remains an ineradicable stain in the history of American justice) was extended over a period of seven years, between the arrest of Sacco and Vanzetti in May of 1920 and their execution in the summer of 1927.

Not satisfied with merely a narration of the facts themselves, Woody drew from them a conclusion that the whole affair was covertly political. The two accused were Italians and had taken part in the struggle for organization of the workers in Boston. Judge Webster Thayer and the local notables were only too happy to take advantage of a double murder to arrest them. No defense, no proof of their innocence would satisfy the court. Didn't one of the judges announce on the first day of the trial that Sacco and Vanzetti were a pair of dirty anarchists and worth putting to death in any case? So it goes . . .

One of the finest songs in this collection is "Vanzetti's Letter," based on a letter written by Vanzetti to his judges. Woody demands, not Vanzetti's and Sacco's pardon, since that would inherently be a recognition of their guilt, but a revision of their trial and their liberation because they were innocent. Rarely has the brutality and hy-

* "Pastures of Plenty," words and music by Woody Guthrie. TRO—Copyright © 1960, 1963 by Ludlow Music, Inc., New York, N.Y. Used by permission of The Richmond Organization and Essex Music, Ltd.

pocrisy of a judicial system been denounced with so much vehemence, the social conscience of the oppressed roused with so much conviction, as in the Sacco and Vanzetti Ballads.

The Dust Bowl Ballads, the Columbia Ballads, the Sacco and Vanzetti Ballads, as well as the songs about the heroes and heroines of the West such as "Pretty Boy Floyd," "Jackhammer John," "Billy the Kid," and "Belle Starr": all these constitute a heroic gesture on the part of the forgotten people, oppressed even after their deaths (for are they not so in the history books?), a living testimony to this other face of America, which suffers and dies, screams and sings to make itself heard, and to which historians and journalists and politicians turn only blind eyes. These songs that we have briefly looked at, today as yesterday, are the surest means of awakening the people of the outside world, without risk of becoming sermons, to what is going on, precisely because they are a product of the *inside* world, of the hearts of the sorry people for whom they speak.

When a politician speaks to us of the Portuguese massacres in Africa, his impassioned pleas are only too often the symptoms of the demagogue, and we tend to treat them as such. But when we see a photograph of a dying child, we see the truth in the agony of his eyes, because it is there in front of us. With the songs of Woody Guthrie and those like him, there is the same phenomenon: this is music that, at its very roots, cannot lie.

The term "protest singer" is a loose one, but certainly some of Guthrie's work would qualify him for the description. But it is necessary to examine just what it means when applied to him (after all, the term doesn't seem to have been in his vocabulary) in case, by the use of it, we get a muddled impression of what he was trying to do.

Since his youth, which as we have seen was extremely hard, Woody had not only involved himself with the misery of the Oklahoma farmers, but also with the whole problem of social injustice that they symbolized. In particular, he didn't have to go far to see the work of the exploiters and oppressors of all types: landowners, police, judges, and bankers, at the encouragement of whom there developed a totally anachronistic system of sharecropping, from which, of course, they themselves, made suitably large profits. When a bulldozer comes to flatten your meager holding under the pretext of developing it for "modern" agricultural exploitation; when, a few months later with thousands of your forcibly evicted compatriots, you find yourself dumped in a jungle camp on the California border without hope of finding employment . . . then your social conscience, even if you are ignorant of the term itself, is likely to develop to rare heights. From there to trying to find the root cause of your misfortunes is only a step. Woody had taken the first step in 1930: he began, here and there in his speeches and discussions, to put forward the idea of "Jesus Christ, the first revolutionary." It wasn't a hippy invention. . . .

Nevertheless, this wasn't enough for him and, several years later, he began to interest himself in Marxism and, even more, in unionism. In his efforts to gain the knowledge that he had been deprived of in his youth, he listened to everyone, observed everything, and read every book that happened to come his way, rejecting nobody and nothing. Reading Karl Marx as much as the Bible, Rabelais, Whitman, or the daily newspaper, retaining nothing but those points that were important and useful in his social activities, he appears to us like a pragmatist who owes his freedom more than anything to his defiance of doctrine. His relationship with the American Communist Party, around about the time he was writing for the *Daily Worker,* is due, we think, to his genuine anxiety for the success of a large organization of the masses rather than a strict faith in the doctrine it was based on. The doctrinaires, for their part, objected to this unorthodox attitude, and—we will come to the story of Tom Paxton—the American Communist Party constantly refused to let him have a membership card.

It is for this reason that Woody's protest songs never mention the name of any particular organization or political party to whom he subscribes. If they had, then they would probably by now have been forgotten. The union, for example, he considers as a union of *all* workers, and by extension of all men: this is the meaning behind "Talking Union," "Union Maid," and especially "Good Old Union Feeling," which song mixes unionism with Biblical references.

And so one sees the same combination of spiritual and physical freedom which we have already discussed in connection with the negro spiritual. But here, and this is one of the great talents of Woody Guthrie, this combination is enriched by a sociological awareness that is lacking in the more religiously oriented spirituals.

Similarly, when Woody protested against war, he did so in the name of all men, as in "I've Got to Know (I'd Like to Know)":

> *Why do your war ships float around my waters?*
> *Why do these bombs fall down from the sky?*
> *I'd like to know, boys,*
> *Yes, I'd like to know:*
> *There's hungry lips askin' me*
> *Wherever I go . . .**

When in 1948 an old and semiderelict airplane carrying a "cargo" of Mexican laborers after the end of the harvest season in California crashed in the Los Gatos Canyon, without survivors, Woody heard on the local radio a commentator who, after having described his grief, concluded, "They were just deportees." He incorporated the term into one of his most famous and today most often sung songs, "Deportee," telling the story of the accident from the Mexican point of view:

> *So farewell my Juan, adieu Roselita*
> *Adios mes amigos, Jesus and Maria*
> *You won't have a name when you ride the big airplane*
> *All they will call you will be deportee †*

Woody Guthrie expressed in their name what these people would only ever be able to mutter confusedly. It is in this sense that we can understand what he meant when he described himself as nothing more than a man who told you what you already knew; when he heard the word "suffering," he would draw forth his guitar, if necessary decorated with a flag which showed which side he was on.

All that he owned, he shared. At the bottom of a page in one of his collections, he wrote that the above song was written by Woody Guthrie and legally deposited at Washington, D.C., under copyright number 75623489108663. Anyone discovered singing it without his

---

* "I've Got to Know (I'd Like to Know)," words and music by Woody Guthrie. TRO—Copyright © 1963 by Ludlow Music, Inc., New York, N.Y. Used by permission of The Richmond Organization and Essex Music, Ltd.

† "Deportee (Plane Wreck at Los Gatos)," words by Woody Guthrie, music by Martin Hoffman. TRO—Copyright © 1961, 1963 by Ludlow Music, Inc., New York, N.Y. Used by permission of The Richmond Organization and Essex Music, Ltd.

prior permission would certainly be a good friend of his, because that's what he'd written it for!

One can easily understand, though perhaps with a slight smile, those who believe that "This Land Is Your Land" (a song today known throughout the entire world, and even by people who have never heard of its composer) is a patriotic song. It is in fact no more or less than a revolutionary song, if one understands by revolution the desire to return to a justice and an honesty that have long been lost: this land is your land, this land is my land, this land was made for you *and* for me. Patriotic songs claim the land for those who already possess it. "This Land Is Your Land" shares it with all.

But Woody Guthrie was not content to condemn, denounce, or protest (his great strength over Bob Dylan's "Guthrian" period). He tried to find solutions and often proposed them. In this respect, his prose writings and his social activities are often more explicit than his songs, which fit very badly into any kind of set "program" that one can devise. Guthrie knew this, and didn't try to pretend that he represented various—unnamed—lines of reasoning. If it happened that he affirmed his hope in his songs (as in, say, "There's a Better World A-Comin' "), he showed at the same time his intelligence by careful attention to reality and objectivity. And in a song like "Sharecropper Song," which ends on a note of hope, the final verse is nevertheless a call to political action.

Sharecropping was a system that he detested above all others. He once wrote that, more than tobacco or whiskey, he wanted to be able to see all the families organizing themselves to work on big farms with modern equipment and without the benefit of an owner whose sole desire was to exploit his laborers.

The professional—for want of a better term—activities of Woody Guthrie were evidently determined by his political views. This is why in 1946 he joined the association People's Songs (president, Pete Seeger; vice-president, Lee Hays) in New York, which defined itself as a new union of progressive songwriters. Their aim: to promote traditional music, to write songs or compile anthologies at the request of unions or communities, to help people to a greater knowledge and understanding via their songs, to make albums of an authentic and genuine nature, and if necessary to send musicians to those parts where people wanted songs and someone to teach them.

More generally, and this with the cooperation of Moses Asch, People's Songs, and Union Records (the label that would become Folkways) published and recorded the works of all those artists whose songs, because of their nature and subject, were unlikely ever to be heard on radio, onstage, or through the commercial record companies. The resultant mass of living documents constitutes an irrefutable defense to the kind of criticism aimed frequently at Woody, his friends, and his companions-at-arms.

For Woody, his part in this association provided an opportunity to reaffirm his faith in the power of songs to communicate. Each song, he believed, spoke in music for a people, and by listening to every kind of song from every people in the world, he maintained that peace could be ensured. He felt he knew plenty about Arab villages, the bombed towns of Sicily, the blitzed cities of Britain, the deserts and jungles of North Africa, but that he knew more about the *people* involved through their songs than through all the words that he had heard spoken in their native languages: In other words, that songs promote international understanding because they break through the barriers of language and culture.

For the same reasons that he worked on behalf of People's Songs, he also refused to have any compromise with show biz, professional "suicide." He sold few records, sang for free on innumerable occasions . . . at the same time as most other folksingers were accepting the established system, the same system that offered even Woody magnificent contracts (on condition, of course, that he dressed better, shaved, cut his hair, improved his "peasant" diction, tarted up his songs with pretty harmonies, suppressed certain rather controversial phrases from his lyrics . . . apart from little details like that, he would be artistically totally free, of course).

We have described Guthrie earlier as a songwriter involved with reality, as a protest singer, and he was a singer who carefully avoided the traps set for him by the professional exploiters of music, because he knew that, in the long term, they would be fatal. He commented on this in *Born to Win* (a revealing title):

> And you must not ever fall into the mistake of believing that the big boys can ruin or "hurt" or "wreck" the folk field, because the more outrightly bloody they become, the faster their warriors will desert from their side to our side. Most of their fighters are

not as solidly convinced as you might believe, and the moment it draws to a clear-cut battle in words or votes or with bullets, then is the time when (as in all other revolutions) the rich are sadly and sorely surprised to see their hired ones pack up and come over onto the side that every child knows is the right side.

A little later, a quote that is instructive to read in our times:

When you ask yourself which of the so-called folk singers live up to the real name, you can cross lots of their names entirely off of your list. Other names you could put lower down on your list. Lots of names you've never heard would have to be first and second on your list.

The last recognition of Woody Guthrie during his own life came in 1966. During the Vietnam War, while Woody for several years had already been totally incapacitated by his illness, and by now incapable of speaking or writing, the Secretary of the Interior, Stewart L. Udall, conferred upon him a "Conservation Service Award." The text of the award contains an expression of gratitude for his songs in praise of the dams of Bonneville and Grand Coulee, in token of which the American government inaugurated at the same time a new hydroelectric power station to which they gave his name. The incongruity of this gesture escaped very few. . . .

We have discussed the convictions and the social activities of Guthrie, which are impossible to consider as other than revolutionary, but one must understand that his hope and his faith resided in an ideal much larger and more profound—from which all the rest flowed. In an article entitled "My Secret" he comments that people often came to him asking if he had a secret, or if he believed in a god, because they wanted to hang around him to await the revelation of some piece of universal wisdom. The only "secret" that he had, the only god in whom he believed, was Love, and God was Love. All is love, love is all, and love conquers all. . . . He then gives a long list, richly lyrical, of all the things he feels that love can do, in a style which instantly brings to mind the Biblical influence which Woody himself would probably have gladly admitted, while also perfectly reconciling it with his ideas of the Socialist, unionist struggle (it is probably here that we have one of the reasons why the American

Communist Party refused to let him have a membership card). Throughout all of his songs, political or otherwise, there runs this theme of love in all its forms, notably:

Self-respect, which one finds exemplified in "My Secret":

There is no known article of duddery, wrappery, bandagery nor of clothing which is one thousandth as pretty, as free, as healthy, and as miraculous as the naked skin of even the worst, ugliest, dirtiest, sickest human being on the face of this earth.

And again these words, from *American Folksong:*

I hate a song that makes you think that you're born to lose. I hate a song that makes you think that you're no good for nothing, no good for nobody, because you're too fat or too thin or too ugly or too young or too old or too this or too that. I'm out to fight that kind of songs until my last drop of blood and my last breath of air.

Sex and women: Also in *Born to Win* there is to be found an extraordinary passage on nakedness and the act of physical love:

I love the very sound of the naked word . . . The best and juiciest of our humanly truths are our naked truths . . . Our greatest feelings are those ideas and inventions which we touch in their most naked places. It is always your places that are not clothed which make you feel your best, your gayest, gladdest, and your happiest, healthiest . . . I work with naked hands and speak my naked words.

So, I ask you and tell you, spread your legs apart now and let me put this several inches of new life and lights into your plowed grounds . . . Let me come slowly enough so as not to do you misery. I will be so light and so easy that you will not even know that I am here in you . . . And I will stay here in you and through you and all here about you till your eyes have closed to the sights of both of us and see only yonder prettier lights which light up the plains and hills in the lands of creation. And let me be man enough to stay here in you till your whole spirit is satisfied and your soul comes down to rest again here where I'm holding you.

Love for children: Woody Guthrie's repertoire is rich in children's songs, which are often nothing more than an excuse for a good laugh ("Car, Car," "Clean-O," "Swimmy Swim," "Bubble My Gum"). In "Why Oh Why" he makes a list of the naïve questions by the adults along the lines: "Because . . . because . . . I'll tell you later . . . Don't bother me now!" *

For his daughter Cathy Ann (accidentally killed before she reached the age of ten), he wrote around the years 1945–46 some words of marvelous tenderness. One day when she had come to disturb him at his desk, to tell him kids' stories, he was leaning on his typewriter trying to find the lines of a new song that would "sanctify the human race"; he pretended to listen while continuing to type, half-dismissing her. Cathy Ann (who was then no more than three) went to dance and sing in the next room. The thoughts surged through her father's head:

> And it flew across my mind when I watched the seat of your britches dance into the front room that I would do right well for myself and for the whole human race if I could put down on paper, film, clay, canvas, wax, metal, or on some windier material, the song you sang for me, and the way you sang it.

One detects that there was more than merely an understanding—there was a *complicity* between Woody and children. Because Guthrie, unlike most "grown-ups," dealt with children as with adults. At the age when they hadn't yet been corrupted by the world of adults, he would help children to express the best in themselves, to discover their personality, their creative potentials, to become in the end free and intelligent men and women. To this purpose, he dedicated to them two collections of songs: *Songs to Grow On* (Woody Guthrie's titles are always explicit). And in connection with them, he noted:

> I know of little three-year-old kids all over the country that can do better than most of these politicians. They at least wouldn't stand around and let you starve, or your home get rotten and fall down on your family, or send your kids off to some war seven or eight thousand miles across the dadgum ocean. (*Sing Out!*)

* "Why Oh Why," words and music by Woody Guthrie. TRO—Copyright © 1960, 1963 by Ludlow Music, Inc., New York, N.Y. Used by permission of The Richmond Organization and Essex Music, Ltd.

All Guthrie's work is based on a scorching reality . . .

All those who knew Woody Guthrie concur in describing him as a direct, natural, and temperamental man, totally without politesse. It is logical, then, that in these circumstances his style of writing and singing are based on his style of speaking (see above, his comments on "naked words").

One of the most noticeable of his traits, talking here of his songs, is his great simplicity, musically and lyrically. Some might dismiss this as "simplistic" or even "primitive." It is necessary to be careful of falling into this trap. As Pete Seeger so rightly pointed out, it doesn't matter which idiot is able to express himself complicatedly, it takes a genius to do so simply. A wise comment, especially when one is speaking of a form of artistic expression that by its very nature must speak to and be a part of people who have no access to culture.

Woody Guthrie wrote as he spoke—naturally, spontaneously, and unbelievably prolifically, as much in his choice of vocabulary and imagery as in the way he managed to present his ideas, and even with grammatical faults. His writing is a surging wave, perfect syntax thrown out of the window in the delirious flow, repetitions and imperfections equally tolerated. He probably never even made a first draft to be brushed up later. For this reason, his production was naturally enormous (more than a thousand songs), of which many were discarded within a few days. Some of them probably are better forgotten, though perhaps it is a pity that we can't nowadays look at the "complete works." But nearly all of his songs had the advantage of being able to be rapidly understood, learned, and remembered by everybody.

Two characteristics of the style of Woody Guthrie appear to me to be particularly worth noting: on the one hand, the onrush of words and ideas that one finds most particularly exploited in his written poetry; on the other hand, a corrosive humor which, reappearing throughout all categories of his work, seemed to play the role of a weapon against the prevalent sadness of life. Often the two would be combined:

> I got cattle in the bank and money out West, oil in my hair, gas on my stomach, water on the brain, and now this Hoover guy to worry the life out of me. (*American Folksong*)

I dried my face in the looking glass
put my lipstick on my nose;
I put my hands into my socks
put my feet into my gloves

I squirted my toothpaste on my hair
I stuck my toothbrush in my ear . . .
I chewed my milk and I drank my toast
I drank down half of a big beef roast . . .

("*Bubble My Gum*"*)

And here is how he introduces another song, "Old Army Mule," dedicated to the mascot of the naval division in which he served during the war:

Folks, I'm gonna tell you about the kickingest mule in any man's army. She kicked over nineteen jeeps, eleven good trucks, two navy subs, three liberty ships, seven invasion barges, four bulldozers, five young tractors, one road grader and a few Army and Navy airplanes of all kinds. (*American Folksong*)

And in one of those footnotes to a song of which he was particularly fond, he asks the serious question:

I went to church and they all sung, Stand Up, Stand Up for Jesus. Then I went to the ball game, and they all yelled, For Christ's sake, set down. I'm just scratching my head and wondering what the Lord wants you to do, stand up or set down.

Not without a certain sense of irony, one thinks of William Wordsworth who, in the preface to *Lyrical Ballads,* wrote:

The principal object, then, which I proposed to myself in these Poems was to choose incidents and situations from common life, and to relate or describe them, throughout, as far as was possible, in a selection of languages really used by men . . . and, further, and above all, to make these incidents and situations interesting by tracing in them, truly though not ostentatiously, the primary laws of our nature: chiefly, as far as regards the manner in which we associate ideas in a state of excitement.

* "Bubble My Gum," words and music by Woody Guthrie. Copyright © 1967 by Stormking Music, Inc. All rights reserved. Used by permission.

Without having taken the trouble to write a preface or foreword of any sort, Guthrie has succeeded in that very aim, where Wordsworth—a quick reading of *Lyrical Ballads* will confirm this—failed.

Huddie Ledbetter, known more customarily as Leadbelly (RCA VICTOR)

Joe Hill, songwriter for the Wobblies

Buffy Sainte-Marie,
one of the Indians
most fervent champions
(DIANA DAVIES / INSIGHT)

Patrick Sky, also a spokesman for the Indian cause
(DIANA DAVIES / INSIGHT)

Woody Guthrie as a young man
(COURTESY OF
MRS. WOODY GUTHRIE)

Cisco Houston, a pioneer of
the urban folk movement, was
commemorated in Tom Paxton's
"Fare Thee Well, Cisco."
(FOLKWAYS RECORDS)

Ramblin' Jack Elliott in 1963 (DIANA DAVIES / INSIGHT)

Pete Seeger, singing during the Poor People's Campaign in Washington in 1968. Seeger has perhaps done more for the folk movement than any other man or woman. (DIANA DAVIES / INSIGHT)

Malvina Reynolds. Her songs include "Little Boxes" and "What Have They Done to the Rain?" (DIANA DAVIES / INSIGHT)

Peter, Paul and Mary in action. (DIANA DAVIES / INSIGHT)

Sis Cunningham and Gordon Friesen, editors of *Broadside*,
and in many ways responsible for the folk revival
(DIANA DAVIES / INSIGHT)

Phil Ochs.
He released one of pop
music's most beautiful albums,
Pleasures of the Harbor.
(DIANA DAVIES / INSIGHT)

Bob Dylan in 1965, around the time of his breakout from the role of folksinger into that of rock star (DIANA DAVIES / INSIGHT)

Eric Andersen, composer of,
among other songs, "Thirsty Boots"
(DIANA DAVIES / INSIGHT)

Joan Baez,
a fine interpreter, in
the days when protest and
poetry on the underground
walls were everything
(DIANA DAVIES / INSIGHT)

Judy Collins, another fine interpreter of both traditional and modern folk music (DIANA DAVIES / INSIGHT)

the urban folk revival

The phrase "the urban folk revival" turns up on record liner notes and in articles—it has even appeared in this book. Certain of the critics see in the expression nothing more than the sudden commercial boom in the early sixties for all those types of songs that are loosely and vaguely labeled "folk." However, the movement had been slowly building up since 1940 through a whole series of artists and popularizers (in the best sense of the word) who, principally in cities like New York, Boston, and Chicago, during these years constituted virtually the "underground" of their epoch.

Certainly a character and a creativity like that of Woody Guthrie, as we have just seen, played a colossal role in the preparatory stages of this revival. But there were other links in this chain. Before we consider the principal ones among them, we should consider the real import of the revival. For the word itself doesn't seem full enough to describe adequately the phenomenon; much more than a folk revival it was, in the words of several American folklorists and critics, a folk *arrival*: the coming of folk to the towns, the awakening of the urban populations to the existence of a popular rural culture. Folk had never been dead—so it didn't revive, it abruptly grew.

Symbolically, one could connect the arrival to a road between the rural states of the South and Southwest and the great metropolises of the northern United States. Along this road, the old traditional singers of the South made their ways toward the towns, where they wished to hear and be heard by the young singers who had arrived in the same towns by the same road, though traveling in the opposite direction, to hear and learn the traditional songs that were the very roots of their own inspiration. The popularity and the consequent commercial success of folksingers around 1960 was therefore merely the product of a long process of spontaneous generation.

Yet again we must mention the pioneering role played by such men, unjustly ignored by the majority of the public, as the Lomaxes, father and son, and Moses Asch. With the resurgence of folk music, they repeated the story of Columbus and the egg: certainly, it's easy to do and anyone can do it . . . just as soon as they're shown how. Their merit lay in sensing, then in promoting, those singers and musicians genuinely representative of their national art, on the borders of a dilemma that then as later would prove fatal to the sense of values of their contemporaries: the future will tell us which of Benny Goodman and Leadbelly contributed the more to the musical history of the United States.

We have mentioned already the activities of Woody Guthrie in company with The Almanac Singers, his friends Millard Lampell, Pete Seeger, and Lee Hays. The name of the group gives some indication of their aims, to sing topical songs, to provide a sort of sung chronicle of the United States. That aim implied the maintenance of constant and active relations with the working classes, particularly the unions. Originally the idea did not seem a new one: we have already encountered the same sort of thing with Joe Hill, Aunt Molly Jackson, and Jim Garland. However, those artists wrote, played, and sang under the aegis and in the service of defined organizations, the Wobblies or the NMU.

The innovation of The Almanac Singers was that they put themselves, for free, at the disposal of all sorts of organizations and unions, not just one. They did not affiliate themselves other than temporarily with those who took advantage of their services, and preserved their freedom of movement and of thought by keeping themselves both unfettered and mobile. In the year of their formation, 1940, they were active in the struggles of the unions and the refugee camps.

In the wake of the war, the activities of The Almanac Singers were united with those of People's Songs, rechristened People's Artists in 1948, of whom they were the "stars." For two years they published a magazine, *People's Songs Bulletin,* containing controversial articles, the musical scores of contemporary songs, and news about events in the movement across the land. (Oak Publications recently made available to the public reissues of *People's Songs Bulletin.*)

With the disbandment of The Almanac Singers, there was

founded in 1948 a new folk group which attained a certain fame in the eyes of the mass public: The Weavers. The Weavers were composed of two ex-members of The Almanac Singers, Pete Seeger and Lee Hays, who were joined by Fred Hellerman (songwriter), Ronnie Gilbert (vocals), and toward the end Erik Darling (banjo) who would later found The Rooftop Singers. During the fifteen years of their existence, The Weavers were the first group to prove that it was possible for authentic folk musicians to have an immense commercial success and, still more, one that lasted (two characteristics generally incompatible with show biz), without ever having to compromise or lower the horizons of their musical taste. Their concerts consistently produced record attendances, while nearly all their records appeared among the top ten in the album charts within two weeks of their release (Peter, Paul and Mary were the only other folk group to have repeated this performance). The most memorable recording success of The Weavers, which revealed to the public at large such songs as "Goodnight Irene" (one million copies sold in 1950) or "Roll On, Columbia," was without question *The Weavers at Carnegie Hall*. Around 1959–60, when The Weavers were at the very peak of their popularity, every American student worthy of the name made a point of purchasing this record.

And thus it was that folk music, born of the "inferior" classes, the subculture of America, made its conquest of the middle class. And it was no more than a beginning . . .

After Woody Guthrie, Leadbelly, and Pete Seeger, Cisco Houston is considered as the fourth "father" of modern American folk music. He was born on August 18, 1918, in Wilmington, Delaware, as Gilbert Vandine Houston, the second of four children of a metallurgical worker. During November 1919 the Houston family moved to Eagle Rock in California. Cisco had a brief schooling there and spent his adolescence in various fairly humble jobs.

During the thirties Cisco, a victim of widespread unemployment, decided to become a comedian: he fell in love with the theater and the movies. He obtained secondary roles in a few Hollywood productions. In search of a more decisive success, he traveled to New York in company with his brother. While his brother got a job as a sailor in the merchant marine, Cisco found no better fortune in New York than he had in the West, and he set out alone back to Los

Angeles. There he took part several times in festivals of folk song and popular theater as well as political and union meetings. In California he explored the Coast and the Sierras, often with Woody Guthrie and Will Geer. At the beginning of 1940, when these two friends decided to return to New York, Cisco joined them.

In 1941, while Woody, Cisco, and Jimmy Longhi served in the merchant marine, Cisco's brother, sailor on another ship that was torpedoed, was reported missing.

At the end of the war Cisco returned to New York with Woody. It wasn't until after the Folkways sessions, in which he accompanied Woody and Sonny Terry, that professional engagements at last began to come his way. Suddenly there were tours, concerts, and recordings, and he made his name simultaneously as a comedian and as a musician. All who met him, even if only briefly, discovered the extent to which Cisco Houston had the gift of humanity, of affecting people, interesting them or advising them, but above all *listening* to them. To one young city singer, who one day confessed his desire to quit his studies to go and find adventure as a hobo, guitar on shoulder, Cisco advised: Certainly, visit the country, but begin at the beginning. Don't feel you have to hit the roads just because Woody, Pete, Lee, and myself did. We *had* to. But everyone wants to live better. That's what we're fighting for. Fight for education, for clothing, and leave the railroads alone.

In 1959 the State Department sent a deputation of singers, Cisco at its head, to India. Sonny Terry and Brownie McGhee took part. This was a magnificent success so far as the exchange of musical ideas between the Indians and the Americans, but for Cisco it was the beginning of the end. Stricken by cancer of the stomach, he knew that he didn't have long to live.

He was never so active as at this time. After a visit to his friend Woody in Brooklyn State Hospital, he explained to Lee Hays that Woody was facing adversity with impressive courage. He hoped that, were he in the same situation of having to struggle for years, he could face it as well as Woody. His own terminal illness lasted a matter of weeks, perhaps months, but he felt that what was happening to Woody and himself was nothing more than an error of nature, diseases that would one day be conquered and not to be compared with the true tragedies of life, Hiroshima or the millions of people killed in war.

Nevertheless, by the grace of God or somebody, Cisco participated in July 1960 in the Newport Folk Festival and made several other recordings for Vanguard (in particular a remarkable collection of Woody Guthrie songs). His last public appearance was at a folk concert in Pasadena. He was unable to make the encore the audience was shouting for, and said farewell to his friends: his illness was by this time torturing him. At the home of his sister Mary Ann, in San Bernardino, California, Cisco died on April 25, 1961.

One must admit that Cisco Houston did not particularly shine as a guitarist nor for his gifts as a songwriter, which pale in comparison with those of Woody Guthrie. But he was a fine singer with a deep voice, and an excellent harmonicist and performer. His version of "900 Miles," much appreciated by young American singers, was in a way his "Hard Travelin'." And among other things, his life-style, his attractive personality, and the richness of his repertoire ensured him a place among those great artists whom we have discussed above who brought folk from the fields to the cities.

And for this we must give him our respect, as did Tom Paxton in 1962 by dedicating to him the beautiful "Fare Thee Well, Cisco." The folk family hasn't forgotten him.

Toward the end of his active life, Woody Guthrie had two friends-of-the-road whom we have already mentioned: Derroll Adams and Jack Elliott. Though they first come to the forefront as companions of the author of the Dust Bowl Ballads, both of them came from very different backgrounds.

Derroll Adams, thirteen years younger than Woody, was born to a farming family near Portland, Oregon. He learned from his parents to sing traditional folk songs and to play the banjo. He also played the guitar and the harmonica, but always retained a preference for the five-stringed instrument. Under Woody's influence he was made aware of the tremendous vitality of topical songs: a survivor of the Korean War, it was only natural that he should become himself a songwriter. And so, about this time he wrote "Portland Town," a song that was both autobiographical and a personal protest against the war. When one thinks of the Commie witch-hunt that Joseph McCarthy was running at the time, one realizes Adams' courage in making this sort of protest.

When Woody Guthrie went into the hospital, Derroll Adams decided to seek his fortune in Europe. First time over, he spent several years in England, and one can see him with Bob Dylan in a scene of the film *Don't Look Back,* which Donn Alan Pennebaker made in Britain in the spring of 1965. Derroll Adams, having in the meantime spent awhile in Paris, finally made his home in Belgium.

One can still occasionally hear Derroll Adams performing in Europe; he was at the folk festival at Lambesc, Bouches-du-Rhône, France. His simple style (brilliant banjo playing though with a far from spectacular baritone voice) and his picturesque sense of humor make him one of the best American singers of traditional type that one can still hear.

In contrast to Derroll Adams, Jack Elliott was of East Coast origin—born in Brooklyn—from a fairly well-off family: his father was a doctor. But when he was only sixteen years old Elliott quit the comforts of home and took to the road, becoming a singer. To begin with his repertoire consisted principally of cowboy songs, which he made his specialty. His fortuitous meeting with Woody Guthrie in 1951 was totally to transform—the word is not too strong—his life. Jack Elliott learned Woody's songs so well that for several years he identified with the writer to the extent of singing and speaking with an Oklahoma accent.

Jack Elliott visited Paris, Belgium, Italy, and Great Britain. The English record company Topic a few years ago rereleased the extraordinary recordings (perhaps the best ever made by any artist other than the composer himself) that Jack made in 1956 of ten Woody Guthrie songs.

Before leaving Jack Elliott, there is an interesting story to tell. In January 1968 there was organized for Carnegie Hall in New York an exceptional concert in memory of Woody Guthrie, with an impressive lineup: Bob Dylan, Arlo Guthrie, Richie Havens, Tom Paxton, Pete Seeger, Judy Collins . . . Jack Elliott, who had returned to the United States after his European adventures, was not invited to take part in the concert: not famous enough. So he threatened the organizer that, if he weren't allowed to play at the concert proper, he would instead bring his guitar and sing to the lines waiting outside Carnegie Hall. The organizer eventually gave in, as justice should anyway have dictated, and the audience was lucky enough to see and hear Jack Elliott sing his homage to Woody Guthrie, one of the most important of the evening though perhaps one of the least noticed. And so it goes. . . .

Among the numerous American publications dealing with music and song, there is one that has played a preponderant role (almost unknown to the general public) in the development of the folk movement and the "revival": it is the magazine *Sing Out!*

Born in the balmy days of 1950 and fathered by several musicians and amateurs of folklore, *Sing Out!* (subtitled *The Folksong Magazine*) was from the start dedicated to the task of placing before the public America's own folklore. One must remember that this was a time when no one but a few specialists like Charles Seeger, Alan Lomax, and Moses Asch was in the slightest interested in folklore. The *People's Song Bulletin* had ceased to appear, so it was left to *Sing Out!* on the one hand to pick up the torch that had fallen, on the other to make the fusion between city and country, between tradition, the collective heritage, and the creation of new songs . . . all of which had simultaneous imperative claims to attention. From the earliest numbers of *Sing Out!* one finds within the pages complete scores of songs both old and new (filling about a third of the magazine); articles on musicians, their vocal and instrumental styles, their homes, their ideas—in short, all the factors that might form or be formed by their mode of musical expression; technical pages that might, for example, give instructions as to how to play a certain piece on the guitar or banjo; news from clubs across the land, an important contribution to the cohesion of the movement and the preservation of the "folk family" feeling that has always existed; reviews of books and records connected either directly or indirectly with the folk movement and the people who form it; and finally readers' letters, whose importance is in general relevant only to the actual time of their writing. Later the magazine developed the interesting tendency to consider foreign artists, such as Jacques Brel, Aristide Bruant, or the Quebec *chansonniers.*

During the twenty-five years of its existence *Sing Out!* has known its ups and downs and survived crises which on occasions have even threatened to destroy it. One must understand the fighting spirit that has always played a large part in the folk movement: consequently the magazine fares badly in terms of the commercialism of the general press, and under the pressures of censure from all directions. From the earliest times, perhaps because of its fighting spirit, *Sing Out!* has been able to attract famous contributors such as Woody Guthrie, Pete Seeger, Israel Young (proprietor of New York's Folklore Center), and Irwin Silber (who was editor in chief). Unfortunately, however, *Sing Out!* devoted as it is entirely to folk music and its devotees, has never been financially or technically able to be distributed properly throughout the vastness of the United States; in its best periods its sales have been around ten thousand copies. Maintaining throughout all difficulties its political ideal of progressive humanism, notably during the Korean and Vietnam wars, apparently hasn't ameliorated its plight; even today, its situation is precarious.

The publication of *Sing Out!* is made possible solely by subscriptions and donations. An attempt in 1968 at commercial distribution to bookstores and newstands failed. The magazine (which to this day has retained its original design, format, number of pages, quality of paper, and so forth, though able to be produced only six times a year) was saved from bankruptcy, fortunately, by a series of benefit concerts organized by clubs across the land who sent their profits to the ailing magazine in New York.

As the same writers and friends contribute articles and news regularly to *Sing Out!,* naturally always for free, about folk events in their various regions, one could say without exaggeration that the magazine appears to be the collective property—just as is the music about which they write—of these writers, who are militants of their type, and that the magazine is at the same time an ancestor and a model of the underground press that has appeared among American youth.

We have already spoken of the "living involvement" of folklore: one couldn't think of a better example of this than *Sing Out!* Speaking the truth and making an affirmation of life in a hypocritical and crime-oriented society has made it, though often at its own great expense, a breath of fresh air in the often cloying atmosphere of the commercial American press; its survival is a miracle, as its thousands of friends know perfectly well while they defend it with the utmost tenacity.

Among the folksingers active before 1940 and still active to this very day the name of Pete Seeger occupies pride of place. After Woody

Guthrie, Cisco Houston, and Leadbelly (who died, respectively, in 1967, 1961, and 1949), there is no reason to disagree with the view of Pete Seeger as one of the four spiritual fathers of modern folk music. However, there is one important difference between him and his three friends: if Woody, Cisco, and Leadbelly were authentic proletarians, come almost by accident to urban life, Pete Seeger was by contrast a city boy from the start, born in the middle classes and later converted (through idealism, certainly) to the cause of folklore.

He was born in New York in 1919. We have already mentioned his father, Charles Seeger, toward the beginning of this book. His mother was a violin teacher. Music, whether it was folk or classical, played an integral part in the daily life of the Seeger family. At school Pete learned to play contemporary tunes on the banjo and ukelele. But it wasn't until 1935, when his father took him to a traditional folk festival in Asheville, North Carolina, that he conceived a genuine love for this sort of music. That passion has never left him.

With the aim of rapidly acquiring a repertoire that was both rich and authentic, Pete Seeger went to the Library of Congress in Washington, where Alan Lomax helped him considerably in his researches. There followed for him an extremely prolific recording career in the two directions that he has always considered complementary: on the one hand traditional songs (of which the four-volume Folkways *American Favorite Ballads* is a good anthology), on the other, contemporary songs.

Pete Seeger did not sidestep social involvement. Around 1940, when he made the acquaintance in New York of Woody Guthrie, he founded with him The Almanac Singers. It was also with Woody that he popularized around this time the practice of having hootenannies. These collective improvised concerts (the idea is of Scottish origin) were to become the basis for the modern folk performance, where everyone present is able to express himself musically if he so wishes. We've already spoken of the involvement of Seeger after his discharge from the Army in People's Songs (People's Artists), as well as of the part he played in The Weavers. Since the foundation of *Sing Out!* in 1950 he has been involved with the magazine in an editorial capacity; in fact, he still writes a regular column for the magazine, symbolically entitled "Johnny Appleseed Jnr.," in which he describes his reflections on contemporary music and social conditions.

He has sometimes been reproached for a sort of Boy Scouts of America character in his concerts and recordings, a criticism of his apparent naïveté. Against that, there are several points to consider:

Above all, the sincerity of Pete Seeger has never been in doubt. His way of life testifies to it—for example, he lives (in Beacon, near New York City, on the banks of the Hudson) in a wooden house that he made with his own hands. Since 1967 (well before the theme had become popular in newspaper and political circles) he has devoted a large part of his leisure time and his income to a campaign publicizing the struggle against the pollution of the Hudson River. To this end, he has a boat aboard which, in the company of folksingers such as Arlo Guthrie, Jack Elliott, and Michael Cooney, he has on many occasions made journeys down the river, stopping at each riverside community to spread the word and collect funds from the inhabitants. One of the finest of his own songs, "My Dirty Stream," is devoted to the Hudson problem.

It must be admitted that he is not a great songwriter. But he has played an indispensable role as popularizer, where the word is used as a compliment. It is he who has most encouraged younger talents since 1960. In one interview Joan Baez said that she and all the rest owed their careers to Pete; Bob Dylan, never a man for compliments, has been heard to speak of the "saintliness" of Peter Seeger. One could hardly count the number of demonstrations and marches in which he has freely participated: the march of the blacks in Washington in 1963, the colossal march to the White House to protest against the Vietnam War at the end of 1969, and so forth. At the beginning of 1970, again in Washington, he led a quarter of a million demonstrators in song, particularly in John Lennon's "Give Peace a Chance," perhaps an unusual choice for a folksinger but, as Tom Paxton pointed out, Seeger has always chosen songs that fit the occasion. And, of course, Paxton is in a prime position to make this point, since Seeger was one of the first performers of Paxton's songs, a service that he had rendered to the majority of important modern songwriters.

The activities and attitudes of Seeger are rooted in an unshakable belief in the power of song and its efficacy to communicate what matters, if it is used intelligently; he has no equal in the ability to rouse an audience to sing together. It is above all to this talent that he owes his popularity and his success, notably during his foreign tours in such differing countries as Kenya, Japan, and the USSR. In order to communicate better with his audience, he makes it a point of honor to learn at least one song of the country in which he is performing.

The role of Pete Seeger in the development of American song is not only as a folklorist and humanitarian. Part of his income is contributed to the struggle for integration in the United States; to the integrationist organizations he has passed *all* the copyrights in his performances and records of songs such as "We Shall Overcome" (probably his greatest commercial success); he refused to copyright the book *How to Play the Five-String Banjo* on the principle that the banjo is a tradition and belongs to nobody—more than the simple integrity of the artist, these gestures show that he has a genuine political commitment. Capable in all circumstances of finding in his professional life and attitudes coherent solutions that are perfectly in accord with the spirit of his music, he is a man who, even from those who for reasons of individual taste are unable to appreciate him as a musician, deserves and receives respect.

In the same way as Pete Seeger, and before the period of the commercialization of folk music that we will shortly be discussing, two women played an important part, though one that is generally forgotten, in the service of the movement: Malvina Reynolds, white songwriter, and Odetta, finest of the black interpreters.

One of the first "contemporary folk" songwriters engendered by the postwar revival—and here is one of the most stunning paradoxes of the United States—wasn't a young man clad in blue jeans but a gray-haired woman, today a septuagenarian, called Malvina Reynolds. It is very natural that she should come to mind here, for Pete Seeger was an admirer of her work from the earliest stages, and also a friend and a faithful interpreter of her songs.

Her spontaneity has become proverbial, as can be seen by the following anecdote. One day she was driving with her husband in their Chevrolet along an avenue in a Los Angeles suburb, and as she drove she looked pensively at the rows of houses, all identical. Suddenly she braked, parked the car at the side of the road, and told her husband to take the wheel. He did so and, as he drove, Malvina wrote "Little Boxes," a satire of the modern construction that produces identical little boxes in which live identical little people. It was to become one of her most famous songs.

Sensitive to the original beauty of nature threatened by the "progress" of twentieth-century civilization, Malvina Reynolds has written a number of very successful songs on the theme, such as "God Bless the Grass," "From Way Up Here," and of course the world-famous "What Have They Done to the Rain?"

As with many others of her songs, "Little Boxes," "From Way Up Here," and "What Have They Done to the Rain?" have been popularized by Pete Seeger, who has often held long telephone conversations with her between New York and California in order to perfect new songs. For her part, Malvina Reynolds has herself made many recordings of her songs, though the fact that these are released by the very small firm of Broadside means that she has not achieved the sort of fame that she deserves.

The career of Odetta, though almost equally far beyond the limelight, has been very different. Born to a black family in Birmingham, Alabama, Odetta Holmes Felious has passed the majority of her life in California. In her youth, as she herself recalls, she did not have the slightest interest in folk music: only *lieder* and certain forms of classical music appealed to her.

However, repeated meetings and ensuing friendships with folksingers and folklorists changed her ways as she discovered that the songs of the American people constituted a remarkably diverse and interesting field, and that her contralto voice (genuinely exceptional as anyone who has ever heard her sing, even if only once, will testify) could be admirably adapted to such a repertoire. And, for a black artist who discovered within herself a latent passion for Marion Anderson and Bessie Smith, what more natural than to turn to the blues?

Odetta therefore began, toward the end of the fifties, to appear more and more often on the programs of various folk clubs wellknown throughout the land, such as the hungry-i and the Tin Angel in San Francisco and, a little later, the old Gate of Horn in Chicago. The latter, unfortunately ruined during 1961–62 by a regrettable "modernization," gave the title to one of her finest albums, *Odetta at the Gate of Horn,* on the Tradition label. Following this, Odetta was to have a prolific recording career, successively with Vanguard, RCA Victor, and Verve-Forecast.

She has sung at numerous folk and pop festivals, especially at Newport, Philadelphia, and Berkeley, as well as at an open-air concert in London's Hyde Park in September 1970. And then there was the concert in New York in early 1968 where Odetta and Harry Belafonte sang together with dozens of children.

She is extremely eclectic: because of her vocal power, her incredible emotionalism, and her excellent guitar playing, she excels as much in the blues as in English ballads or the songs of Bob Dylan, to whom she devoted an entire album in 1965. By her modest attitude and above all her effectiveness in the musical and social folk movement in America, she is an example that most other folksingers would do well to emulate.

The formidable eruption, perhaps one could even say explosion, of soloists and groups in English and American pop during 1965–66 brought into current usage the idea of the birth of the "white blues." [1] One could be forgiven for imagining that those artists regarded as principally bluesmen—Canned Heat, Mike Bloomfield, and Johnny Winter in the United States; Eric Burdon, Eric Clapton and John Mayall in Great Britain—were the first whites to perform this music professionally. In fact—and this doesn't in any way reflect upon their merits—they were preceded in the genre by a good number of other instrumentalists and singers, a few of whose names will be found in the ensuing discussion.

In 1963 Barry Hansen, critic of the very specialized *Little Sandy Review,* pointed out in an article that from that date on it seemed inevitable that the majority of blues that one would hear would be sung by whites. Over the previous years it seemed that the young blacks had totally lost interest in this "outmoded" musical form. No young blues player of any importance had appeared during the previous decade, and, as the old blues players were dying out one by one, it looked as if black blues were in a precarious situation. Nowadays the majority of the blues public was whites and, sooner or later, they would constitute the greater part of the performers—just as had already happened with Dixieland music.

Fifteen years later, even though Hansen's prediction hasn't been

---

[1] On one of their albums, the Bonzo Dog Doo Dah Band includes a song entitled, "Can Blue Men Sing the Whites?"

entirely realized (many great black bluesmen have disappeared, but at the same time there has been the emergence of Taj Mahal, among others), it must be recognized that the great majority of new blues is of white origin. The white artists who were responsible for this situation were still very much integrated into the urban folk music scene (represented essentially by Greenwich Village) in 1963. Among them, and right from the beginning, were "Spider" John Koerner, Dave "Snaker" Ray, and Tony "Little Sun" Glover who, clad in their picturesque nicknames, formed the remarkable trio of Koerner, Ray & Glover.

Another person important to the origin of the white blues was Eric von Schmidt, who has always incorporated, as much onstage as in his records, equal doses of genuine feeling and an admirable sense of humor. This sensitive musician, who was living in Cambridge, Massachusetts, at the time (the end of 1961) that Bob Dylan recorded one of his songs, "Baby Let Me Follow You Down" as a token of friendship, has since moved with his family to Florida.

Never put off by the pop revolution, he has continued to record and present onstage what seems good to him. The idiom of the blues comes naturally to him, and he has done much to popularize several white musicians, all of whom work in the genre. This last point is important, and we will come back to it later.

In New York there were to be found many other white bluesmen. It's only necessary to think of the activities of Bob Dylan in this field alone. In the early days he gave evidence of a fantastic talent, both as vocalist and instrumentalist, for the interpretation of a traditional black repertoire. His first album is still a precious document in this respect; many of his personal recordings, made available through the famous bootleg albums, even more so. Moreover, Dylan has accompanied numerous other blues artists, sometimes using a pseudonym such as "Bob Landy" to avoid contractual complications. (He is currently out of contract, and uses his own name.)

But the most popular of the white blues artists in those early days was unquestionably Dave Van Ronk, who adorned many fine evenings in the Greenwich Village cafés. A very fine guitarist, Van Ronk, whose greatest success was and still is "Cocaine Blues," is especially memorable for the timbre of his voice, which is hoarse and anguished. After trying his hand in groups like the Hudson Dusters, he seems to have nowadays returned to the solo playing that suits him best.

One must also accord particular mention to Paul Butterfield, who was born in Chicago in 1941. Remaining there, Butterfield frequented throughout his youth the blues clubs that then proliferated. In the circle of masters like T-Bone Walker, B. B. King, and Buddy Guy, whom one could hear at any time in the Chicago clubs, Paul Butterfield had one of the best blues schoolings possible. When he had acquired sufficient techniques and experience, he quite naturally formed his own group, the Paul Butterfield Blues Band, with notably Mark Naftalin and Mike Bloomfield. Butterfield is almost unquestionably the finest white harmonicist in the world, and many credit him with having founded the first American heavy rock band. Without later being able to recapture the remarkable inspiration of their earlier days (particularly after the departure of Bloomfield), as on the album *East-West,* the group nevertheless crystallized an idea that was soon to have many imitators.

In mainstream pop, numerous white soloists have shown themselves capable of singing with the same amount and type of feeling as the black musicians, though the structure of the songs themselves (rock or ballad, for example) may be very different from the blues. If the facts of life change, then music should reflect those changes and our criteria of appreciation should follow suit—only logical. Therefore these "whites with black voices" may give us the impression of the blues for various reasons but rarely because the song itself is constructed in the traditional twelve-bar way. This is perhaps because they are born of races that have been oppressed in the same way as the blacks (Indians: Buffy Sainte-Marie; or Puerto Rican: José Feliciano); others have intelligently modeled themselves on a black original (Skip James for Al Wilson, the lamented singer of Canned Heat, or in one sense Bessie Smith for the equally lamented Janis Joplin). Still others have successfully imitated (a process quite different from plagiarism) the black bluesmen through having led during their youth an adventurous or miserable life just like their black models (this seems to be true for Bob Dylan—though see Anthony Scaduto's biography of him—and is certainly true for Johnny Winter), and/or through their admirably suited vocal mastery (like Stevie Winwood and, to a lesser extent, Joe Cocker). The comparison of the voice of a white like Cocker with that of a black like Richie Havens, in, for example, "With a Little Help from My Friends"—after all, however you look at it, the Beatles song is in no way a blues—is well worth making.

The increasing success from about 1965 on of popular music derived more or less directly from the blues, but being played by white artists for a predominantly white public, often ignorant of the origins of the music it was listening to, poses moral, social, and political problems. One can consider the number of blues by black writers that have been rediscovered or arranged more or less successfully by white groups; also the immense popularity of these groups, the considerable wealth earned through their concerts, and the appearance of their records on the hit parade. To cite one famous example among many, the Rolling Stones, who owe much to Buddy Guy and Junior Wells, invited them as token of a rather late and suspect recognition to share the bill with them during a recent tour of the Continent. This debt of white pop to black blues, the general public (and it seems that the notion of the "general public" exists also in the pop music world) has never had enough information at its disposal to understand fully. Several white musicians, and perhaps still more their employers, have more than once omitted to make the most elementary acknowledgment to their black inspirers (even though there are happy exceptions like Cream). One needs no more proof than the absence, or at least the distinct rarity, of black bluesmen invited to appear in the programs of pop concerts and festivals.[2] That this particularly subliminal form of segregation, even though it be no more than embryonic, should still exist in the circles that overtly claim to fight all forms of segregation is an offensive contradiction and one that must be vigorously denounced and opposed.

The American folk vogue of the 1960s was naturally marked by the foundation of many large festivals devoted to folk music and all the forms derived from it. These were the ancestors of the pop festivals that would follow. The most famous of these was the Newport Folk Festival.

Inaugurated in 1959, the Newport Folk Festival knew vicissitudes and went through crises. Organized and presented, as was its jazz sister, by George Wein, it was from 1963 distinguished particularly

[2] More recently, in Britain at least, this trend is beginning to be reversed.

by its noncommercial operation. The first two festivals, in 1959 and 1960, were considerable financial successes with a net (after taxes and deductions) of $180,000 for the two years together. The first task for the Newport Folk Foundation—an administrative body that directed the festival and the activities that flowed from it—was to re-invest these considerable sums in projects that would be profitable to folk music in general.

In 1959, the first Newport Folk Festival had given birth to the talent of Joan Baez, that of 1960 had seen one of the last perfor-mances of Cisco Houston. After a gap of two years, in 1963 George Wein took up the challenge with new ideas, starting with the assis-tance of the active members of the foundation, notably Pete Seeger and Theodore Bikel, soon to be joined by Peter Yarrow and Judy Collins.

In an interview with Peter Lyon in *The American Folk Scene,* George Wein explained how the project took form in Seeger's home during 1962. There had been plenty of mistakes made in the 1959 and 1960 festivals, and Wein had several ideas as to how to correct them for the future. So he got in touch with Pete Seeger, who not only knew every folksinger but was also respected by all of them.

He decided, with general consent, that the festival should be ad-ministered by the artists themselves, and that each should work for a union minimum—about a hundred dollars per set—rather than for his or her usual fee. The substantial profits would be invested, as we have said above, in projects profitable to the promotion of folk music. These included the purchase, preservation, and preparation of recording equipment for collectors and ethnomusicologists, assis-tance for the publication of collections of songs, financial aid to the organization of many regional festivals that were unable to attract stars, and the setting in motion, during the off season, of concerts in cities like Philadelphia, Boston, and New York.

The formula of the Newport Folk Festival always oscillated be-tween two sorts of presentation, incompatible in the eyes of the carp-ers, complementary to the more optimistic. One type is in the form of workshops that were held during the afternoon around twenty or so little stages scattered across the field. These specialized workshops were created with the aim of presenting to the public all the forms, all the divergent styles, of folk songs and music: bluegrass, rural blues, electric blues, music of the Indian tribes, songs by contemporary writers, Louisiana Cajun music, harmonica playing, Autoharp playing, dulcimer playing, songs of the sea and of sailors, Appalachian ballads, political songs . . . and so on for a considerable list. For the folk purist the workshops, each limited to an audience of about a hundred, were a dream come true: these alone could permit a natural contact, in a genuine and informal atmosphere, between audience and artists. These latter wouldn't hesitate to improvise special requests on demand. And in a couple of days spent circulating the workshops, the amateur could discover and better understand the folk music of the United States, in a sort of living panorama, than he could ever do through even the best collections of songs.

The other sort of presentations was the evening concerts on the big stage equipped with powerful sound system and spotlights, before an audience of perhaps twenty or thirty thousand. These are the concerts that one reads about in the press or on the covers of records, the recitals that were discoveries (Arlo Guthrie or Leonard Cohen in 1967), confirmations of power (Johnny Cash in 1969), or catastrophes (Bob Dylan in 1965).

The combination within the single festival of the workshops with the big concerts is characteristic of the two orientations of the folk revival in America, though at the same time symptomatic of the dilemma that faces folklore in the industrialized society: should one try to safeguard a certain purity, faithfulness to tradition (in spirit at least, if not in the letter), permitting the participation of all in a collective creation, but thereby condemning folk to minority interest only, however active or progressive it becomes; or should one, in contrast, sacrifice quality to quantity, presenting music on a grand scale and giving it a national appeal with the aid of press and publicity, though simultaneously the inevitable onslaught of the star syndrome and the infiltration of a show-biz mentality? To what extent is there a middle course?

George Wein and his colleagues never pretended to have discovered a *single* universally satisfactory solution to this problem. The result was the discontinuing of the festival in 1970 because they felt the need to debate a new presentation, to redefine the orientation of a festival that they felt no longer corresponded to the realities of the folk or the lore of contemporary America.

Perhaps it will take the realism of a George Wein combined with the humble authority of a Pete Seeger to assist the organizers of those colossal pop festivals that have more recently been the butt of the international press, before they either stagnate in the impasse they have reached or drown in an excess of ambition.[3]

Although the folk music specialists and lovers have conscientiously ensured and proved that their favorite music hasn't suffered, but has rather profited from its revival and arrival in the cities, the record and concert industries naturally didn't take long to perceive the promise of a new and ample source of income. As in so many other cases, the great power of the Establishment engendered parallel interests in the public and singers in "folk song" (the quotes are deliberate) with the sole aim of exploiting the market that had opened up. Unfortunately, not everyone has the integrity of The Weavers; it is impossible always to make it into the top ten without compromising one's music and, in the case of folk, without losing sight of the primary definition of music *for* and *of* the people.

From about 1957 on there was a veritable orgy, totally anarchic, of groups who, protected by the benevolent label of "folk," invaded the concert halls, universities, and jukeboxes. Day-old groups, generally second-rate, whose principal accomplishment was the rapidity of their success (and subsequent demise), sprang up like mushrooms. Their promising names—The Tarriers, The Ramblers Three, The Folkswingers, The Limeliters, and other varieties of "Roving Gamblers"—were unable to hide the amazing paucity of their inspiration and ability, and their sole aim (though never admitted) of becoming rich and famous.

So one understands better that, a little later, the arrival of a Bob Dylan or a Joan Baez in the middle of such an ocean of clichés was heralded as a virtual Second Coming. The majority of these routine folksingers are fortunately no longer with us. The Kingston Trio, founded in 1957, whose hour of "glory" was achieved with their record of "Tom Dooley" which had the unbelievable sale of 2,600,000, were one of the early arrivals. They were followed in

[3] Before leaving the Newport Folk Festival entirely, it's worth noting that a young American moviemaker, Murray Lerner, devoted to it a long film entitled simply *Festival*. This film, which was much appreciated by the international critics during its presentation at the Venice Festival in September 1967, is a montage of extracts from the Newport Festivals of 1963, 1965, and 1966. One can see, among others, Bob Dylan and Donovan and Joan Baez and Peter, Paul and Mary and . . .

their turn by the New Christy Minstrels, a ten-strong troupe (that to their credit included two blacks) that was adequately refined to ensure that no trace of freshness or originality remained: their theme song, entitled "Green, Green," more recently recorded by Trini Lopez, had a dramatic life-span of some months.

One could fill several pages with examples of others. But it's more interesting to talk instead of another group who, though very much in the commercial vein, nevertheless left behind them something of value: The Brothers Four. Students at the University of Washington, Bob Flick, Dick Foley, Mike Kirkland, and John Paine formed in their spare time a group, as did many others of their young American contemporaries. "Having fun with a song" was their aim: modest, doubtless, but in no way reprehensible. The big problem was that they met up with Mort Lewis, Dave Brubeck's manager, who went wild about The Brothers Four. There followed a record contract with the all-powerful Columbia, and a few months later (in the summer of 1959) their first "smash" (not a word that turns up very often in a book about folk music): "Greenfields." Translated into God knows how many languages, it was recorded in as many countries by diverse types. This pretty tune for months dominated the lips of millions of people who never heard the original version.

Certainly the music of The Brothers Four didn't owe much to authentic folk, and much more to the new sort of folk–show biz. One must nevertheless acknowledge the several musical qualities that their successors so painfully lacked: in particular, Mike Kirkland's banjo playing and the bass voice of Dick Foley contributed toward the original sound of The Brothers Four, a sound that, it must be admitted, was pleasant to hear. And, on occasion, they did not hesitate to interpret certain important contemporary songs, such as Ewan MacColl and Peggy Seeger's "Spring Hill Mine Disaster" or Bob Dylan's "Long Ago, Far Away." And finally, in a time when Peter, Paul and Mary were as yet unknown, and when The Weavers had disbanded, The Brothers Four performed the service of picking up the torch of folk music and letting its light be seen by millions who, without them, might never have had the idea, nor perhaps the courage, to listen directly to the music of Leadbelly, Woody Guthrie, or Pete Seeger. A large number of people, initially attracted to but eventually bored by the records of The Brothers Four, had the curiosity to go back to its sources, where they had the joy of finding at last something that perhaps came closer to the truth. . . .

It's an ill wind that blows nobody any good: the eruption of commercial folk groups gave birth to the excellent trio of Peter, Paul and Mary. University products, personal friends of Bob Dylan, and all three of city origin, Peter Yarrow, Paul Stookey, and Mary Travers had the good fortune to arrive at exactly the right moment, and benefited from the principle of natural selection whereby the more mediocre eliminate themselves and only the best show themselves capable of surviving.

Unquestionably, Peter, Paul and Mary were the best interpreters of this kind of song. Their first record (released in the United States at the beginning of 1962) already reflected the perfect vocal cohesion of the three, which has been described as "the two cellos and the voice of an angel." Also obvious since the time of their first recording was the influence on them of a repertoire that is unquestionably traditional, though modernized by the use that they made of it. One thinks of the epoch of "Where Have All the Flowers Gone?" and "If I Had a Hammer," put in circulation by the efforts of Pete Seeger (once again we note his definitive role), following whose example the young trio contributed toward introducing the songs to the large protest and political-justice movements. One has no need here to emphasize the participation of Peter, Paul and Mary in the 1963 March on Washington or the presence of Peter and Mary (we are not concerned with the reasons for Paul's absence) in the street demonstrations of the Yippies in Chicago in August 1968. During their visit to Paris in June 1970, they confessed to one of our colleagues their difficulty in retaining contact with the "Woodstock generation."

Peter, Paul and Mary's desire for contemporary relevance has been certain since 1963 when, in their third album, they recorded two of Dylan's earliest songs: "Don't Think Twice," and notably "Blowin' in the Wind," the song that gave them a national audience and which, through its appearance in the hit parades (though its effect was beyond that), revealed the nascent talent of Bob Dylan.

Certainly Peter, Paul and Mary could never be thought of as a part of the avant-garde; nevertheless, they have in their way contributed toward the progress and coming-of-age of topical pop music. And this is perhaps not the least of the paradoxes that have come to them while they yet remain faithful to the musical formula to which they initially adhered: three rich and mellow voices, two acoustic guitars, and the double bass of Dick Kniss. All the same, on certain of their later albums (particularly since *Album 1700* released in the fall of 1967), they have made obeisances toward contemporary music by adopting from time to time one or two modern instruments: here an organ ("Weep for Jamie"), there an electric bass or drums ("I Dig Rock and Roll Music," "Rolling Home").

Their stage act hardly varied after the time of "Blowin' in the Wind": harmony combined with humor, spontaneity, and vocal and instrumental beauty. Each plays a determining role: Mary, with the voice of an enchantress, alternates dramatic tension with mischievousness; Paul, the comedian, the ruthless mimic and sound effects specialist, who nevertheless can retain all solemnity when the occasion demands; and finally Peter, the spirit of the group, by turns producer, chief jester, and, during foreign performances, interpreter. The group, stamped as it was with a genuine freshness, never gave the impression of tiring of its polished formula, for, as all their friends say, Peter, Paul and Mary never were satisfied with second best; in their perpetual search for improvements, after each concert, they adopted the habit of going over point by point every detail that could still further be perfected. With a remarkable sensibility, they knew how to work with all seriousness yet without giving an impression of taking themselves too seriously.

Peter, Paul and Mary did not run the risk of becoming old-fashioned, even obsolete, for the formula and the spirit to which they remained faithful are not the product of the preoccupations of fashion. Among other things, their dedication to stability (as proof the fact that they remained under contract to the same recording company from their beginnings) steered them clear of the troubles that have been the lot of practically every other commercial folk group. If one day they announce that they have split up, that will only have been the result of a well-thought-out decision.[4]

[4] It's worth noting as a footnote that one of the nicest albums of 1972, when the group did disband, was Paul Stookey's *Paul and . . .*. On it he interprets not only his own songs and those he has cowritten, but also Woody Guthrie's "Gabriel's Mother's Hiway." —P.B.

At the time of which we are writing, American folk music was going through a commercial phase which, in "syruping" it, in lowering it to the detestable ranks of "hits," and in regarding it with the same scorn and casualness as the rest of show biz, put the whole of folk music at peril. It appears that—and we do not know if it is due merely to chance—the death of *spurious* folk music, around 1965–66, was a parallel phenomenon with the birth of modern pop music, which to a great extent supplanted it. This also has come through a period where it has suffered the attacks of big business and the popularization forced on it by the masters of commercial music, ill-directed because it is extremely fast-moving and all the time detrimental to the innovatory character of the music and the ideas behind it. It is today still far too soon to say if present-day pop music will be improved, destroyed, or remain simply indifferent to these tentative signs of revival. But perhaps the recordings made prior to this era of modern pop, during the era of the folk revival, will help it to decide upon its future.

What were, for folk music and even more for its public, the symptoms and the consequences of the commercial gallop that came about for a decade or so? They can be seen through the taking over of both the practice and the word, "hootenanny."

The hootenanny came to prominence during the politico-unionist movement of the 1930s, and little by little was imported into cities like New York after 1945. This was helped along by Woody Guthrie, Pete Seeger, and the people of *Sing Out!* The hootenannies, with their "Communist" connotation, were around the beginning of the 1950s the object of the attacks of McCarthyism, and their artists and audience were put on the blacklists.

In April 1963, however, at the height of the commercial fashion for folk music, one of the biggest American TV companies, ABC, created a weekly program, claiming to be folk music, and entitled "Hootenanny." This program, destined for the consumption of millions of viewers, had little in common with the free-participation collective sessions that had been the origin of the word "hootenanny." On the contrary, ABC's broadcast opened the doors of success to phony musicians who were prepared to disinfect their music, make it "polite," and eliminate from it anything that might trouble the middle-class American conscience. In a word, "Hootenanny" was the king of bad taste, conformity, and "apolitics." One learns—not without surprise—that a singer like Pete Seeger was refused the right to take part in the program on the incredible pretext that he would not draw the public! As a mark of protest and in solidarity with Seeger, other singers who had no difficulty in getting invitations to perform boycotted the program. Even The Kingston Trio joined this action.

Parallel with the "success" of this ABC series, the season 1963–64 saw the release of nearly one hundred albums entitled *Hootenanny with . . . ,* which revealed the "art" of the commercial groups whose albums they were.

At the end of 1964, while announcing the end of the hootenanny programs on the ABC chain, Irwin Silber, in *Sing Out!,* described it as the end of an era in which there was a fundamental contradiction:

> In the year of its success, folk became the sesame word that opened bank accounts to the strum of a banjo. Folk became the panacea of our age, making us all feel young, virile and regular again. The irony, of course, is that success and folk music are, by rights, at opposite extremes of the American spectrum. Folk music, after all, is the voice and expression of generations of ordinary folk who were on familiar terms with hard work, poverty, hunger, and homemade culture. They kept their art alive outside the pale of professional show-business and despite the impact of successive Establishments. Success, on the other hand, is the "American dream", the middle-class confusion of illusion and reality, the pot of gold at the end of the rainbow clutched tightly in the hands of the beautiful blonde with the torrid torso and the hint of nymph.

Irwin Silber's analysis does not least reflect the paradox of a situation that had been realized, not without disquiet though with differing reactions, by the thousands of sincere disciples of folk music. For this music, at its best, does not only represent a form of artistic expression valuable in itself: if this were all, it would tend to become a sort of "pure" art with all the dangers inherent in that. On the contrary, from every angle—its creations, its performance, its being listened to, and its being commented upon—it demands in its internal logic a global vision of the human condition, a way of evoking its own epoch, a way of life. For Israel Young, not only the proprietor of Greenwich Village's Folklore Center but one of the builders of the folk revival in the urban scene, folk music represents a sort of popular life ideal which is no longer feasible in America. This means that the combination of authentic folk music and commercial music is an impossible one, in the same way that Marxism and mysticism are mutually exclusive.

The declaratory allure and the political and social engagement of numerous folksingers, famous or obscure, represents nothing more than the demands of fashion or a desire on their part to appear to be in the forefront of things; it must be realized that the folksinger's life, commanded as it is by an instinct for at least survival, is a declamatory *act* in itself.

That said, what is to happen to folk music and, even more important, what positive good has it done for the people affected by it? In the light of the last few years, one can describe the situation in terms of the following:

First, the effect of traditional music, collectively created, on the American musical scene has been equivalent to the transfusion of fresh blood into the veins of a moribund culture. For the first time, because of it, the leaders of opinion and the makers of cultural images have implicitly permitted that pop music *also* can reflect, even though to a limited extent, a certain amount of social realism.

Second, authentic folk music and its interpreters were stimulated and confirmed in their convictions and revitalized for at least a generation to come (as in the case of Doc Watson and his son), just at the moment when "modern" life menaced their extinction, their "natural" death.

Third, and this last point is of interest to the general public rather than merely the enthusiasts, several "great names" that issued from folk, such as Bob Dylan, Joan Baez, Paul Simon, or Donovan, have been in their turn absorbed by the current of modern pop music, which they have contributed toward creating. For in the meantime there has been born a new factor, inherited from the folk revival: the new generation of songwriters, which culminates with the work of Bob Dylan, and which by his example invites each of us to become, not only an heir or a listener, but also one of the members of an eternal process of collective creation and re-creation.

If the years 1955–60, when one comes to look at them, were decisive ones for the American folk revival, contrarily they did not see the birth or even accession to fame of any notable songwriter. Only the veterans such as Pete Seeger or Malvina Reynolds continued during this period to compose and perform new works that reflected the hopes, tensions, and indignations of the moment, and in that stayed faithful to a tradition of which the guiding principles were laid down by the Wobblies, the years of the Depression, Woody Guthrie, and The Almanac Singers.

Around this time, a resurgent movement of songwriters, all more or less dedicated to the pacifist, political, or workers' struggle, was coming to the fore in Great Britain. Among the principal figures of this resurgence were Matt McGinn and, above all, Ewan MacColl. This latter, as with Matt McGinn and others, derived his musical inspiration from the pattern of the traditional ballads of Scotland, from which land both originated. Over the years, MacColl has written and recorded an impressive number of songs in company with Peggy Seeger, Pete's half-sister, whose contribution has been to juxtapose the Scottish influence with that of the Appalachian hillbillies. The combination of Ewan MacColl / Peggy Seeger has composed notably a number of ballads on the theme of the miners, of which "Spring Hill Mine Disaster" remains one of the finest examples.

From this promising situation for British folk music there resulted a sort of inferiority complex on the part of urban folk music circles in the United States. Returning from a trip to England at the end of 1961, Pete Seeger and his wife Toshi discussed with their New York friends their feelings on this question. In New York only Bill McAdoo, who had published a collection in 1959 called *The Bosses' Songbook* as well as recording his compositions for Folkways, seemed to any extent to translate into song the aspirations of his young contemporaries. All the same, the popularity of Bill McAdoo was at this time no more than local, and it was not until the publication in February 1962 of the first number of the magazine *Broadside* that one could see the signs of a serious movement, on a national scale, of young American songwriters.

The creation of *Broadside* was the result of three hopes: to revive the radical American tradition of political and topical singers; to prove to the skeptics that the United States *also* had singers and songwriters of real talent; and to combat by practical action the dominance of commercialism by offering to young writers the opportunity of publishing a type of work which the record firms and the established music publishers, with their predilection for apolitical material, would not consider.

Putting their words into action, the creators of *Broadside* gave it from the beginning a policy and an administration that were as anticommercial as possible: the authors remained proprietors of their works, and no music publishing business was created to work in parallel with *Broadside*. The magazine was prepared with whatever was available; gratuitously transcribed by hand from tape recordings, the songs were then mimeographed with the help of an old machine, and the sheets collated and stapled by hand. Photographs were considered too expensive, so the illustrations in *Broadside* were limited to the reproduction of extracts from newspapers and the artwork of amateurs. In the guise of an editorial office, the apartment of the creators of *Broadside,* Gordon Friesen and Sis Cunningham, was used. These two, assisted by their daughters, Pete Seeger, Gil Turner, and sometimes passing young songwriters (Bob Dylan visited frequently), got together regularly as a sort of editorial committee to decide which songs and articles to publish. Some of the writers were personally known to the editors; others, on the contrary, lived outside the New York region and simply sent their songs in by mail.

For a production cost of forty-five dollars, Number 1 of *Broadside* had a print run of three hundred copies, of which one hundred were immediately bought by Israel Young, an adept at spotting a good thing, who put them on sale in the Folklore Center. The other two hundred were sent as review copies to a number of luminaries in the world of song (singers, journalists, specialists, and so forth).

During the winter of 1961–62, Gil Turner (who had been active in the antisegregationist struggles in the Southern states, where he had many friends and relations) presented his "Hootenannies" each Monday night at Gerde's Folk City, one of the most famous folk clubs in Greenwich Village. The singers who appeared there were not paid; but, if the management liked their performance, they were engaged for a week and they would be paid for this. Gil Turner made it his duty to put them in touch with *Broadside* and encourage them to publish their new compositions. For its part, the editorial "staff" of *Broadside* had the merit of respecting the liberty of these ambitious young singer-songwriters, by keeping at a distance the political and commercial pressure groups, by limiting the space accorded to established authors, and by avoiding the formation of a clique at the heart of the magazine. This last point is important because, with the exception of Bob Dylan, all the famous songwriters initially associated with *Broadside*, Phil Ochs and Tom Paxton at their head, "passed the hat" when performing their songs in the Greenwich Village cafés.

The following year, the circulation of *Broadside* having tripled, Gil Turner took the second step necessary for the growth of the new movement: to give the songs life. In sum, it was not enough that they could be read, they had to have at least a hope of being heard, learned, and broadcast—through the medium of the record. So Gil Turner directed some recording sessions in which took part, notably, Bob Dylan (under the curious pseudonym of Blind Boy Grunt), Tom Paxton, Phil Ochs, Eric Andersen, and Pete Seeger. The record label "Broadside" was created for the occasion, and the double album that resulted from these sessions, *The Broadside Singers*, was distributed to the record shops by the Folkways company.

So to a great extent it is to the constant efforts of the *Broadside* crew that one owes the birth, the coming to fame, and the evolution of a "new generation" of contemporary American folk music. To begin with, Bob Dylan himself.

dylan

A complex individual, an exceptionally gifted artist who is exciting and baffling, mysterious and mundane all at the same time, Bob Dylan is probably the most difficult of all American songwriters to analyze. When talking of the man and his work, one cannot apply the hard-and-fast rules that can be used to delineate other artists. It is worth listing just a few of the things that make the task practically impossible: the frequent radical changes in Bob Dylan's attitude, style, and subject matter, as if by some sort of permanent self-analysis and self-criticism; the more or less laconic or equivocal remarks that he contributes in the rare interviews he grants; the high emotions and diversity of opinion on the part of audiences, critics, and other singers (genius or impostor? traitor or prophet? seeker or obscurantist?—or even all of these at the same time?); his capacity for disconcerting his loyal followers as much as his detractors; the remarkable speed and complaisance with which the leaders of popular opinion created the myth, the "living legend," the "idol" that is Dylan. Cheering or depressing to you as they may be, these are a few of the symptoms of the existence of a phenomenon. And whether or not one appreciates his work, one is obliged to recognize that in Dylan there lies an immensely original talent, coupled with a tremendously strong persona, both of which have exercised for a good number of years a profound influence on the pop song in particular and pop music in general, both in the United States and abroad.

Bob Dylan can claim, among other prizes, the one for being the songwriter about whom the most ineptitudes have been written and said. We have to tread very warily then, and yet there are a few advantages which we have when discussing Dylan: it is possible that, on the one hand, the sole fact that we are judging an American cultural phenomenon from the shores of the Old World will give us at least a fragile objectivity; and that, on the other, our distance from the focus of it all may allow us to escape the inevitable temptation of being swept along with the current of the times. However, even supposing all this, one must remember that for a number of years yet, with the birth of each new Dylan work, the conclusions drawn between the covers of this book about his imagery or his creativity are bound to be rendered invalid sooner or later. For, like the civilization and the cultural context in which he works, the evolution of Bob Dylan has been extremely rapid, his outward facade (at least as far as we are concerned) often confusing, and his future quite unpredictable. Even his past is uncertain, for he has always been evasive in talking about it—no doubt for the same reason his stage name is a pseudonym adopted out of respect for the Welsh poet, Dylan Thomas.

Rather than repeat the myth yet another time, a chore that would in no way help us to appreciate works that are complex enough in themselves, we will restrict ourselves to a brief presentation of the principal facts that seem necessary to enable comprehension of a contemporary poet whose importance, for every reason, cannot be ignored.

Robert Zimmerman, to give him his real name, was born on May 21, 1941, in Duluth, Minnesota. But it was at Hibbing, northwest of Duluth, that he spent his childhood. Hibbing was already on the decline; the local iron mines, to which it had until recently owed its prosperity, had been almost exhausted and unemployment was becoming a serious problem. When the north quarter of Hibbing became completely depopulated, the Zimmermans moved to the southern part of the town where they succeeded in making a comfortable living. Nevertheless, the family environment and a fatalistic obsession turned the young Bob toward other things; at the age of ten, he ran away from home for the first time, ending up in Chicago. It was there that he came across folk music, in the form of an old black street singer with whom he spent three months. A friend of the street singer gave Bob the precious gift of a half-size guitar, which, after his (forced) return to Hibbing, he learned to play. Always an autodidact, he set to work also on the harmonica, the piano, and the Autoharp. At the age of eleven he took up smoking, and at twelve he ran away from home for the second time, meeting in Evanston (a suburb of Chicago) one of the great living black traditional blues singers, Big Joe Williams. Williams exerted the first stylistic influence on the music of Bob Dylan.

Dylan ran away from home plenty of other times (seven before he was eighteen, he says), interspersed with usually forced returns to Hibbing where, at the age of fifteen, he wrote his first song. It was dedicated to Brigitte Bardot, the sight of whom in a film had captivated him. Youth excuses much. . . .

At nineteen, having been on the road through Illinois, Dakota, New Mexico (where he discovered the Indian tribes and their music), Kansas, and California, Bob obtained his first professional singing engagement. This was at the Gilded Garter, a strip club in Central City, Colorado. Naturally enough, the audiences were considerably less interested in the songs than in the antics of the women onstage. At the end of ten or twelve days Bob, finding the experience understandably somewhat unsatisfying, abandoned the Gilded Garter and went to the University of Minnesota. He arrived at Minneapolis in the spring of 1960. Nobody knows quite what he hoped to learn, but he tangled with a number of academics, none of whom seemed to appreciate his anticonformist dialectic. Out of spite, he cut many of their classes.

On the other hand, the six months that he spent studying in Minneapolis gave him the opportunity to try out his music in front of a more enlightened public. During the summer of that year he played and sang regularly in a local club, the Ten O'Clock Scholar, where the young people organized mini-concerts and hootenannies. Among others, one could find there Jon Pankake and Paul Nelson, themselves students, who were soon to become music critics and to found the *Little Sandy Review*. They described the talents of Bob Dylan as "promising." Zimmerman-Dylan didn't stay there long, and in the autumn of 1960, without regrets, he formally gave up his studies and traveled to New York.

New York was the cradle of the folk revival, where the future seemed to smile on every young man with a yen to sing and play the guitar. But most important of all, Bob went to the hospital where Woody Guthrie, whose records he had been listening to for months, was dying. Naturally, he had by this time discovered almost all of the giants of folk music, both black and white (as for example Jimmie Rodgers, Hank Williams, Jack Elliott, Jesse Fuller, Leadbelly, Big Joe Williams, and Big Bill Broonzy), but the influence of Woody Guthrie on his musical and lyrical style was to eclipse all others for the ensuing three years.

Arriving in New York at the end of autumn, Bob instinctively made his way to Greenwich Village, where to begin with he had great difficulty in being allowed to sing in the clubs. Competition was rife, his music judged as "too rustic," engagements rare and badly paid. Poverty-stricken, he was forced to spend many nights sleeping in the filthy stations of the New York subway, the world of the bums, the addicts, and the rest of society's dropouts. From this tough period sprang two of his foremost compositions of 1961, "Talkin' New York" and "Hard Times in New York Town." During all this there was a consolation straight out of his dreams: often he was allowed into Woody Guthrie's hospital room. Unable to write, sing, or play, Woody was still able to see in Bob the birth of an exceptional talent and gave him both advice and friendship. Woody also made to him an important point: he (Woody) was not a "god" or a "prophet" as Bob Dylan had thought, merely another human being. Bob took the lesson well and, after a visit to Woody's bedside, wrote for him the touching tribute, "Song to Woody."

In the spring of 1961, Bob gave a much-noted performance at the Ten O'Clock Scholar back in Minneapolis, and Jon Pankake and Paul Nelson, who still went there, waxed wild about the musical progress that he had made. Their report in the *Little Sandy Review* described the change in Bob Dylan as "to say the least, incredible." In six months he had learned to produce from both his harmonica and his guitar an enthusiastic, bluesy, fiery music, and he had absorbed, they continued, during his meetings with Guthrie not only the inimitable syntax of the great Okie musician, but also his musical color, his diction, and his inflection.

Returning to New York, Dylan continued to sing around the clubs, sometimes at the Gaslight, sometimes at Gerde's Folk City. It was at the latter that his music began to be taken seriously. Robert Shelton, the well-known critic in the folk world, devoted to him in *The New York Times* (September 29, 1961) a veritable eulogy which concluded with the judgment that the highly personalized fashion with which Dylan had grappled with folk music was still in the process of evolution; he had absorbed his influences like a sponge. From time to time, Shelton felt, the drama that Dylan sought descended to melodrama, and his stylization was in danger of becoming gross, but nevertheless his musical interpretation and his marked originality of inspiration were remarkable for someone of his age. As always, Shelton found Dylan evasive about his antecedents and his birthplace, less concerned with where he had been and more concerned with where he was going—which, Shelton predicted, was straight to the top.

As a part of our "pocket history" it is worth noting Dylan's very first professional recording. This was for Columbia at the beginning of October 1961, and consisted of providing harmonica accompaniment to a young Texan singer, Carolyn Hester, on three tracks. Despite his distrust and basic contempt for the press, he was certainly happy at this stage to show Robert Shelton's article to Carolyn Hester's producer, John Hammond, whom he invited to come and hear him at Gerde's Folk City. But John Hammond, already primed by his son who was himself a folksinger and who knew Bob Dylan's work well, saw no need to bother with that and instead offered him a record contract without preliminary audition.

Recorded in New York in December 1961, Bob Dylan's first album was released in March 1962, having as its only title his name. For reasons which will be explained below, only two of the thirteen songs on the album ("Song to Woody" and "Talkin' New York") were from his own pen, the eleven others being almost all garnered from his traditional repertoire. From the very first track, "You're No Good," the listener is plunged into the embrace of a blues that is savage, ironic, and quite brilliant: from both vocal and instrumental viewpoints, *Bob Dylan* contains several admirable tours de force, something which one doesn't find on most of his later albums, where both melody line and accompaniment are simpler. Perhaps the fact that most of the songs were not his own meant that they lent themselves more easily to becoming technical showpieces.

Always in the world of blues there is the whiff of death, and here Dylan seems to be thinking about his own. There can be no doubt that the fear of death was one of his principal preoccupations at this time, as is suggested by the choice of songs on this album; three among them ("In My Time of Dyin'," "Fixin' to Die," "See That My Grave Is Kept Clean") speak directly and in the first person of death, while five others ("Man of Constant Sorrow," "Pretty Peggy-O," "Highway 51," "Gospel Plow," and "House of the Rising Sun") deal with heroes or heroines living in the shadow of death. With respect to the problems of the authenticity of white bluesmen which we have discussed in the previous chapter, it is interesting to note how Dylan considers himself different from the others, and he has several times given his views on this. What he feels gives the true blues singers their stature is the fact that they are capable of stating precisely all the problems that they have, yet at the same time can look at these as if from the outside, in this way freeing themselves; in general the people making records are singers trying to get *into* the blues, forgetting that the old singers used them to get rid of their sorrows. In this respect it is interesting and instructive to compare Dylan's version of "House of the Rising Sun" with that of Eric Burdon and the Animals.

Bob Dylan sold eight thousand copies in the first year of its release, earning for the young artist the unanimous enthusiasm of the folk world. Woody Guthrie, who was well enough to listen to the record, sent to Dylan a simple but significant appraisal: "It's a good 'un, Bob!"—which represented for the young singer the finest of compliments. The *Little Sandy Review* was no less vehement. Nevertheless, while predicting for Bob Dylan an extraordinary career, Jon Pankake and Paul Nelson expressed a reservation which, in the light of what was to come, takes on a prophetic value: they hoped that Dylan would set himself apart from the protest singers, continue writing songs in the traditional genre, and develop the mastery of his difficult, delicate, and highly personal style.

Bob Dylan was not then to follow the counsel of his old friends, as is shown by his second album (*The Freewheelin' Bob Dylan,* released in the United States in 1963), which demonstrates his talent as a songwriter, and above all as a *topical* songwriter, one who concentrates on current events and takes a stand on topical events.[1] Yes, protest was the word of the day, and at least five of the songs on this album come into that bracket: "Blowin' in the Wind," "Masters of War," "A Hard Rain's A-Gonna Fall," "Oxford Town," and "Talking World War III Blues." Had it not been for the production team at Columbia, even more protest songs would have found their way onto *Freewheelin'*.

[1] Only two of the songs on *Freewheelin'* ("Corrina, Corrina" and "Honey, Just Allow Me One More Chance") were not by Dylan. After this it was not until the release of his album *Self Portrait* in 1970 that he recorded songs by other people.

We must go back in time a little to find the genesis of these songs.

Bob Dylan was already writing protest songs at the end of 1961 and wanted to record several of them on his first album. Unfortunately Columbia, as with most of the large recording companies of the time, still did not believe in the commercial value of protest songs, especially on political themes. This respectable company far preferred albums to be collections of well-known standards than have them contain anything controversial. The public was fond of folk songs, and so they were offered the traditional. Looking forward to happier days in the recording field, Dylan consoled himself by continuing to write songs for his own satisfaction, on all the themes that inspired him, to perform them onstage, and to try and get them published. The first printed publication of any song of Dylan's was "Talkin' John Birch Society Blues," which appeared in *Broadside*'s first issue in February 1962. During this period Dylan was writing songs at an incredible rate, sometimes as many as five in a single evening! The best of them were almost always first published in the pages of *Broadside*. Dylan himself plugged on all possible occasions the various songs which, for want of commercial recordings, never acquired fame beyond a certain modicum: "Percy's Song" (a very long and beautiful ballad in which he recounts the conviction of one of his friends after a car accident and Dylan's vain intervention on his behalf in front of the judge), recorded by the English group, Fairport Convention; "Ballad of Donald White" (telling of a convict who, after his release, cannot readapt himself to the life of a "free" man and asks to be returned to prison); "Who Killed Davey Moore?" (about a boxer who was killed during a fight, a song which was released in France by Graeme Allwright); examples abound. . . .

During the year 1962 something happened that forced Columbia to reconsider its position with regard to singer-songwriters. Bob Dylan had written lyrics to a tune at the same time attractive and easy to sing, posing a series of questions on the future of humanity, very general questions that all invoked the reply: "blowin' in the wind." Bob tried it out with success at Gerde's Folk City and it was heard by his Greenwich Village friends, notably Gil Turner and Peter, Paul and Mary. The latter were so enthusiastic over "Blowin' in the Wind" that they recorded it as the final track on their third album, *In the Wind.* By the beginning of 1964 this album (which contained two other Dylan songs, "Quit Your Lowdown Ways" and the famous "Don't Think Twice") had achieved the decisive million copies sale, and "Blowin' in the Wind" had on many occasions been sung by hundreds of thousands of people on civil-rights marches. It had become a symbol of the movement, of the same order as, say, "We Shall Overcome."

After this, Columbia no longer had any objections to Bob Dylan recording his own compositions, among them those "with a message." He needed no more encouragement: besides several songs of a more personal nature (like the beautiful "Girl from the North Country," "Down the Highway," "Don't Think Twice," "Bob Dylan's Dream," and "I Shall Be Free"), it is certain that the majority of people who bought *Freewheelin'* did so because of the five protest songs already mentioned. As well as "Blowin' in the Wind," particularly notable is "Masters of War," a highly vigorous if rather naïve condemnation of armaments manufacturers.

But "A Hard Rain's A-Gonna Fall" is a far more important work and one of his greatest successes in combining the styles of several epochs. Following an eminent folk tradition, the melody and even the basic idea are taken from an old English ballad, "Lord Randall." A youth who has returned from exploring the world explains in the first couplet where he has been, in the second couplet what he saw there, in the third what he has heard, in the fourth whom he met, and finally, in the fifth, what he is going to do now. Dylan, with an artistry that goes beyond poetry, describes his apocalyptic visions of a world that is insane, cruel, and ready to explode. This song was written in the fall of 1962 at the time of the Cuban missile crisis which sparked off the fear of atomic war in the minds of the entire world and, to an even greater extent, in the minds of Americans, because of their proximity and involvement.

After "Oxford Town," a satirical little song about segregation in the small towns of the Deep South, "Talking World War III Blues" restates, stretched over more than six minutes of grating humor, this psychosis about the Third World War. Dylan chooses to laugh about it: he recounts what he has seen in a dream, with himself as the sole survivor in a deserted New York after a nuclear attack. But perhaps it's a hollow laugh. [Some years later the British songwriter Mick Softley, in his rapidly remaindered album *Songs for Swingin' Survivors,* used the same sort of technique, though without dressing his story line up in the guise of a dream. P.B.]

"I Shall Be Free," the fifth track on the album, is another of those comic, frantic improvisations, where the playing of the harmonica provides a happy counterpoint to the highly heteroclite imagery (Brigitte Bardot, President Kennedy, Mr. Right, and so forth) which Dylan pulls in and at the juxtaposition of which he excels, as he gives free rein (and this during the studio session) to his abundant imagination.

Returning for a moment to the lovesongs on the album: In "Don't Think Twice, It's All Right," Dylan accuses a woman whom he has loved of expecting too much from him, and demands that she set him free. This is a theme which we will find repeated many times in Dylan's work.

During the studio sessions for *Freewheelin'* Dylan recorded many other tracks which, for various reasons, Columbia didn't include. Of these lost titles, two at least deserve particular mention, "Talkin' John Birch Society Blues" and "Mixed-up Confusion." The former is an extremely satirical, acid talking blues which, in a style reminiscent of the better moments of Woody Guthrie, ridicules the members of this right-wing extremist group and their obsession with "Commie hunting." [2] Since the popularity of Dylan was rapidly growing—*Time* and *Newsweek* had devoted articles to him—he was invited to perform on the well-known CBS television program, the "Ed Sullivan Show," planned for May 12, 1963. Dylan had announced to both Ed Sullivan and the producer that it was his intention to perform "Talkin' John Birch Society Blues"—and both of them had given their agreement. But when he arrived at the studio for rehearsal on the afternoon in question—it was to be his first appearance on the tube—an executive of CBS, after having listened to the song, told him that it was too controversial and asked him to choose a different one. Dylan retorted that, quite frankly, he really wasn't in the mood for singing any other. The intervention of Ed Sullivan was of no avail, and Dylan refused to sing on the broadcast.

The sleeve of *Freewheelin'* indicates on the back that five studio musicians, a rock-and-roll band as-it-were, accompanied Dylan in "Don't Think Twice, It's All Right" and "Corrina, Corrina." In fact, the musicians are totally absent from the first of these tracks and only just audible on the second. But during the same session Dylan recorded with them a rock track, "Mixed-up Confusion." This, ac-

[2] This song is still only available on bootleg albums. —P.B.

companied on the B Side by an electric version of "Corrina, Corrina," was issued by Columbia as a single (probably in the hope of making it a chartbuster) but was returned by the shops after a couple of weeks for the incredible reason that it wasn't selling!

There are a few points arising out of this. Firstly, that Dylan, with his rapid musical evolution, was decidedly too far in advance of the times; secondly, that Dylan, still seen at this time as the new Woody Guthrie the publicists had made him out to be, sought with "Mixed-up Confusion" to show his own originality; thirdly, that this track, with a sound that portended that of the *Bringing It All Back Home* album two years later, could have featured on *Freewheelin'*. And that might have changed the whole course of modern pop music.

It was at the Newport Folk Festival in July 1963 that Bob Dylan, whether he wanted to be or not, decisively found himself the "leader" of the movement born out of the American protest song. On the exceptional program were blues singers like the Reverend Gary Davis, and Mississippi John Hurt, new and promising singer-songwriters like Tom Paxton, Phil Ochs, and Peter La Farge, and established names like Theodore Bikel, Pete Seeger, Jack Elliott, and Joan Baez.

However, the performance of Bob Dylan during the closing concert on Sunday evening eclipsed all the rest. In the eyes of thousands of avid students, Dylan had become an active sympathizer with the civil-rights movements for black integration, movements like CORE, SNCC, and Martin Luther King's SCLC. He had sung for free at their meetings on many occasions and had made a militant tour of the Southern states; in a scene in the film *Don't Look Back* one can see Dylan with a group of blacks, singing "Only a Pawn in Their Game" with tears in his eyes. During his performance at Newport a crowd estimated at more than thirty-five thousand people, delirious with enthusiasm, sang with him "Blowin' in the Wind" and listened to the new compositions that were to figure on his forthcoming album, *The Times They Are A-Changin'*.

The day after this memorable festival, *Freewheelin'* began to sell at the formidable rate of ten thousand copies per week, reaching by the end of 1963 the total of a hundred and fifty thousand sales. One could reasonably suggest that the success of this album encouraged the record companies to look more carefully at the possibilities of recording other singer-songwriters, even those who had previously been "too controversial." To back this up: the spring of 1964 saw the release of the first albums by Tom Paxton, Phil Ochs, and Mark Spoelstra on Elektra, and by Patrick Sky and Eric Andersen on Vanguard.

By this time Dylan was on his third album for Columbia, *The Times They Are A-Changin'*, which was released in January 1964. Although songs on political and social topics are dominant in this album (seven out of a total of ten), the tone is not at all the same as on *Freewheelin'*. More mature (no longer is there the naïveté that tends to spoil, for example, "Masters of War"), he has also become much more serious: the photograph on the cover, in black and white, shows Dylan with a wry and quietly pained expression.

The first side opens with the song that gives the album its title, "The Times They Are A-Changin'." A particularly aggressive Dylan tells the senators, congressmen, business magnates, potentates, doctors, and all other "adults" of America and the rest of the world that they are about to be swept away, for "the times they are a-changin' " and they shouldn't criticize the things they don't understand.

"Ballad of Hollis Brown" (the tune of which is very simple and reminiscent of, among others, Woody Guthrie's "Pastures of Plenty") is one of those story songs that Dylan has always handled so well. The story line, dramatic in itself (an out-of-work laborer kills his wife and children because he has no way of feeding them, then kills himself), is made more poignant, even oppressive, by the abstraction with which it is sung.

"With God on Our Side" is the keystone of the album, at the same time one of the longest, one of the most personal, and one of the best known of Dylan's political songs. After an introduction in which he tells us that his name and age are of little importance, but that the country he comes from has God on its side, the following verses are a narration of the principal wars that have marked human history. Declaring that in each both antagonists have had God on their side, he asks, who are the traitors? Who is to blame? And who are the victims? And in the last couplet he leaves the listener free to decide for himself—for even Judas Iscariot had God on his side.

"North Country Blues" is, despite its title, less a blues than a long ballad of the traditional English type; and it was certainly inspired by

Dylan's recollection of the coming of the Depression to Hibbing following the closing of the iron mines. A mother tells about her miserable life as a miner's wife, the closing of the mine, unemployment, the hunger and the cold that came in its wake, the death of her husband, and finally, in the last verse, the pathetic result, that her children are leaving her to go elsewhere because there's nothing to keep them there—just the same way as Bob Dylan himself left Hibbing to seek pastures anew, leaving his mother behind. The situation is without hope. As in "With God on Our Side," Dylan has no miraculous remedy to propose; he refuses even to point a moral, but confines himself to involving us in a drama which belongs to all men: the quest for an impossible Utopia when hope has been deceived. More than any other, it is this quality of universality that gives to "North Country Blues" its greatness, its macrocosmic position, its rank along with Guthrie's "Tom Joad" or Brassens' "Pauvre Martin" as a contribution to modern mythology. If Bob Dylan has genius, this is where we find it.

Dylan returns to the theme on Side Two of the album with the same desire to enlarge the debate on the human situation by taking one case in particular as a "worked example," with two songs that share as their point of departure a racial murder. "Only a Pawn in Their Game" is concerned with the killing at the beginning of 1963 of Medgar Evers. This particularly sordid crime caused a considerable stir at the time among progressive Americans. On the subject of the police and the white racist populations of the South, Bob Dylan points out, in the phrase that gives the song its title, that Medgar Evers was only a pawn in their game.

The clarity of his political judgment is even more obvious in "The Lonesome Death of Hattie Carroll." Hattie Carroll was a fifty-one-year-old chambermaid with ten children, who was murdered, in the Baltimore hotel where she worked, by being repeatedly slashed with a cane by William Zensinger, a large landowner from Maryland. His high-up friends in the local administration rigged the trial and eventually quashed the sentence. Dylan tells the story with a crudity, a realism, and an unprecedented violence which makes "The Lonesome Death of Hattie Carroll," in the eyes of many, the finest of his protest songs.

Bypassing "When the Ship Comes In," a rather labored repetition of "The Times They Are A-Changin' " that certainly adds nothing to Dylan's glory, we carry on to look at the three "personal" songs on this album, forerunners (if only the fans of Dylan-the-Protestor had taken notice) of the next step that his creativity was to take. They are "One Too Many Mornings," "Boots of Spanish Leather," and "Restless Farewell."

The first two are love songs or, to be more exact, songs about the end of a love affair. Not long after he arrived in New York, Dylan made the acquaintance of a New York student the same age as he, Suze Rotolo, the pretty blonde on the cover of *Freewheelin'*. She, unfortunately for Bob, left to pursue her studies in Italy for a year, a departure that he had already sung about in "Down the Highway" on *Freewheelin'*. The theme of the sorrow of the lover left behind is developed with bitterness (and artistically much more competently) in "One Too Many Mornings" and "Boots of Spanish Leather." This latter is particularly poignant, especially as the tune is a variation of "Girl from the North Country." The girl, as she leaves for Spain, asks the man if he wants her to send back some sort of a souvenir from there to remind him of her; he replies that all he wants is to see her come back as soon as possible, that he doesn't want anything from Spain. But much later, when he has been told in a letter that she isn't coming back anymore, he tells her that yes, he would like a souvenir: boots of Spanish leather. (According to the people who knew her in New York in 1961–62, Suze Rotolo often wore high leather boots, well ahead of the fashion.)

"Restless Farewell" anticipates (the kind of forecast it is easy for posterity to understand) Dylan's future desertion of songs with a "message" in favor of songs for and about himself. As he says in the song, it has all been written; he's sorry if in the past he's committed faults or hurt people, but it was out of ignorance. Now he says farewell to a past that he does not regret. This desire to apologize to his earliest followers, who cannot understand or who do not wish to admit his right to evolve, is found again in plenty of his later songs, particularly on his next album.

In August 1964 Bob Dylan's fourth album was released, *Another Side of Bob Dylan,* and we could term it "the album of the breach."

The title emphasizes the change that we have already noted, and effectively this change is encapsulated in "All I Really Want to Do," the opening track on Side One: with a rapid tempo, a lyric filled with wordplays and puns, it contains the first erotic allusions by Dylan in any of his songs. "Black Crow Blues" is also something of an innovation, but in musical terms as it is the first time one hears Dylan accompanying himself on the piano. Unfortunately, the track is otherwise of little merit. "Spanish Harlem Incident," with a similar inspiration to that of "All I Really Want to Do," needs a little clarification: to the great disappointment of those who tried to find in it another social song, it is about neither an incident nor Spanish Harlem. This is one of the first symptoms of his later tendency toward mystery, giving to many of his later songs titles that seem to bear no relation whatsoever to the lyric.

"Chimes of Freedom," a long ballad which, it must be admitted, is musically rather boring but is extremely interesting on the plane of ideas, is a vigorous plea for the liberation of the individual (not for that of society). Dylan seems ill at ease in his role of militant leader, pestered as he is by journalists and those of his fans who attempt to dictate his course. However, it would be a year or more before he came to have the total contempt for many who spoke or wrote about him, favorably or otherwise.

Noting in passing a strange musical perfume, a climate redolent of the Latin sun in "To Ramona," we come to the two comic pieces of the album, "I Shall Be Free #10" and "Motorpsycho Nitemare." The former is a sort of talking blues, like a repetition of "I Shall Be Free" on *Freewheelin',* with a new lyric. Unfortunately, the vocals in "#10" are nowhere near as good as in the original. (Incidentally, both of them took for their inspiration a track by Leadbelly, "We Shall Be Free.")

"Motorpsycho Nitemare" is possibly one of the best songs on the album. Told in the first person, it is the story of a young man on the road (no prizes for guessing whom) who is put up for the night by a farmer. There, is, however, a condition attached to this: no messing around with the farmer's daughter during the night, and of course he has to milk the cows in the morning. The usual story. During the night, while he is wisely sleeping, he is awakened by the knock of the young woman who has come to see him. The father appears and berates the youth, who replies with the only political allusion on the record—he loves Fidel Castro and his beard—and rapidly rushes from the house. Can one see here any political thought whatsoever on the part of Dylan? Or even a simple evocation of the conflict of the generations? Possibly, insofar as the two are tied together. Whether or not there is greater depth to the song, "Motorpsycho Nitemare" has its place beside the best of American comic films.

"My Back Pages" is, in contrast, a serious song, perhaps even the key to the rest of the album. Dylan, with admirable frankness and clarity, performs an excellent self-criticism. As evidenced here, he has given serious thought to the political and social problems of the world around him and has allowed his songs to be used as tools by others. Now, feeling he has deceived himself or allowed himself to be deceived, he is disillusioned and decides to think only about the problems and subjects he fully understands—his own problems—saying he was so much older then but is younger now. Those who doubt the sincerity of Dylan would do well to listen again to this excellent track and realize the severity with which he treats himself.

There remain three songs: "I Don't Believe You," "It Ain't Me Babe" (which is the last track on the album), and "Ballad in Plain D." All three have in common the theme of impossible love, and the difficulties (certainly something close to Dylan at this time) that two lovers have in communicating to each other their hopes which are obviously very different. While the two former titles show the author's burning relish for rock (while on tour in England he had discovered and fallen for the music of the Beatles), "Ballad in Plain D" remains, at least in formal terms, well within the folk bracket. Here he confesses, in astringent terms, that he hasn't had the time or even the desire to make poetry out of his role at the end of a love affair.

Because of the clean break he had thematically (also in form and in essence) made with the past, *Another Side of Bob Dylan* was treated badly and little understood by the critics. They complained about or mocked the long poem in free verse (not very convincing, it's true) which is on the back of the sleeve. In Dylan's defense he was sorely pressed for time for production reasons, and had to record in a single twelve-hour session fourteen new songs (of which three were rejected) which he hadn't yet properly practiced. At this stage of his evolution Dylan needed, to make himself better understood, more convincing vocal and instrumental performances than ever before. Moreover, the acoustic guitar and the harmonica, which play a dominant musical role throughout the album, give it in spite of everything a definitely folk appearance, contrasting bizarrely with the content of the songs. All this left the critics in a confused heap . . . but only for a few months.

With the release of *Bringing It All Back Home* in March of 1965, doubt was no longer possible, and the stage was set for months of passionate polemic. For it is here for the first time that Dylan had recourse to the intensive use of a rock band (electric guitar and bass, drums, and so forth) which would make him, looking back from much later, appear to be the inventor of a new form, christened "folkrock."

The general idea of *Bringing It All Back Home* is simple, though at the same time almost frightening: Dylan takes us on a dreamlike tour of the world, which he sees by turns as chaotic ("Subterranean Homesick Blues"), even hallucinogenic ("Bob Dylan's 115th Dream," far longer than the original "Bob Dylan's Dream" in which we encounter not the friends of Dylan, but an America peopled by spiritual dwarfs), shockingly cynical ("Maggie's Farm"), cruel ("It's Alright, Ma [I'm Only Bleeding]"), or simply ridiculous ("Gates of Eden"). This last song is one of his most remarkable achievements in that domain of humor used as an antidote to the folly of "teachers" of all sorts, each of whom attempts to explain the world through the spectacles of his own truth (let's face it, it's a sin we all share). Dylan seems completely convinced that the world in its absurdity is quite inexplicable: now he wants to do no more than describe (and in what terms!) his visions. He's run out of certainties.[3]

Does this mean that Dylan refuses to create any longer, that all that is left for him is suicide? Is there nowhere left to run? There *is* a refuge—in laughter, as we've already noted regarding "Gates of Eden." And after that there is, all the better, the music itself: the flights of imagination and, through those flights, salvation, escape of some sort. And Dylan makes clear to us the possibility in "Mr. Tambourine Man," a hymn to the intoxication of music (if one is content to explain this song on the superficial level only, that of the words themselves—and this interpretation is perfectly satisfactory), or

---

[3] In fact, if we followed to the letter the despairing lesson of *Bringing It All Back Home,* we would have replaced the whole of this chapter with the simple explanation: "Bob Dylan exists, but we have no right to discuss him. We would advise the reader instead to go and listen to all his records."

even—for those who like to find a deeper meaning—to the intoxication of wine, colors, smells, or LSD (without taking up a position for
or against this last suggestion, there is no particular evidence for its
being true, though one could imagine it of the Dylan of 1965). In
sum, of course, it doesn't really matter what's in the bottle, so long as
it's Dylan who's passing it around.

Another suggested refuge is love. Contrary to what was happening on *Another Side of Bob Dylan,* he seems to be going through a
good patch in *Bringing It All Back Home:* the photograph on the
sleeve (showing Dylan with a young but elegant brunette relaxing in
a room that has a certain touch of lived-inness [4]) gives one a fore-
taste; and, during the record, on the two occasions that Dylan leaves
the ferment of his subconscious to speak to us in words strong and
plain, it is to tell us of the woman he loves, and with whom he seems
extremely happy: His love speaks like silence, one song begins
("Love Minus Zero / No Limit"), and later ("She Belongs to Me") the
realization that his woman has everything she needs—she's an artist,
she doesn't look back. This woman doesn't spend her time trying to
explain the world or wishing she could change it and seems able to
communicate to Dylan a share of her serenity. And through Dylan,
to the listener. . . .

A word in closing on "It's All Over Now, Baby Blue," the necessarily final track of *Bringing It All Back Home.* Who is "Baby Blue"?
As often with Dylan, there are plenty of explanations offered, most
of them thoroughly contradictory. Certain among them would credit
any novelist.[5] Others, more plausible, postulated a woman whom
Dylan had left (a logical view in the first place because of the lyrics)
or even that the song was for a whore who was dying. Most of the
remainder of these theories consider Baby Blue to be a projection of
Dylan himself, a repeated farewell to his old character, as well as to
the public who worshiped that old character. "It's All Over Now,

---

[4] The brunette in question is actually Sally Grossman, the wife of Dylan's manager.
—P.B.

[5] In the course of a long and very interesting interview given in *Broadside* in July 1968,
Alan Weberman, the self-styled "Dylanologist," gave vent to his theory: to him, Dylan
has never ceased to be a protest writer; however, because of his poetic evolution, his
protests have become more subtle in their expression than they were in *Freewheelin'*
and have reached what might be termed a "second stage." Baby Blue, in Weberman's
view, is in fact a "symbol of capitalism." In the laborious interview in *Rolling Stone* of
November 29, 1969, Bob Dylan, questioned about Weberman, said this was nonsense.

Baby Blue" also constitutes the last of a trilogy of farewells, the previous ones being, of course, "Restless Farewell" and "It Ain't Me Babe"; we will see when we come to our discussion of the 1965 Newport Folk Festival the relevance of this point.

Bringing It All Back Home was naturally slammed by all the usual folksy types, critics, and fans: Dylan had betrayed the cause, politically and artistically. Not content with having given up writing political and sociological songs, look at the way he was corrupting the pure stream of folk with vulgar pollutions of rock 'n' roll, backings that had—horror of horrors—a commercial sound. He was described variously as a prostitute and a Fascist.

In *Sing Out!*, if Irwin Silber gave credit to "It's Alright, Ma" (in which he saw a cry of denunciation for a world where corruption seems always to be the master), he certainly didn't hold the same view about the album as a whole. He felt that it was the unfortunate realization of a cult that had made Dylan a megalomaniac and a parodist of people better than himself. In fact, it's obvious that if the album is a realization of anything, it is of Dylan's own personal existence (hence the title) and as a corollary a refutation of his role as a vanguard of the trendies and an idolized prophet; we have already mentioned his permanent self-criticism.

Nevertheless, at the same time as his earlier fans were publicly dismembering him, the new-style Dylan was succeeding in reaching a public quite different from his earlier one: a younger audience, less pseudointellectual and more spontaneous, and—the commercial success of *Bringing It All Back Home* being the proof—infinitely more numerous. Greenwich Village could sulk, but American students went wild. And Great Britain took the new Dylan straight into its arms as he made, in the spring of 1965, a long, delirious, and exhausting tour of the country, during which Pennebaker filmed most of the scenes of *Don't Look Back*. Many British pop musicians, such as the Beatles, Alan Price, and Stevie Winwood, made special efforts to meet him. Among American musicians, Joan Baez, Odetta, and Phil Ochs understood his evolution and attempted to defend it from attack.

Despite all this oil on troubled waters, storm broke out again in July 1965 at the Newport Folk Festival. Dylan was top of the bill at the closing concert, and large numbers of folk purists, come to Newport with the secret hope of seeing him return to the straight and narrow of his "honesty" of 1963, packed the place. The "trapeze art-ist" (one of the nicknames which, for scorn of the title of "poet," he had found himself with) wandered onto the Newport stage clutching an electric guitar. At the sight of this sacrilegious instrument the crowd had coronaries in all directions. During the third song, booed and hissed, Dylan stopped. The shouts took their course—"You've betrayed us!"—"Go back to the 'Ed Sullivan Show'!"

Dylan left the stage. Peter Yarrow (of Peter, Paul and Mary) in-tervened in a conciliatory way, coming to the mike to tell the crowd that if they quieted down Dylan would reappear. A few minutes later Dylan returned to the stage, tears in his eyes, carying his bat-tered old acoustic guitar, to give a dramatic rendition of "It's All Over Now, Baby Blue."

But it was the end, for a long while, of the old-style Dylan. Sev-eral other turbulent concerts confirmed it, notably the one at New York's Forest Hills stadium where the spectators, divided into two armies—the "old" and the "new"—had a grand brawl while Dylan, without batting an eyelid, continued his recital.

As Dylan put it, they could carry on disapproving to the end of time. But there was more truth in his music than there was in their disapproval.

With the release of *Highway 61 Revisited* in August 1965, the rupture was finalized. This album has, even more than the one that preceded it, the imprint of modern pop music to the extent that, unlike *Bring-ing It All Back Home,* the rock imagery is visible in the album photo-graph: Dylan is decorated with a black leather jacket, under which he is wearing a T-shirt emblazoned with the Triumph trademark.

On the musical level, two great American musicians play on the album: Al Kooper on organ and Mike Bloomfield on guitar. And the whole album raises again the question of exactly what is meant by the term "folkrock" (noting in passing that, as one might have guessed, Dylan himself disagrees with the term being used at all). The point is quite an important one, since later (in connection with *John Wesley Harding* and *Nashville Skyline*) people were going to talk about Dylan "going back to the roots." This notion, on hindsight, ap-pears erroneous since, even at the height of his "folkrock" period, Dylan was drawing on the same essential sources, rooted as they are in tradition.

Examples? Woody Guthrie for one. Who else could have evoked the title song of the album, "Highway 61 Revisited"? Highway 61 crosses the United States from north to south and is traversed by huge numbers of bums and hitchhikers of all descriptions (among them, at one point, the young Robert Zimmerman), and the song makes clear that everything happens on Highway 61. One also notes that on his first album Dylan had a blues entitled "Highway 51." Again, on this album is the definite influence of the traditional negro blues, and there is a quite brilliant example of bottleneck blues playing, worthy of any of the old Mississippi bluesmen. In fact, one finds traces of the blues throughout the entire album, whether it be from a purely formal point of view—as in "Tombstone Blues"—or where songs have captured the spirit of the blues, though formally otherwise. One example is "Just Like Tom Thumb's Blues," a depressing tale set in a brothel in the Mexican town of Juárez, but perfectly transportable to Memphis or New Orleans; another example is "Queen Jane Approximately," where the singer sends the mysterious Queen Jane an invitation, couched in highly erotic terms, to "come see" him—the correlation with something like John Lee Hooker's "Let's Make it, Baby" is obvious.

Another source of inspiration that Dylan has always drawn on is the traditional British (usually Celtic) ballad, with its rigidly rhythmical musical phrases repeated ad infinitum, its continual resurgence and its interminable verses. On this album both "Ballad of a Thin Man" and "Desolation Row" are of ballad type and certainly, even if unconsciously or indirectly, carry on the ballad tradition. Even "Like a Rolling Stone," the highly successful single taken from the album, though it is a rock 'n' roll song, bears the imprint of the same spirit. It's not too important what sort of coloring or instrumental arrangement Dylan has given these songs: their essence of balladry remains. The leopard and his spots . . .

Thematically and lyrically, there are to be found everywhere throughout Dylan's work images drawn from Scripture and references to Biblical personages and situations. Are these perhaps due to his Jewish origins? Throughout, from "A Hard Rain's A-Gonna Fall" to "The Ballad of Frankie Lee and Judas Priest," priests, children, sermons, mountains, and deluges are never too far from the surface of his mind. The first verse of "Highway 61 Revisited" sets the scene, in extraordinarily comic terms, of Abraham receiving from God the order to kill his son; in "Ballad of a Thin Man" and "Desolation Row" his apocalyptic vision is ubiquitously haunting. The whole world is involved willy-nilly in the chaos that Dylan inhabits: unless you join him on Desolation Row he doesn't even want you to send him a letter.

There are also, throughout *Highway 61 Revisited*, flavorings of other poets: in particular, of course, Allen Ginsberg (Dylan himself points to the album as being strongly influenced by Ginsberg); imagery reminiscent of Baudelaire (think of the possible correspondences between "L'invitation au voyage" and "Queen Jane Approximately," or more especially the feelings of companionship in disgrace which permeate both "Fleurs du Mal" and "Highway 61 Revisited"); from Rimbaud (who was Dylan's favorite poet), and even from the surrealists. On this last point, there are the images of Einstein disguised as Robin Hood and of T. S. Eliot engaged in a literary argument with Ezra Pound in the captain's tower on board the *Titanic*.

In May 1966 *Blonde on Blonde*, Dylan's first double album and a natural progression from *Highway 61 Revisited*, was released. Most people rate this album as the ultimate culmination of Dylan's work. One must be constantly careful of falling into the trap of naming a "best work," but . . .

A technical detail, not much noted at the time, emerges in retrospect as significant: *Blonde on Blonde* was recorded at Nashville with the assistance of numerous musicians whose more common field was country and western, such as Charlie McCoy on harmonica and Kenny Buttrey on percussion.

In essence the album is very close to *Highway 61 Revisited;* in fact, one rediscovers on the later album almost all the principal components present in the earlier: blues either in the flesh ("Pledging My Time") or in spirit (as with most of the tracks, but particularly "Memphis Blues Again"); eroticism ("Visions of Johanna," "Just Like a Woman," "Absolutely Sweet Marie," and above all the highly celebrated, marvelous "I Want You"); derivations from the British ballad form, especially the monumental eleven-minutes-plus "Sad-Eyed Lady of the Lowlands" (the low pitch is particularly Scottish). Rarely can any woman of dreams have been described with the savage beauty of "Sad-Eyed Lady of the Lowlands."

However, all these components do not by themselves suffice to explain why *Blonde on Blonde* is a landmark in the history of pop

music, unless as a repetition, however able, of the formulas that originated in *Highway 61 Revisited*. In what other way does it have importance? I've already said that it was Bob Dylan's first double album
but, even more important, it was *the* first double album (so far as I
can determine) ever released by a modern songwriter. For the first
time, the notion of the album as a work in itself emerges, a notion
previously reserved for "classical" music (perhaps a bourgeois notion, but nevertheless important), but now making its incursion into
the world of modern song. This album is a whole, it has a construction: an introduction, a development, and a conclusion. The era
when an album was built up merely of a bundle of tracks set down in
any old order was nearly over.

One is expected to write, I'm afraid, of both *Highway 61 Revisited*
and *Blonde on Blonde* as an "affirmation of *life*." I think, however, it's
more important to realize that both albums are a cry from the heart
for the *survival* of the individual who knows full well that, as Paul
Nelson has it, anything that an individual hasn't accomplished, the
rest of the world can't either. Dylan invites us all to become creative
artists. Which makes perhaps finally, and paradoxically, *Highway 61
Revisited* and *Blonde on Blonde* the two albums of Dylan, and possibly
of the entire "folk revival," most deeply part of the folk tradition.

Much later, other giants of both the pop and the folk scenes
(such as Joan Baez, Richie Havens, the Beatles, Simon and Garfunkel, and Pink Floyd) followed Dylan's example in their own way.
And they would be the first to admit that they had learned from that
songwriter who, in his youth, had come to New York to recover the
spiritual heritage of the dying troubador of the dust storms, Woody
Guthrie.

But the wheel of fortune cannot be dodged. Not long after the
release of *Blonde on Blonde* Bob Dylan vanished for a period of total
retreat and absolute silence that lasted more than a year. What had
happened? The official reason advanced was that he had had a bad
motorcycle accident; this accident did in fact take place, and Dylan
was confined to a hospital for a few weeks. But there was a more
serious problem: during 1965 he had on several occasions admitted
to drug-taking. Without being able to say exactly what kind of dope
he was on, it is certain that for about two years Dylan was
dangerously close to losing his physical and mental health. One need
do no more than look at the pale photograph of him on the sleeve of

Blonde on Blonde or listen to the strangely hazy timbre of his voice to convince oneself. The reports of his friends would tend to confirm this impression: Richard Fariña (who was close to Dylan as the brother-in-law of Joan Baez, the "Johanna" of "Visions of Johanna") remarked that, whereas some people burned the candle at both ends, this wasn't enough for Dylan: he wanted to set fire to the middle as well, so that more people could see it. It is thus more than likely that a drastic cure continued long after the wounded motor-cyclist had recovered from his injuries.

These circumstances explain why it was not until January 1968 that Dylan's next album, *John Wesley Harding,* was released. The wait was worth it since Dylan seems to have pulled himself out of the abyss and cured of his illness. His voice is much clearer, his diction has become much more intelligible, and the whole album has an air of freshness about it.

Musically, the straightforward folk style is once again dominant: the acoustic guitar, the plaintive passages of harmonica, and the Guthrie-style melody lines predominate. Apart from acoustic guitar and harmonica, the only other instruments used are, occasionally, the piano, steel guitar, and the excellent percussion of Kenny Buttrey.

The title track tells the story of John Wesley Harding, a friend to the poor. The lyrics are filled with obscure allusions bound to appeal to the peculiar detective skills of A. J. Weberman, who sees in them fascinating parallels that could apply perfectly to the old-style Dylan: Dylan sings no more than the truth; his remarks hurt no one but hypocrites; [6] his action is right on the spot in the depths of Mississippi, where Goodman, Schwerner, and Chaney were murdered, and where Dylan sang for the blacks in 1963. All just troubling coincidences?

"As I Went Out One Morning" (again according to Weberman, with whom on this occasion we agree) is straightforwardly autobiographical, though transposed into symbolic terms. The facts: in 1964 Dylan was invited to a cocktail party at the Americana Hotel, New York, by the Emergency Civil Liberties Committee to be awarded

[6] Though, according to Anthony Scaduto's *Bob Dylan,* he hurt a lot of honest people quite badly; as for example Phil Ochs, when Ochs made the mistake of saying that he honestly thought "Can You Please Crawl Out Your Window" was a bad record. —P.B.

the Thomas Paine Award as recognition of his work and influence. He turned up but was visibly turned off by the whole spectacle of radical chic (luxury hotel, fur coats, bulging buffets, and all that). Seeing that these representatives of a movement theoretically dedicated to easing the plight of poor unfortunates were in fact nothing more than the worst bourgeoisie, Dylan created a furore ("I have a little of Lee Harvey Oswald in me," he confessed. "In spirit we were all at Dallas on the twenty-second of November.") He left, refusing to accept the prize (he eventually accepted it after long negotiation). The story is told symbolically in "As I Went Out One Morning": As the narrator went out one morning to breathe the air around Tom Paine, he met a fair damsel. He offered her his hand but she took his arm (that is to say, he offered them his help, but they wanted the whole of him), and he knew that very instant that she meant to do him harm. In the end, Tom Paine himself intervenes to apologize for the actions of the "damsel" (that is, the committee) to Dylan, and tells him he is sorry for what she's done.

A sort of mystical dream, "I Dreamed I Saw St. Augustine" is sung in an ironic tone which seems to be in the way of a new rejection of the world, with the writer participating in the dream, as in *Bringing It All Back Home*.

"All Along the Watchtower" is a highly successful song with a superb rhythm (think of the incredible version of it given to us by the late Jimi Hendrix). The lyrics are no less impressive:

> *"there must be some way out of here"*
> *said the joker to the thief*
> *"there's too much confusion here*
> *I can't get no relief.*
> *businessmen they drink my wine*
> *ploughmen dig my earth.*
> *not one of them along the line*
> *knows what any of it is worth."* *

Are these the words of a man who has sold out to the Establishment?

"The Ballad of Frankie Lee and Judas Priest" is probably the best known, the most talked about, and also the most intriguing (though some would say the most overrated) of the twelve songs on the

---

* Bob Dylan, "All Along the Watchtower." Copyright © 1968 by Dwarf Music. Used by permission of Dwarf Music and B. Feldman & Co., Ltd.

album. Frankie Lee is guessed to be the Dylan of 1965–66, and Judas Priest . . . who else but Al Grossman, his old manager? The song lashes back again at the "judges," the "critics," the "purists" who attacked Dylan way back in sixty-five. A messenger asks the narrator if he's Frankie Lee: there's someone waiting for him who calls himself Priest. Always an irony, at the same time admirable and provocative. The moral of the last verse pleads in favor of what is to come, and requests good sense—don't confuse Paradise with the house along the way. So, don't judge others by your own criteria.

If Frankie Lee isn't Dylan, who else can he be? The conviction is strengthened by the prose poem (again of Biblical flavor) that adorns the back of the album. Three kings are speaking together. The first king has a broken arm, the second, a broken nose; the third, who is poor, says to the other two: "The key is Frank." The three kings go to find Frank, tell him that there is a new Bob Dylan album on the market, which of course contains nothing but the Dylan songs themselves: they assume Frank is the key to their understanding. And Frank admits that he is. He gives them a demonstration, by breaking an ampule and a pill, and the three kings return satisfied: on the road, the arm of the first and the nose of the second are miraculously cured, and the third has become rich.

"Drifter's Escape" again sets the scene of Dylan faced by his judges. This time they have formed a tribunal. But at the end, while everybody is kneeling to pray, the drifter chooses the moment to escape . . . on his motorbike, one assumes.

"Dear Landlord," which contains a brilliant piano part played by Dylan himself, seems to be a supplication addressed to those who would like to make him their puppet. At any rate, the last verse of the song ends:

> *and if you don't underestimate me*
> *I won't underestimate you.**

For "I Am a Lonesome Hobo" there is little need for interpretation for, even if the lyrics are taken quite literally, the autobiographical sense is preserved. The same is true of "The Wicked Messenger" and "Down Along the Cove," two of the other songs on the album.

---

* Bob Dylan, "Dear Landlord." Copyright © 1968 by Dwarf Music. Used by permission of Dwarf Music and B. Feldman & Co., Ltd.

But with "I Pity the Poor Immigrant" the sense is not nearly so easy to come by. Weberman, with his ill-directed Marxist obsessions, sees in the "poor immigrant" the American soldier forced against his will to fight in Vietnam. For our part, we feel that the immigrant is none other than Dylan himself, the lyric, for example, at one point applying to the continuous self-delusion of the drug addict.

It is tempting to consider "I'll Be Your Baby Tonight," which closes the album, as nothing more than an invitation to loving. And certainly it is, on a superficial level. On the second level, it was to take a further year for the explanation to become clear; in fact, we have already noticed instances of the last song on a Dylan album being the forerunner of the next album (think of "Restless Farewell"). The sound of "I'll Be Your Baby Tonight" is tranquil, intimate, as if Dylan is trying to speak (in a gentle voice) to his listeners of all sorts, traditionalists and progressives at last reconciled, asking them to restore to him their trust. Perhaps this is why one should listen particularly to the words of this song:

> *kick your shoes off*
> *do not fear*
> *bring that bottle over here*
> *I'll be your*
> *baby tonight* *

From all points of view, *John Wesley Harding,* despite its apparent simplicity, is an album extremely rich in surprising revelations, and even more in enigmas. It is a return to protest but in a more mature form, disguised homage to Woody Guthrie, autobiography, a record of memories (in his hospital bed, the patient / addict must have had plenty of time to think about his own past) or of healed wounds. There were to be fifteen months for us all to practice our detective skills before the release of Dylan's next album and the start of his next "scandal": *Nashville Skyline* and what came after.

It was in April 1969 that *Nashville Skyline* came on the scene. It is perhaps still too early to evaluate this album objectively and certainly it lacks, particularly on a lyrical level, the complexity that would

* Bob Dylan, "I'll Be Your Baby Tonight." Copyright © 1968 by Dwarf Music. Used by permission of Dwarf Music and B. Feldman & Co., Ltd.

require any form of analysis. Let us be satisfied then with noting the principal characteristics of the album.

It was recorded in the same Nashville studios with the same band of session musicians, apart from a few minor changes of personnel, as *John Wesley Harding* had been. Among other things, it is worth noting a new recording of "Girl from the North Country" sung as a duo with Johnny Cash (a number of commentators frankly admit that they prefer the earlier version). All in all, the tracks are very much under the influence of country and western, and not always with advantageous results. Instrumentally, the Hawaiian guitar is too insipid; lyrically, Dylan does not hesitate to plagiarize clichés from the worst kind of C & W, along the lines of "the moon is shining bright" and all that. But one must give justice to Dylan and the other musicians on the album: technically, the performance on *Nashville Skyline* is perfect from the first note on Side One right through to the last note on Side Two.

But the novelty that is perhaps the most spectacular part of the album is the change in Dylan's voice—it has suddenly gained a clarity though, unfortunately, this sometimes deteriorates into a reedy affectation. In *Rolling Stone,* November 29, 1969, he explained that this change had come about because he had given up smoking. His new voice certainly adds an extra dimension to his beautiful love songs, tender and lacking all pretension, such as "Lay Lady Lay" or "Tonight I'll Be Staying Here with You." On other occasions ("One More Night," "To Be Alone with You") it soon becomes pretty nauseating.

The general atmosphere of the album is relaxed and companionable, with many references to a tempestuous past (save perhaps in "I Threw It All Away") or a world of chaos as a contrast to a new life; in good health, rich, married, the father of a family, Dylan has rediscovered a tranquillity of the body, heart, and spirit which one could describe as "well earned." We are delighted for his sake, but the dearth of inspiration on the album leaves us unsatisfied. On *Nashville Skyline* the highway is now bedecked with pretty flowers, little birds sing sweetly in all directions, beautiful young women abound; but it's the road that goes around the writer's perfect house in the country, and that's a long way from where we are.

At the end of August 1969 he created another furor on the occasion of the famous Isle of Wight rock festival. Although he hadn't appeared onstage for months, Bob Dylan accepted an offer to appear at the festival for the modest sum of some £20,000. A crowd estimated at rather more than two hundred thousand people (some of whom had flown especially from places as distant as the United States, Canada, and Japan) waited patiently for him to appear. Accompanied by his five friends who form that excellent group, the Band, Dylan gave a superb performance before abruptly leaving the stage and, without warning, disappearing from the scene—at the end of only an hour's performance. With all respect to the liberty of the artist, the crowd was unnecessarily insulted by his action: one could retort to Dylan that "If you don't underestimate us, we won't underestimate you." [7]

Is it true, then, that Dylan has degenerated into a money-maker, a petulant superstar? It is impossible, even today, to answer a question like that. We've already talked about the dangers of making any absolute statement about a man as mercurial as Dylan (one can counteract his behavior at the Isle of Wight by thinking of his unexpected free performance at the charity concert organized by George Harrison to raise funds for the refugees in Bangladesh: it was a magnificent example of Dylan at the very acme of his powers), and there is no way in which any commentator can clarify the situation, write down on paper the character that is Dylan. For all that, there are small signs that provide intriguing pointers as to where his head's now at: for example, his replies to various of the questions in that *Rolling Stone* interview. Asked about his musical tastes, in particular concerning artists as diverse as Ray Stevens, Stevie Winwood, Joan Baez, and the Jefferson Airplane, his response was practically identical in every case: he liked them, he'd liked them right from the very beginning. And, on professional matters, he announced his desire and intention to devote his time to managing and directing "show-business" (his term) artists. We must wait to see, when his intentions are realized, what Dylan will make out of his new role.

June of 1970 saw the release of his second double album, *Self Portrait*. However much time and devotion are spent listening to it, and

[7] Cf. the report on the Isle of Wight Festival by Philippe Koechlin in *Rock & Folk*, no. 33, pp. 35–55.

however much leeway one gives to the creative impulse of the artist, it is still hard to find a motive for the recording of this album: laziness? The review of it in *Rolling Stone* summed up the attitude of most critics and most of the public. The review opened with, "Say, what is this shit . . . ?" Is Dylan mocking that section of the rock world that he thinks too pretentious? Is he spitting in the faces of his critics? Was he at the mercy of political or commercial pressures, as some reporters have it?

Whatever our questions, the only thing that we can base our judgment on is the music itself. There are several distinctive traits on the album: the title, *Self Portrait*, is perfectly appropriate. Making, I suppose, some sort of point to the listener (maybe, "Where am I in 1970?"), he presents to us a catalog of his talents, his musical tastes, and his personal preferences.

Only a few of the tracks are the product of Dylan's own pen. Most of the twenty-four songs on the album are either traditional or by other contemporary songwriters. Eight of the tracks are of an unprecedented banality, and perhaps the lowest point of the whole collection is a travesty of "The Boxer," Paul Simon's touching song about a man exploited and ruined by the fight game. The style and spirit of the album (there are fifty session men—all, of course, technically perfect) belong less to the world of modern rock music, more to the world of show biz.

Dylan, certainly conscious of and probably reveling in the complaints and protests he has engendered among successive generations of his followers, here reaches the heights in his rejection of his role. In short, there are ten good tracks among the twenty-four on the album (my particular favorite is a phenomenal version of "Days of 49," a traditional song about the gold rush), ten worthwhile pieces of Dylan at his best. If these ten had been released as an album on their own, one might have been able to sing his praises anew, but not when they are littered with the rest of this heterogeneous nonsense.

With *New Morning*, released in October 1970, there was at last a rebirth of hope, though the album is hardly the revolutionary innovation that one might expect from its title. It adds nothing to the glory of the author of *Blonde on Blonde*, the album of Dylan's with which it was most compared, though it must be admitted that certainly is is better than the average album released in those times and even more certainly an improvement on his previous two releases.

One of the best points about the album is that Dylan had regained that deeply sarcastic, gloomy mastery of the voice that illuminated *Blonde on Blonde* (for example, "Time Passes Slowly," one of the highlights of *New Morning*). On a lyrical level, though "Day of the Locusts" is certainly lyrically successful, the remainder of the tracks are generally mundane with occasional moments that cannot be described as other than embarrassing. Nevertheless, it must be admitted that there are one or two bright lights, good new ideas or fine turns of phrase, that shine through the fog. But these are in the nature of first drafts, as in "Father of Night," an extremely simple-minded song that suggests, albeit tentatively only, that the writer may just have been interested in mysticism.

If one doesn't pay too much close attention to the lyrical weaknesses there are some very nice songs on the album ("nice" is the most fitting word for them). Perhaps the best in this way is the first track on the album, "New Morning" itself. Here Dylan is at his happiest, and it's a far cry from the kind of rose-colored-glasses happiness evinced by *Nashville Skyline*. If you like, he is rejoicing in the spiritual and bodily communion he has with his lady, both watching as the new day breaks. If one really wants to find a deeper meaning in everything, then one could say that it is in fact Dylan speaking to his audience, saying, look, the pair of us can trust each other—forget what's gone before, everything is reborn with the passage of time. But this is probably to read far more into a good commercial pop song than was originally intended to be there.

One could endlessly criticize *New Morning,* but it has to be admitted that it was well received by the critics and that large sections of the public consider it the best of all Dylan's albums. Why this should be so, it is rather hard to say. Perhaps because it is the first time that Dylan had united, on more than the occasional track, a genuine feeling of happiness with music that is really, often extremely, good. *Blonde on Blonde* was lyrically and musically staggering, *Nashville Skyline* showed Dylan in a relaxed, content mood, but it is on *New Morning* that for the first time he achieves a synthesis of the two.

It was in early 1974 that Dylan's next album proper was put on the market. (In the interim *More Bob Dylan's Greatest Hits* and *Dylan* had been released, the first being a mixture of tracks from earlier albums and previously unreleased tracks, the second an ungainly hodge-podge of offcuts that had lain around in the Columbia studios.) *Planet Waves* is an exceptional album, showing a return to Dylan's earlier style, and with it, to his earlier power. Symptomatic of this is the fact that the only musicians on the album are Dylan himself and the five members of the Band who, if you remember, were years ago Bob Dylan's backup group for live performances.

It's hard to pick out any track in particular—"Going Going Gone," "Hazel," "Something There Is About You," "Forever Young"—all clamor for detailed attention. But perhaps the one that is most interesting for our purposes, in the light of what we have earlier said, is the last track on the album, "Wedding Song." As Dylan puts it:

> *it's never been my duty to remake the world at large*
> *nor is it my intentions to sound the battle charge.**

It might seem, from what has been said, that the career of Dylan has been one littered with twists and turns, one which has never had any cohesion, any sense of direction. This is perhaps at least partially true, but it is also most certainly partially an oversimplification. At least one prime characteristic of the writer flows all the way through his work, from *Bob Dylan* to *Planet Waves:* the fact that he is a natural rebel.

His rebellion may change its nature, from the early days of political protest, through the musical rebellion of electrifying folk and refusing the role forced on to him by his early fans, the personal rebellion of writing about himself rather than about the problems of the world, the rebellion against being expected to sing new songs that are just like the ones that have gone before, the rebellion against being expected to record his own songs only. . . . And of course one cannot evaluate the influence that this has had on the young of today, particularly in America and Britain: if you like, the freedom of thought, the enlarging of horizons that are possibly more important than political freedom. And in so doing he has asserted his own freedom.

Perhaps it is for the future to pass the final judgment on the life and work of Dylan—if judgment is necessary. And perhaps it is for the future also to pay him the only token of respect that finally is of any importance whatsoever: that of having understood him.

the new generation

Following closely in the footsteps of Dylan, the reborn folk movement swiftly brought other first-rate singer-songwriters into the public eye. In this respect, the first name that must come to mind is that of Tom Paxton. Before his memorable triumph in front of two hundred thousand spectators at the Isle of Wight Festival in August 1969, Tom Paxton's career had followed a long and difficult road.

He was born in Chicago in 1937, where he lived until he was eleven years old. In 1948 the family moved to the little town of Bristow, Oklahoma. Three months later his father died. But apart from that, he seems to have enjoyed a very happy adolescence: he played the trumpet in an orchestra, a little football, basketball, read Kenneth Roberts, James Oliver Curwood, and Jack London (who still remains one of his idols). He had his first unhappy love affair and had his share of expeditions to the principal's office.

In time, he went to the University of Oklahoma and enrolled as a student in the school of dramatic art there, studying for four years. At that time his idol was James Dean, and he would spend hours having what he thought were splendid nostalgias. As he puts it, "Never underestimate the capacity of a man to make an ass of himself!"

It was around this time that music began to replace the theater as Paxton's prime preoccupation. In the company of his fellow students, he would spend fruitful and ecstatic hours listening to the great folk commercial successes of the day, such as Ed McCurdy's *Blood, Booze 'n' Bones* or *The Weavers at Carnegie Hall*. And with the aid of his guitar and a collection of Burl Ives songs, which the student Paxton very swiftly learned to perform, he decided to become a songwriter. But Paxton wasn't content merely to copy his first influences, and added his own personal experiences; it wasn't long before he had plenty of personal experiences from which to draw.

During his period of military service, which he was fortunate enough to complete in the interim period between Korea and Vietnam, he discovered at firsthand the inhumanity of war while working on the exercises which he was forced to undergo as a young conscript: the operation of the tommy gun, of the bayonet, and the grenade, which inspired his famous song, "The Willing Conscript."

In 1962, returning to civilian life, Tom Paxton had found his vocation as a professional songwriter. He started to publish his songs in *Broadside* and frequently performed in the Greenwich Village folk clubs like the Bitter End (to which he was to return faithfully many times in the future) and the Gaslight; often he would install himself in these clubs and work on his new songs. Milton Okun, the musical director of The Brothers Four and Peter, Paul and Mary, was one of the first professionals to spot the talent of Tom Paxton and encourage him to keep singing and writing. Tom developed the habit of phoning Okun to sing him the first drafts of new songs. And at the beginning of 1964, after his success at Newport, Elektra released his first album, entitled *Ramblin' Boy*.

At the beginning, he confesses, he saw himself as the new Woody Guthrie; but in due course he realized that he was something rather different. Nevertheless, *Ramblin' Boy* (as one might guess from the title alone) is indisputably stamped with the example and the spirit of the "school" of Guthrie. Thus we can understand the presence of social themes throughout the collection, as in "A Job of Work" (about the loss of pride in a man who can't get a job) and, even more, in "Standing on the Edge of Town," where the narrator of the song tells of his life bumming around trying to find odd jobs here and there.

In "High Sheriff of Hazard" he tackles the great Kentucky mineowners and their collusion with the government and the local police. But, although the song is framed in humorous terms, the political drive is never far beneath the surface.

Other problems of the collective nature of society are dealt with, but Paxton treats them almost always in terms of the individual. For example, "When Morning Breaks" is less another war song, more the apprehensive reflections of a young soldier who must leave the next day to go to the front, all told in the first person. And when

Paxton denounces (without losing his humor) the follies of the American educational system, he does so by telling of a young boy relating to his father "what he learnt at school today":

> *I learnt our government must be strong*
> *it's always right and never wrong . . .**

But one of his finest satires concerns the New York paper, the *Daily News,* which he sees as a symbol of the brutalization of the masses by a journal with the conceit of describing itself as "the people's." As Paxton says on the back of the album, you don't need to satirize it, just quote it. In the song, all the worst elements of American reactionary society emerge and, because of their juxtaposition, the final effect is extremely funny: at the end of each revelation there comes the invariable response that he knows because he read it in the *Daily News.*

All the time, Paxton remains the realist. Without ever particularly carrying banners, he merely diagnoses the symptoms of the sickness of America. This was probably a lesson learned from Bob Dylan (he credits Phil Ochs with having taught him how to laugh about it at the same time), and it is not hard to see traces of "A Hard Rain's A-Gonna Fall" in "A Rumblin' in the Land."

Another omnipresent theme in Paxton's work, and one in which he is faithful to the folk tradition that was the forerunner of his songs, is that of voyages, of the size of the earth, of aimless wanderings, symbolized by the quasi-mythological highway: "Ramblin' Boy" is the song of his that provides the most typical example, but others on the album reflect better the classic dualism axiomatic to this strain of folk song: on the one hand, the irresistible appeal of nature, expressed in "I'm Bound for the Mountains and the Sea"; on the other, in the magnificent standard, "I Can't Help but Wonder Where I'm Bound," he draws attention to (speaking from personal experience, it seems) the dangers of aimless vagabondage.

By turns political and, in complete contrast, intimate, common throughout all the themes of Tom Paxton is a particular feeling of tenderness (the famous "The Last Thing on My Mind" is one of the finest examples); the man can recoil in revulsion from something, but he cannot hate. This characteristic is, as Tom Paxton would be the first to admit, one result of his lifelong admiration for the works of Jacques Brel.

His second and third albums, *Ain't That News!* and *Outward Bound,* both on Elektra, continued his development along the lines started in *Ramblin' Boy:* a very genuine though totally nonpartisan political and social sense, an attachment to all that seemed to him solid and durable. Hence, many of his songs are dedicated to his wife, Midge, such as "Hold On to Me, Babe" and "Every Time" (as well as the beautiful "My Lady's a Wild Flying Dove" on his first album); hence also his frequent recourse to tunes, rhythms, and backings of a traditional type, to which he splices more modern lyrics—as in "King of My Backyard" and "All the Way Home"— though adding for his own part a deep desire to preserve the certainties of life. It is in this way that the work of Tom Paxton diverges totally from that of Bob Dylan: though perfectly conscious of the injustices and the follies of the world around him, he nevertheless refuses to see it through despairing eyes.

At the beginning of 1966 Tom Paxton came for the first time to sing in London (at the request of a British admirer). In the cellar of an obscure London pub, before an audience of about sixty, he gave his first English performance for the modest fee of £30. He was nevertheless highly satisfied with his experience in England and promised to return: remember his tender farewell, "Leaving London." Much later he was to be asked in an interview what, in his opinion, was the best decision he had ever made during his career. His reply came firmly that in his opinion the best thing he'd ever done was go to England, that it had been something of great importance to him, the finding of a public that understood his songs better than the American public itself.[1]

In July 1968, after a brief retreat into the background to write some new material, Tom Paxton reappeared spectacularly with, simultaneously, an appearance at Greenwich Village's Bitter End and the release of his new album, *Morning Again.* The title seems to announce a renaissance of musical inspiration (cf. Dylan's "New Morning") on the part of the author of "Ramblin' Boy." Listening to it, one can even talk in terms of a new beginning. During his withdrawal from the public eye, Paxton made innumerable important discoveries: in the first place, he listened with profit to some of the

[1] Interview with François Ayral in *Pop-Music,* no. 9, May 28, 1970.

finest pop musicians to emerge during his earlier period; he realized the necessity for the principal representatives of urban folk music to evolve toward more complex musical forms; and finally, he had the experience of being on the bill with Jacques Brel at the latter's farewell concert at Carnegie Hall at the end of 1967. Even though Paxton speaks hardly a word of French, he was intensely affected by Brel's songs and considers him to be the finest songwriter from any country in the world (he rates him higher even than Bob Dylan).

Despite these innovations, Paxton, his conception much clarified, nevertheless remains faithful to the tradition that he entered at the start: hence the extraordinary, satirical "Talking Vietnam Potluck Blues," a classic spoken blues to the sole accompaniment of his guitar, which deals with pot smoking in the U.S. Army (and suggests that they may have found the way to end the war peacefully). This received the biggest ovation of all at the Isle of Wight Festival in 1969 but was stamped on by the censors of most of the radio and TV stations in America itself. The whole of *Morning Again* demonstrates a slight moving away from strictly traditional folk idioms toward pop music proper. On the album he uses brass, percussion, cello, flute, guitar, and electric bass to provide backing. On not all of the songs is a proper equilibrium maintained in the use of these instruments—since, after all, it was his first tentative essay into a new sphere. Nevertheless, there are several promising successes on the album: "Clarissa Jones" is a fine rhythm song, and "Now That I've Taken My Life" is an excellent drama a la Brel.

In November 1968, at the suggestion of a group of his French followers, he gave in Paris his first French recital, at the Centre Americaine on the Boulevard Raspail, before an audience of four hundred. The novelty for him, of course, was that he had never before performed in front of a non-English-speaking audience. He repeated the experience in May 1970 at the Salle de l'Olympia in a more convincing manner still: although the audience was thin (a Saturday in Pentecost at half-past midnight!), the audience applauded for more than two hours.

His more recent albums (*The Things I Notice Now, Album Number 6, How Come the Sun, Peace Will Come,* as well as a live album called *The Compleat Tom Paxton*) represent a logical continuation of the road he started with *Morning Again. The Things I Notice Now* is an exceptional attempt to unify several genres: jazz is there ("The Things I

Notice Now"), but also a renaissance sound ("Wish I Had a Trouba-
dor"), sophisticated folk songs ("I Give You the Morning" and "All
Night Long"), rock 'n' roll ("Bishop Cody's Last Request"), and a
Brelian song ("About the Children").

But the most astounding track on the album is without a doubt
"The Iron Man." We have here, in effect, far more than simply an
orchestrated song, but a veritable song-symphony, in several movements, lasting for more than fifteen minutes. It is probably because
of this latter fact that "The Iron Man," too long to be played on conventional radio stations, remains essentially unknown to the great
majority of the public, on top of which the complexity of the orchestration prohibits Paxton from performing it onstage. Despite these
handicaps, with "The Iron Man" the song-symphony is born.

It is remarkable that, all the different genres used being apparently immiscible (at least until the release of this album), the
result is a work of music and poetry that is totally homogeneous, the
piano of David Horowitz complementing perfectly the excellent
acoustic guitar work (it's a Martin) of Tom Paxton himself.

Having come to the maturity of his creativity, to a superbly satis-
fying balance of music and lyrics, Tom Paxton explores in his *Album
No. 6* new areas of inspiration. In "Whose Garden Was This?" for
perhaps the first time he sings from the heart in the most poignant
terms of the disillusionment of a man who has habitually refused to
despair. An antipollution song of the first order, showing Tom Paxton to be a writer of realism, it depicts a future when people can no
longer remember that once upon a time prairies were green, oceans
blue, and birds flew. But the emotion that pours from "Whose Garden Was This?" (the melody, too, being important here) is so over-
powering that it could be transferred to any of man's destructive
follies. The same theme is repeated in "Dogs at Midnight," but probably with less success.

"Forest Lawn," "Annie's Going to Sing Her Song," and "Molly
Bloom," above all the last, give to Side One a more easygoing manner (and, for Paxton, loving and laughter are inseparable). Side Two
opens with a homage to John Lennon: "Crazy John." Here again,
Paxton's tenderness as he speaks of Lennon is incredible.

"Saturday Night" introduces a new technique in satirical song:
the use of two melodies superimposed on one another, the first one

of great anguish, the second destroying voluntarily the grim atmosphere to produce comic levity (we have already mentioned Paxton's lyrical juxtaposition as a comic effect in connection with "Daily News"). But the second high point of the album (the first being "Whose Garden Was This?") is certainly "Jimmy Newman." An American soldier at the front—one presumes it is Vietnam, but the author has the subtlety of never naming it—attempts to awaken his friend Jimmy Newman: they're coming to take them home; but still Jimmy Newman sleeps obstinately on. Paxton's voice becomes progressively more frantic: Jimmy's going to miss the plane. And although the words are never said, we know that Jimmy Newman is sleeping for the last time. One sees that "Jimmy Newman" (like "When Morning Breaks" in 1963) is much more than a song about the war: it is at the same time a drama (because war or its suppression depends solely upon human will) and a tragedy (because we are all, even during times of peace, preparing for death). Tom Paxton succeeds, by personalizing the cruelties of war, in shocking the listener far more than any statistics of dead and wounded could ever do.

More recently, he has continued the same logical progress as shown through these three albums. But with time has come a maturity that is a little more difficult to appreciate immediately. In his mixing of genres he has become more practiced, but with this he has lost a little of the rough excitement of freshness that was present earlier. There are a few exceptions: on the album *Peace Will Come,* for example, the title track is barely more than a chant, with Paxton multitracking his voice, that is yet effective where more complex songs might have failed; and on the same album there is "Jesus Christ (SRO)"—the letters standing for "Standing Room Only"—which tells how at last Jesus has become a box-office smash: his daddy always knew he could make it big!

And where does he go from here? It is much less difficult to predict for Paxton than for someone like Bob Dylan. For Paxton, both the man and his music, has the special characteristic of stability. He has never pretended to be a revolutionary singer but is satisfied with being merely a commentator on his times. Smoking his pipe and strumming his guitar serenely, solid as a rock, he replies faithfully "present" to all those who call his name. Without ever forgetting his past, he has matured his art to a degree of downright honesty that compels respect.

Unlike Tom Paxton, Phil Ochs is practically unknown in Europe and Britain. This is a severe loss on the part of the countries involved, since Ochs is one of the prime figures of the urban folk revival and one of the finest, most innovative songwriters of recent years.

He was born in 1940 in the border city of El Paso, Texas. But, like many other American families, his moved to a different state, Ohio, where he spent the most part of his boyhood and adolescence. As with most boys of his generation (he was fifteen in 1955), he conceived his first musical passion for the rock 'n' roll of Bill Haley, then Elvis Presley and Jerry Lee Lewis, all of whom caused a considerable stir in their time. But, several years after his sojourn into rock fandom, over the horizon came the folk revival: the young Ochs, dividing his time between the study of journalism at Ohio State University, learning the guitar, and writing articles for various of the student magazines, discovered in his turn the attractions of the folk song and moreover, by extension, its contemporary importance, its uses to express directly the problems of the moment, its truth. At this time it was inconceivable that the mission of protest could be entrusted to rock 'n' roll or pop music, and repeated listening to Pete Seeger, The Weavers, Odetta, and even The Kingston Trio began to give Phil Ochs new ideas.

Skeptical about his own future and above all about the possibilities of freedom of expression, however limited, through writing articles for other people's newspapers, Ochs decided to create his own, *The Word.* His friend Jim Glover, with whom he shared a college room, shortly lured him away from the world of the university—to the profit of the world of song. He formed his own group, the Sundowners, and they started to perform for thirty dollars a week in a club in Cincinnati where he met Bob Gibson. At the beginning, the Sundowners considered themselves to be a commercial group occasionally performing songs with political relevance. But the first song Phil Ochs wrote, "The Cuban Invasion," achieved a success denied to all their others, encouraging its author to continue in this vein. That was in 1962.

Another songwriter, John Wynn, passing through Cincinnati, introduced to Ochs the magazine *Broadside,* and he decided to take his chance in New York. Ochs followed the usual course: sojourns in the South among the Kentucky miners and black militants, songs published in *Broadside,* frequent appearances at the Greenwich Village clubs, discovery at the Newport Folk Festival, and so to a recording contract.

Some months before Tom Paxton's *Ramblin' Boy* was released on Elektra, Phil Ochs's first album came from the same company. The title was significant: *All the News That's Fit to Sing,* an allusion to the well-known slogan of *The New York Times,* "All the news that's fit to print." His style, from the moment that he starts playing, is incisive, sometimes cynical. At this time he had a lot in common with Tom Paxton who, expressing above all the right of the individual to be free, refused to be considered as the voice of any particular party or ideology. In the meantime, while individual and collective liberty are the objects of public mockery, he replies with his guitar.

With a voice often passionately angry, he sets about all the windmills that the press and public opinion seem to have missed. What are the principal themes of his work at this time? No surprises: war and racism. At this time the escalation in Vietnam was just beginning, and in "Talking Vietnam" (a talking blues performed with dazzling satiric verve), he excels in describing humorously what is not in the slightest humorous. A young GI who has profited vastly from his training tells how "maneuvers" is the word that they have been taught to use—very useful when they get lost. He then meets Syngman Rhee, Madame Nhu ("the sweetheart of Dien Bien Phu"), and the ghost of President Diem. The song closes with his presence at a television press conference, where he tells the assembled journalists that he doesn't have a country for which to give his life.

As was Bob Dylan, Phil Ochs was much affected by the Cuban crisis, and it inspired in him "Talking Cuban Crisis," another spoken blues with the same dazzling fire as "Talking Vietnam" and which is certainly every bit as good as the talking blues Dylan was producing at that time. Since 1962 Americans have not been allowed to leave their country for Cuba without a special visa that is extremely hard to obtain. Some, like the journalist William Worthy, who launched a campaign against the restriction of freedom of movement, protested and continued traveling to Cuba. Phil Ochs dedicated a ballad to this apostle of reconciliation. Pointing out that the only route to Cuba passes by the CIA, he puts into the mouth of the government the paradoxical concept: if you live in the free world, that's where you *must* stay!

For dramas on a more personal level, Ochs's voice becomes serious, as when he sings of the death of the crew of a submarine which foundered while on maneuvers ("The *Thresher*"), or when he evokes (in "Knock on the Door") the anguish of men living under a dictatorship, whether it be of the right or the left.

With the increase of racial strife at demonstrations concerning which he often assisted, notably in Mississippi, Phil Ochs (like Dylan) in "Too Many Martyrs" devoted his attention to the murder of Medgar Evers.

But the best song of all on the album is certainly "Lou Marsh," the story of a young New York Youth Board street worker, who was accidentally murdered in a confrontation with four members of a street gang. Phil Ochs sets the scene to a throbbing melody of rare beauty. Spanish Harlem, fists, boots. And every shadow perhaps not empty.

Despite his corrosive humor, alternating with a genuine sense of drama, Phil Ochs, on the grounds of his first album (which acknowledges Woody Guthrie among others in "Bound for Glory") is vulnerable to criticism on two important points: one, that the quality of his tunes (with some brilliant exceptions, such as "Lou Marsh") and his guitar playing does not match the quality of his excellent lyrics and ideas; two, lacking the finesse that we have observed in the works of Dylan and Paxton, he moralizes sometimes with an oppressive flat-footedness.

Again with Elektra, his second album, *I Ain't Marching Anymore*, reaffirms all his good qualities and all his faults: humor ("Draft Dodger Rag," "Talking Birmingham Jam"), a sense of the dramatic ("In the Heat of the Summer" and a venomous indictment of the electric chair, "The Iron Lady"), a special humanitarianism, ("That Was the President," in memory of John F. Kennedy, and "Ballad of the Carpenter," in token of friendship for Ewan MacColl, met while the latter was touring the States); but also, unfortunately, examples of rather inferior moralizing ("Links on the Chain," "Here's to the State of Mississippi"), sometimes degenerating into a dubious pathos ("Days of Decision"). Musically, if one deplores certain of the tunes, one must on the other hand respect at least two of the others: that of "In the Heat of the Summer" and, still more, that of "The Highwayman," a poem by Alfred Noyes which had haunted Ochs since his childhood. Nevertheless, *I Ain't Marching Anymore* remains essentially an anthology of sung journalism—though thereby giving to both journalism and song a breath of fresh air, which both had much needed.

His third album (his last on Elektra), while it confirms all the characteristics of Ochs that we have discussed, makes new ones evident. In the first place, its live recording (*Phil Ochs in Concert*) shows us to what extent he is an artist far more at ease onstage than in the studio, because of the feeling of direct contact with his audience . . . and his remarkable talent as a comedian. To sing for free dozens of times in the middle of a crowd, in the streets, at meetings, among picketing strikers, and at demonstrations is a unique education in the "sensing" of an audience, making it laugh or angry with equal skill. And above all, certain of his spoken introductions ("Santo Domingo," "Ringing of Revolution") confirm what we have already suspected—Phil Ochs avoids taking himself too seriously. Another notable element in his evolution: though he remains, in direct contrast to Dylan, still interested in political and sociological subjects, he also has started to write songs on more lyrical subjects ("There But for Fortune," "Changes") and more personal ones, on topics such as religion ("Canons of Christianity") or death ("When I'm Gone").

To be a poet and lyricist or a political activist? This was to become the great dilemma for Phil Ochs, tossed from side to side in his public performances and his private life alike between these two opposing careers, a dilemma he found irreconcilable. Perhaps Ochs didn't have the strength of character comparable with those who, like Woody Guthrie, lived for their political and social involvement throughout their active life, or who, like Dylan, are prepared to ignore the dictates of their audience and follow their own course. Whatever, from 1967 the creativity and the professional activities of Phil Ochs take on an elusive resemblance to a zigzag.

The first step: Phil Ochs's fourth album was released in November 1967 under a newly founded label, A & M, controlled by Herb Alpert. Its title, *Pleasures of the Harbor,* is in itself an announcement that Ochs has become concerned with more lyrical themes, and a brief listening to the album confirms this. Ochs has made a definite decision to start anew, and to such effect that we have no hesitation in naming *Pleasures of the Harbor* as one of the most beautiful pop albums ever released by a singer-songwriter—more than adequately arranged, it is true, but without the benefit of a backup group. Five of the eight songs on *Pleasures of the Harbor* are of a duration between six and nine minutes. Ochs was the first songwriter to follow Dylan's example, breaking through the legendary three-minute barrier with a sovereign contempt, even though at the same time he was thus ensuring that the songs were unlikely ever to be broadcast on the radio.[2] These songs have become far more intimate and timeless than those that went before. In this way the title track, "Pleasures of the Harbor," is a visual description, almost cinematographic in its technique (the progression of the verses evokes in the listener a strange sense of traveling), of the adventures of a seaman between the docking of his ship and embarkation, adventures that you are invited to share:

> *Soon your sailing will be over*
> *Come and take the pleasures of the harbor* *

"I've Had Her" seems on the surface at least to be a résumé of the past love life of the author. In an interview I once asked Phil Ochs if he ever thought of love, and he replied laconically, "Yes, indeed, but in small doses." [If one digs deeper into this song it is less a history a la Casanova but very much more an analysis of the mentality that considers Woman as merely a sex object. While one can sympathize with the disillusionment of the narrator, one has to realize that he has brought it upon himself through his own egocentricity. "I've Had Her" is one of those songs that is like an onion: one can peel away layer after layer and still find more beneath. The same is true in particular of one of the other songs in this album, "The Party," discussed below. P.B.]

Does all this signify that Phil Ochs has said good-bye to protest?

---

[2] But even without this problem of length, the songs of Phil Ochs were unlikely anyway to be played over the radio. Ever since the release of his first album he has figured prominently on the blacklists of many U.S. radio stations.

* "Pleasures of the Harbor," words and music by Phil Ochs. Copyright© 1966 by Barricade Music, Inc. (ASCAP). All rights reserved. Used by permission of Almo Music Corp. (ASCAP) and Rondor Music (London), Ltd.

Not at all. But his protest is now moving in directions that he has not previously explored. Quite clearly, Phil Ochs has realized that one must be more than a man of reason to be a good songwriter. His psychology has become more penetrating, and, no longer content to point to a single evil and set it up for our consciences to ponder, he seems to wish to attack the very roots of that evil: the mentality of the classes, of those who call themselves "the silent majority." Hence "The Party," which plunges us right into the heart of the superficial fashionable life:

> *the hostess is enormous*
> *she fills the room with perfurme.* . . .
>
> *and she offers you a drink*
> *she promises to speak to you*
> *if you promise not to think.* . . .*

Reviving the satirical verve that shone through his earlier successful spoken blues, Phil Ochs tackles in "Outside of a Small Circle of Friends" the indifference that we show to our fellowmen. In this particular instance a small group of friends watch from the window of their apartment while discussing in a patronizing way the problems of the world. Just in front of them, in the bushes of Central Park, a woman is being raped and stabbed; a few blocks away, in the ghetto, "the rats have joined the babies that are sleeping on the floor"; on the highway cars are crashing and people dying; young "immoral" people are arrested because they prefer smoking marijuana to drinking beer,[3] but pornographic magazines can be sold on the open market. . . . At the end of each verse the question arises: should one do anything about it? But no, the excuses are rife: it would be useless, or the police are there for that, or even it would be bad form to spoil the game of Monopoly that's in progress, and anyway

---

[3] I have only twice ever heard a Phil Ochs track played on British radio, and once it was this one. The verse beginning, "Smoking marijuana is more fun than drinking beer" was carefully spliced out of the song so that it was hard to notice that it had been removed unless one knew the song. No mention of this was made by the disc jockey, Kenney Everett. —P.B.

* "The Party," words and music by Phil Ochs. Copyright © 1966 by Barricade Music, Inc. (ASCAP). All rights reserved. Used by permission of Almo Music Corp. (ASCAP) and Rondor Music (London), Ltd.

I'm sure it wouldn't interest
anybody
outside of a small circle of friends *

The lethargy and indifference of these people (and aren't they ourselves?) are accompanied by a Dixieland jazz backing which combines to make "Outside of a Small Circle of Friends" one of the most intelligent and yet one of the most simple-seeming protest songs ever written.

But the newly acquired finesse of Ochs culminates in "The Flower Lady" (a description of a journey through a modern American city where everyone is going about their various occupations ignoring the flower seller) and even more in "Crucifixion," a shattering tableau of the decadence of American society; apart from a lyric of exhilarating poetry, one notes the addition of a full electronic score, very much in advance of the popular music of 1967 and probably unparalleled in popular music to this day.

In September 1968 a very curious album was released: *Tape from California.* Ochs seems in part to be reverting to his roots, in particular in a long ballad dedicated to Joe Hill, using Guthrie's "Tom Joad" melody and recorded with the aid of Jack Elliott; Ochs himself describes this track as the most ethnic he has ever recorded. "When in Rome" could well be considered as an extension of "Crucifixion": lasting more than thirteen minutes, accompanied only by Ochs's solo rhythm guitar, it allegorically describes the present situation in the United States. The style is not without resemblance to that of "A Hard Rain's A-Gonna Fall" (the lyric takes the form also of narration in the first person), with the difference that by now the flood has come. One can quote the refrain of "When in Rome":

and all the high-born ladies
so gentle and so true
have been handed to the soldiers
when in Rome do as the Romans do †

The lyricism of *Pleasures of the Harbor* reappears in "Floods of Florence" and perhaps more in the title track, "Tape from California," while with "The Harder They Fall" Ochs returns to his satirical vein. Moreover he never forgets the war ("White Boots Marching in a Yellow Land") and permits himself the declaration inherent in "The War Is Over." But he abandons any form of journalistic reference by which reason his work becomes universal rather than specific.

Released in the spring of 1969, *Rehearsals for Retirement,* with a very rock arrangement throughout, is a very successful but extremely depressing album. Ochs has been impressed very strongly by various of the events that have taken place in the world: the assassination of Martin Luther King, followed by that of Robert Kennedy; added to which is the Soviet invasion of Czechoslovakia in the autumn of 1968, the rejection of the French by Mexican students, the occurrences in Chicago at the Democratic Party Convention, and the spectacle of Hubert Humphrey sweeping away the nomination from Eugene McCarthy, whom Ochs had supported for several dreamlike weeks. When he returned to New York ten days later, he was defeated and disillusioned. The *coup de grâce* for him was at the end of 1968, with the election of Richard Nixon as President. It was at that time, we think, that Phil Ochs's ideas became actively revolutionary. The title as much as the sleeve of *Rehearsals for Retirement* gives the impression of the last will and testament of a songwriter.

The songs themselves alternate between melancholy ("The Doll House," on which the imprint and even the complexity of Dylan is undeniable) and total disillusionment ("My Life," "The World Began in Eden but Ended in Los Angeles," "Rehearsals for Retirement"). A very moving ballad on the wreck of the submarine *Scorpion* (reminiscent of *Thresher*), "The *Scorpion* Departs but Never Returns," brings home to us exactly how far Phil Ochs has come since the days of *All the News That's Fit to Sing.* For all that, satire is not absent from the album ("I Kill Therefore I Am"); Ochs knows that he should remain faithful to his own aims but, at present, he is more interested in his own personal experiences ("William Butler Yeats Visits Lincoln Park and Escapes Unscathed"). And then, finally, there is the revolutionary side to the album. Before announcing to us the dawn of a new era in "Another Age," he affirms lyrically in "Pretty Smart on My Part," the first track on the album, that they can try to trap him or arrest him but, when he feels a little stronger, he will join in the struggle to assassinate the President and form a government of the people.

The following year the album *Phil Ochs' Greatest Hits,* totally barren of the subversiveness of "Pretty Smart on My Part," was released and is new proof of Ochs's indecision, though also of his sincerity. The title of *Greatest Hits* is no more than self-mockery on his part, irony that his records have never sold very well (on the back of the jacket a gaudy slogan announces that "50 Phil Ochs Fans Can't Be Wrong!"), and satire on the American show-biz syndrome with its love for such timewasters as gold records (on the front of the jacket Phil Ochs, with an Elvis Presley lick to his hair, is defiantly clutching an electric guitar and wearing a suit of gold). The general style of the disc, even on close listening, is hard to pick out (the more severe say that it is totally incoherent): the traditional-sounding "Boy in Ohio," an autobiographical song accompanied by guitar, violin, and harmonica; "Ten Cents a Coup," a satirical song attacking the fallacies of the American "democratic" system of election—

> *I dreamed Nixon died of a suntan*
> *there was only Spiro left*
> *when swearing in*
> *he fell on his chin*
> *he'd assassinated himself* *

—rock 'n' roll in the style of his earliest heroes, with echoing voice and the lot ("Basket in the Pool" and "My Kingdom for a Car"); pop music a la Phil Spector, with choirs of female voices in the background ("One Way Ticket Home"); mellow country and western with an agreeable preponderance of violin ("Gas Station Women" and "Chords of Fame"), which is great if you like that kind of thing; he even takes lessons from the classics, being accompanied by a harpsichord in the rather velvety but nonetheless beautiful ballad, "Bach, Beethoven, Mozart and Me" (the calm before the storm?). And then there are the two high spots of the album. Firstly, an admirable five-minute ballad, accompanied by piano only, entitled "Jim Dean of Indiana." To a slow, hesitant tempo, with an infinite sadness

* "Ten Cents a Coup," words and music by Phil Ochs. Copyright © 1971 by Barricade Music, Inc. (ASCAP). All rights reserved. Used by permission of Almo Music Corp. (ASCAP) and Rondor Music (London), Ltd.

and an incredible emotional range, this ballad recounts the life and death of James Dean. The subject is a good one and deserves to be so treated: Phil Ochs gives to the actor the homage he deserves. Secondly, a longish, classical influenced song called "No More Songs," an explanation and a key to Ochs's indecisions over the years, a belated apologia for the album. With a full orchestral score and Ochs's voice at its very mellowest, he explains that once he saw his dreams in song, but that now the dreams are dead and the songs are all gone.

We have spent some time studying the work of Phil Ochs, in whom we see one of the finest of American singer-songwriters born out of the urban folk revival. If he hasn't got the delirious vocabulary of Dylan or the stability of Paxton, Ochs has other fine qualities: in particular a sort of despairing energy which, even while he communicates emotions of the gloomiest nature (*Rehearsals for Retirement,* "No More Songs"), forces him to persevere along the bright highroad that he has followed: writing, singing, communicating, never hesitating to risk his safety by descending to the level of the street and, sometimes, arriving in prison. If there are heroes in modern American folkrock, then, like Len Chandler, Phil Ochs surely deserves to be so described.

And, when the chips are finally counted up, are not the indecisions and even the self-contradictions of Phil Ochs the mirror of that strange country in which he somehow survives? [4]

Bob Dylan, Tom Paxton, and Phil Ochs, to whom we have devoted some dozens of pages, are generally considered to be the three most important voices to emerge from the American urban folk revival in the sixties. During the dozen years or so that all three have spent steadily and prolifically writing and recording, they have matured and improved until now they are the three names synonymous with the early days of the revival (even if, in the case of Ochs, the name is not known far beyond the devotees of the genre). Nevertheless, the movement that gave them birth was also the stimulus that engendered self-expression in numerous other artists who, writing their own songs in the folk tradition, have prolonged that tradition and given it depth, so that the torch is no longer carried by merely the

---

[4] As this book was going to press Phil Ochs committed suicide. A family friend said, "Mainly, the words weren't coming to him any more." —P.B.

creativity of a few artists, but became a national, even international, phenomenon of a generation.

For various reasons, one has more or less lost track of the writers discussed below. However, since they have been responsible for excellent songs, gained their own public, and attracted emulators, they naturally deserve their place in this chapter.

Born in Pittsburgh, Eric Andersen gave up his studies in his home city to come to Greenwich Village, at the suggestion of Tom Paxton, to seek his fortune in the winter of 1964. For the year preceding that he had been writing songs. One of his first was in the form of a homage to his homeland, "My Land Is a Good Land," in the same vein as Phil Ochs's "Power and the Glory" or, even more, "This Land Is Your Land" by Woody Guthrie, to whom Andersen's song was dedicated. Between his leaving Pittsburgh and coming onto the New York folk scene, Andersen had traversed the United States in the most adventurous fashion imaginable in order to complete his knowledge of life, living as a vagabond in the Guthrie tradition—stations, freight trains, and all that. Deliberately, he started his trek without a cent in his pocket. All of this went toward providing him with the inspiration to write songs about the life-style he had adopted, and still more about the people who had been his companions.

On the back of the sleeve of his album, *Today Is the Highway,* he summed up his view of the world and its people: he was interested in victims, fugitives, hookers, thieves, criminals, immigrants, bums, cowards, and perverts.

Eric Andersen recorded on Vanguard two albums, both excellent: *Today Is the Highway* and *'Bout Changes 'n' Things.* On listening to them one finds a spirit of romanticism ("Everything Ain't Been Said," "Time for My Returning", "Violets of Dawn"), of love ("Looking Glass," "Come to My Bedside," "The Girl I Love"), which has the passion of genuine goodwill ("Song to J.C.B.," dedicated to an old black bluesman who had lodged with him), and the essence of wandering ("Today Is the Highway," "Dusty Boxcar Wall," "Plains of Nebrasky-O," "Bay of Mexico," and above all the famous "Thirsty Boots"). Certainly the influence of Woody Guthrie has made itself strongly felt in the last-named song, as it has on Andersen's social sensibility ("The Blind Fiddler" tells the story of a miner blinded by an underground explosion) and on his tenderness toward children ("Bumblebee," derived directly from "Why Oh Why?").

The voice of Eric Andersen is able to express marvelously the full gamut of human emotions. As Robert Shelton described it, he has a fine baritone voice, strong and buoyant, sometimes echoing the styles of Tom Paxton and Bob Dylan, reminiscent on occasion of Elvis Presley singing at his gentlest. Eric Andersen is also a remarkable stylist with the guitar (one needs only to listen to "Dusty Boxcar Wall" or "Champion at Keeping Them Rollin' " to accord with this viewpoint).

At the moment when, by grace of Bob Dylan, the style known as folkrock took flight, Eric Andersen for his part made a second start by recording in identical order all the songs on his second album with the addition of a rock backing (*'Bout Changes 'n' Things—Take 2*). Having left Vanguard, he signed up with Warner Brothers for a new album, *Avalanche* (June 1968), which, in spite of the undeniable high standard of the songs therein, is spoiled by the musical arrangement; without doubt the intimacy of Andersen's vocals is far more at ease with arrangements of a more traditional nature, and one can still listen to his earlier work with unalloyed pleasure.

About the same date as the emergence of Eric Andersen (1964–65), Mark Spoelstra appeared as a brilliant young folksinger. The title "folksinger" applies better to him than it would to, say, Phil Ochs or Tom Paxton to the extent that Spoelstra was not content merely to interpret his own songs composed around contemporary themes; he remained at the same time much attached to both the black and the white traditional repertoires, and notably indulged his own passion for the blues with a strong predilection for the twelve-string guitar which he made his specialty, and worthily so. Gentle and tender, lacking the choler of a Phil Ochs (but not his determination), the voice of Mark Spoelstra was particularly suitable to convey the emotions of his pacifist songs, written in a poetic, symbolic style, which earned him the admiration of, among others, Joan Baez and Richard Fariña.

At the age of twenty, having opted out of military service on the grounds that he was a registered conscientious objector, Mark Spoelstra was given the choice of spending two years in prison or the same period of time working with the social welfare services in California. He naturally chose the second course, and served in a Fresno school. David Anthony Lee, a little boy at this school with whom Spoelstra had struck up a friendship, was run over by a car at the age of six and thus inspired one of Spoelstra's finest ballads, the famous "Just a Hand to Hold."

As well as "Just a Hand to Hold" one notes on Mark Spoelstra's first album (*Five and Twenty Questions,* released by Elektra at the beginning of 1964) one of the most impressive of all pacifist songs, presented in the form of a dream, ever engendered by the peace movement: "White Winged Dove." It deals with the question of bellicose education, the reverence for firearms inculcated by many American parents into their children. While with the title song of the album, "Five and Twenty Questions," he poses twenty-five questions to the representatives of the adult world, questions that they seem always to try to ignore: the song deals at length with the indifference and the isolation of each one of us in a world inundated by the media—a long and courageous indictment.

In 1965 Spoelstra recorded a second album, *State of Mind,* which confirmed his talents both as a twelve-string guitarist and as a songwriter, combining to make him an attacking personality, an artist fitting perfectly into the spirit of the folk revival and yet at the same time eminently original.

Fred Neil has in common with Mark Spoelstra a specialization in the twelve-string guitar and a marked preference for self-expression in the blues idiom. But that wasn't where it all started for him: by 1963 he was writing his own songs and released on the Elektra label an excellent first album, *Tear Down the Walls,* recorded in company with Vince Martin. "Tear Down the Walls," the song that gives the album its title, is a vibrant appeal for the liberation of all, and one remarks in it an interesting symbolic relationship between music and liberty. This idea used by Fred Neil is by no means merely a piece of wishful thinking, and one recalls the phrase used by a black militant in Alabama who, while justifying a series of demonstrations in his hometown where the crowd sang for hours on end, remarked that "you can't put your confidence in a delegate who doesn't love the music of his people." Which all goes to show that, whether one likes it or not, all the different types of musicians *are* of political significance. . . .

But if Fred Neil sang for the liberation of all, he found his peak in more introspective creativity. His second album, *Between Bleecker and MacDougal,* recorded this time without the aid of Vince Martin, proves it. Maturing in the flourishing Greenwich Village environment, he here evokes the famous Bleecker and MacDougal streets (think of Paul Simon's excellent "Bleecker Street" on *Wednesday Morning 3 A.M.*) where he has found himself out in the cold with his guitar, attending a nonexistent club engagement. As with so many others . . .

Wearied perhaps by the turbulent atmosphere of New York, Fred Neil retired to a farm in the South, and at the end of 1969 made a dramatic reappearance with the song "Everybody's Talkin'," written especially for John Schlesinger's film *Midnight Cowboy.*

One can also cite in this first wave of writers-composers-interpreters, contemporary with the appearance of Bob Dylan, a singer who played a large part in the origination and success of the magazine *Broadside:* Gil Turner. For a long time he has been known and admired as the composer of one of the best, most intelligent, and most *communicative* of all songs written by a white for the black integrationist movements, among whom he can count numerous friends: "Carry It On." For many years "Carry It On" formed an integral part of the repertoire of the black demonstrators, in the same way as did "We Shall Overcome," "Oh, Freedom!" or "Blowin' in the Wind."

Patrick Sky, Peter La Farge, Buffy Sainte-Marie, Julius Lester, and Len Chandler, all of whom we have earlier discussed in this book, are also among the genuine personalities, the original artists struggling toward some positive form of action, who owe at least part of their success to the welcome accorded to them by the pages of *Broadside.* But as much as *Broadside* played its part, it was not only because of it that they reached their audience: it is not only Nina Simone and Harry Belafonte who have never forgotten their roots.

With Pete Seeger and Bob Dylan, Joan Baez is certainly the artist who has done most to bring the whole scene of contemporary American folk to the attention of the rest of the world, even to those sections of the public that had not previously shown any signs of interest in song. Rather tentatively, but affectionately rather than ironically, one could say that Joan Baez was almost "part of the furniture." To achieve the status of the madonna of folk song which has been accorded to her, Joan has done so by being not a writer of songs but a judicious selector of those of others, by her crystalline interpretations, by her voice which is quite without equal (though that is a natural talent), all adding to make her immediately remarkable. Her spectacular but eminently sincere pacifist activities have done the rest.

Born in 1941 to parents on one side Mexican, on the other English, Joan Baez passed her childhood in New York, Palo Alto in California, and Boston. As an adolescent she learned the guitar while continuing her studies at college. As early as the end of 1958 she was singing in public in the folk clubs of Boston, such as The Unicorn, and, a little later, the Gate of Horn in Chicago. (It is worth mentioning that Boston and Chicago were certainly the two principal centers after Greenwich Village of the urban folk revival.)

It was in July 1959 that Joan Baez first made her sensational appearance on the scene during an evening concert at the first Newport Folk Festival when Bob Gibson, a commercial folksinger very much in the public eye at the time, spontaneously invited her to join him onstage. The reaction of the spectators and the critics, literally flabbergasted by her vocal performance, was instantaneously enthusiastic. Representatives of the major record firms, no doubt sensing the big deal, were not very far behind. During the following months, Joan Baez received dozens of requests to appear at major concerts in all parts of the United States and offers of wonderful recording contracts, notably on the part of Columbia. However, she proved the extent of her own wisdom by, rather than jumping onto a commercial bandwagon which she possibly would have been unable to control, plugging her ears to the sounds of these sirens until eventually, at the beginning of 1960, she signed up with a (at the time) very small record label, Vanguard. It was largely due to the popularity of Joan Baez in the years to come that Vanguard achieved its considerable commercial success.

The first two albums by Joan Baez are almost exclusively devoted to British or Spanish traditional ballads, with among other influences those of black and South American folk music. It is important to recognize that she excels in this traditional repertoire, even though she does not treat it (as we have already noted in our earlier discussion of hillbilly music) in the customary folk manner; preferring doubtless a certain plastic perfection to genuineness, Joan Baez in these two albums places all her reliance on her voice. In general, this reliance is not misplaced: "Silver Dagger," "Henry Martin," "El Preso Numero Nueve," "Lily of the West," "Silkie," "Barbara Allen," or "Old Blue" are unalloyed joy to hear. On the other hand, on some occasions her confidence leads her to catastrophe in exaggerated crescendos and utterly artificial, almost ridiculous, vocal feats and pretensions to a bel canto of the lowest level, as in "Fare Thee Well," "Rake and Rambling Boy," and "Wagoner's Lad."

Her third and fourth albums, both recorded live (*Joan Baez in Concert* and *Joan Baez in Concert, Part 2*), mark an evolution of her repertoire: certainly she demonstrates a predilection for traditional British or Spanish ballads. Venerable songs such as "Geordie" or "Jackaroe," and the extraordinary and passionate "House Carpenter" and "Matty Groves," for their part continue to charm us and move us, and are even reborn in our minds through her interpretations. Folklore purists, lovers of the grating, nasal ethnic voice with a certain "respect for tradition" can decry as scandalous her treatment. It doesn't matter: by courtesy of Joan Baez, with her limpid diction and without—thank the lord—sophisticated arrangements, the American middle classes began to understand their country's folklore at a time when none of the country's commercial groups could help them do so. Moreover, if Joan Baez was not being strictly responsible to the authenticity of tradition, then she was at least being responsible to herself; and this is just as important.

We mentioned an evolution in her repertoire: the two *In Concert* albums signaled in effect the beginnings of Joan Baez' involvement in the domain of contemporary songwriters. Part 1, still looking back to her earlier work, provides us with only three examples, but these are highly successful: they consist of the standard "Pretty Boy Floyd" by Woody Guthrie; a satirical song about Prohibition, "Copper Kettle"; and the beautiful song by Malvina Reynolds, "What Have They Done to the Rain?" This last evokes the dangers of nuclear fallout, but through the extremely poetic image of a little boy walking in the radioactive rain. Laconically Joan introduces the song as the gentlest folk song that she knows; its protest is not a gentle one, but the sound of it is gentle.

In Part 2 the tendency toward modernity is clearer: of the fifteen songs on the album five are contemporary, either through the actual moment of their writing or through the way in which Joan interprets them ("Battle Hymn of the Republic"). In the interim she had made the acquaintance of Bob Dylan, both as the writer and as the man. Very quickly they had become friends, and started the habit of inviting each other onstage during their concerts. At the 1963 Newport Folk Festival they sang "With God on Our Side" together. For two or three years, in fact, the rumor was rife that they were married. But let's leave that to the pop press. . . .

By this time Joan Baez was the most celebrated female folksinger around, even in other countries. In France, for example, where a public, bourgeois and without much English, faithfully went out and bought each of her records, she was certainly becoming a useful piece of propaganda for folk music in general; it was above all by grace of Joan Baez that a good part of the French general public learned about, among others, the existence of Bob Dylan or the struggles of the American blacks. "We Shall Overcome" is a rallying song to action. With Joan Baez, white agent for the black message, it took on a new international dimension. The role fitted her like a glove: she was to be seen in the 1963 March on Washington, where she was revealed as one of the most certain elements to cause understanding between races.

It's worth pausing a moment to look a little more closely at Joan's pacifist role. In effect she has deliberately refused to follow any particular party line. Her activities have been confined to nonviolent indirect action: peace marches on which she has been arrested, refusal to pay a percentage of her taxes corresponding to the percentage of the United States budget devoted to the maintenance of the military, the foundation and financing of a school of nonviolence in California, and so forth.

By 1966 the recorded work of Joan Baez (including the album *Farewell Angelina*) reflected almost faithfully the golden age of the folk revival. Almost, because she was not representing certain of the people contributing to *Broadside* whose songs would legitimately have fitted into her repertoire. From Phil Ochs, the only song she sang was "There But for Fortune," a beautiful melody, and one well adapted to Joan Baez' vocal qualities, but hardly the most significant feat of the intellect.

One finds the album *Farewell Angelina* particularly rewarding for several reasons. The first resides in the quality and balance of the songs chosen: the traditional ("The Wild Mountain Thyme," "The River in the Pines," "Ranger's Command") alternating with compositions by Lee Hays ("Satisfied Mind") and Donovan ("Colours," which Joan had sung with the composer during the 1966 Newport Folk

Festival), an English version of "Where Have All the Flowers Gone?" and, to complete the survey of foreign influences, the French "Pauvre Ruteboeuf" set to music by Léo Ferré. But, once again, it is in Bob Dylan that Joan finds the most important contribution, by including four of his songs on the album. The first side starts off with three of them one after the other: "Farewell Angelina," which it is said was written especially for her, "Daddy, You Been on My Mind" (neither of these two have been officially put on record by their composer), and "It's All Over Now, Baby Blue." The second side closes with an extraordinary version—one could say, the standard—of "A Hard Rain's A-Gonna Fall." The other factor that renders this album particularly memorable, in my opinion, is the excellence of the vocal, instrumental, and technical execution.

We are here in the presence of a perfectly mature artist in full possession of all her talents. *Farewell Angelina* is the last album of Joan Baez which can be viewed logically from beginning to end.

With the release at the end of 1966 of the album *Noël* the great Baezian singing machine began to come off the rails. At the time that Bob Dylan, whom Joan still admired, was in the process of revolutionizing pop music, she seems to have had difficulty, musically speaking, in adapting to the times that were a-changing. To judge by her albums, the standards of her performances at this time were up and down like the teeth of a saw. *Noël* represents on her part a tentative struggle to be free of the role of "madonna of folk" which had been built up for her: it contains the songs of Christmas that are universally known (such as "Silent Night"), stamped with the musical cultures of different lands. These songs are accompanied by a classical orchestra. The effect, curious but not entirely unpleasant despite several ghastly errors in the arrangements, exerts a certain charm. One could only conclude, nevertheless, that it was a whim on the part of Joan Baez. . . .

Things became worse with *Joan,* the album released the following summer. Indeed, the selection of songs included is excellent, with, apart from a splendid seven-minute English traditional ballad ("The Greenwood Side"), names among the credits like that of Paul Simon ("Dangling Conversation"), John Lennon and Paul McCartney ("Eleanor Rigby"), Tim Hardin ("The Lady Came from Baltimore," "If I Were a Carpenter"), Donovan ("Turquoise"), Richard Fariña

("Children of Darkness"), and even Jacques Brel ("La Colombe") and Edgar Allan Poe ("Annabel Lee"). Alas, the orchestra under the direction of Peter Schickele, apparently more at ease performing circus music than accompanying songs, does not rise to the occasion. The brass in particular are ill directed, and the voice of Joan Baez, though always beautiful, is suffocated by the murky environment. Among other things, she lacks completely the necessary flame, impetuosity, and finally conviction: magnificently triumphant through ample ballads, her voice shows itself strikingly unable to cope with songs requiring a more imperative rhythm ("Eleanor Rigby") or an immediate sense of drama ("La Colombe"). All of which goes to make *Joan* an album well worth forgetting.

Baptism, subtitled "A Journey Through Our Time," is a poetic album, where songs alternate with orchestral pieces and the recitation of poetry that is often well chosen (poets like Rimbaud, Joyce, Prévert, and Lorca, for example). Once again, Joan Baez seems here to be trying to escape from the folksinger tag. The album is interesting and has many devotees, but it hardly represents significant progress in the musical plane.

With the double album *Any Day Now,* released at the beginning of 1969, Joan found once again the correct balance between voice and instrumentation which she seemed to have lost. It must be admitted that the chosen program, sixteen songs by her friend Bob Dylan, is particularly appropriate for her voyage of rediscovery. One passes a benevolent ear over several of the unfortunate aspects of the album (a slight excess of lyrical flight in "Tears of Rage," sung a cappella, or the doubtful incorporation of a choir into "I Shall Be Released") and remembers only the better moments, happily numerous: the perfectly rendered drama of "Boots of Spanish Leather," the dream eternally reborn of "Sad-Eyed Lady of the Lowlands," and even the declaration that Joan Baez *can* adapt her voice also to more rapid rhythms, as in "Drifter's Escape" and above all the unforgettable "Love Is Just a Four-Letter Word." We can remark in passing that she is backed by astoundingly good musicians, retaining only the part of country and western that is its human truth and without a moment of affectation, among whom emerges a guitarist of exceptional ability, if not of genius: Steve Stills.

David's Album (December 1969) causes doubts again. Here the most questionable characteristics of country and western take pride of place, starting with the choice of the songs themselves. If one feels strongly about the notion of returning to the simple pleasures, to rural life (as contrasted with the corruption of the cities), should one in 1969 have sung titles that insist oppressively on the protection of one's home, harping on the green grass one would like to be walking on ("Green, Green Grass of Home"), above all when the songs are accompanied by a panoply of imitation Nashville cowboy instrumentation? We can see, with three exceptions, nothing but platitudes in *David's Album*. The three tracks that are worth listening to are "Glad Bluebird of Happiness" with its impressive verve; the duo with Mimi Fariña on "Poor Wayfaring Stranger," and the vocal performance by Joan on "Just a Closer Walk with Thee," extremely representative of the affection felt by the singer for spirituals. Apart from that, the album doesn't do much to bolster her reputation. Some have advanced the theory that the inclusion of a commercial orchestration of this type permits Joan's message to be heard (and accepted?) by the whites of the Southern states; this argument seems to us to be unfortunately illusory.

The release of *One Day at a Time* in April 1970 did nothing to alleviate our perplexity as to why a singer who has played an integral part in the urban folk revival should abandon it for clichéd country and western, on the planes of both music and politics; for this is what she continues to do on this album. Buffy Sainte-Marie, also distracted for a while by this experience, wisely returned with *Illuminations*. Joan Baez seems to delight in it.

Not so the listener. Certainly, one can say, she is free to sing and play the type of music she wants to, especially if she does it well (for lovers of country and western will probably appreciate *One Day at a Time*). However, the case of Joan Baez is unlike that of, say, Bob Dylan with *Nashville Skyline*. At least for him the change in his music corresponds to a change in the man, his life, and his ideas. He is still coherent. Joan, on the other hand, follows—with faith and an admirable perseverance— a political pacifist activity that involves the rebuttal of a certain section of Americana—exactly that part which is communicated aurally in country and western.

The form of a work corresponds to the essence of the thought in which it had its origin, so one cannot happily allow, in *One Day at a Time*, that Gil Turner's "Carry It On" is fairly treated by the addition of an arrangement a la Buck Owens. One detects here, fundamentally, an inherent contradiction, all the more regrettable since Joan Baez is sincere enough to pay physically for her beliefs. One must not forget her spells in prison, nor the sentencing of her then husband, David Harris—to whom is dedicated not only *David's Album* but also one of the songs on *One Day at a Time*—to three years' imprisonment, during the course of which he frequently participated in hunger strikes.

The incursion of Joan Baez into the repertoire of the Rolling Stones ("No Expectations") is no more convincing than the rest. A single exception, but an exceptionally fine one, to the general pool of severity we are creating (but aren't we always most critical of the ones we love?) she has called "Sweet Sir Galahad." It is (and here one sees a definite promise of further evolution on her part) a song composed by Joan herself. One cannot listen to her singing "Sweet Sir Galahad" without feeling that there still exists the personal touch that graced *Farewell Angelina*. And, through this song, we know that the great Joan Baez, though nearly always hidden behind a jumble of debris and choirs, is still alive. She has confirmed it to our pleasure at the festivals at Biot and the Isle of Wight during the summer of 1970, and to a certain extent in her more recent albums.

It is the trees that hide the forest. In the domain of songwriters, it is clear today that the exceptionality of Bob Dylan has unwittingly been the cause (and probably the only one) of masking from the view of a huge public other American songwriters whose careers we will be discussing in later pages. In the same sort of way, it is in no way derogatory to affirm that the success of Joan Baez on an international level for a long time hindered Judy Collins (above all in France, where no one will take the risk of bringing her over and putting her onstage) from being heard and appreciated to the extent of her true worth, outside of a small circle of specialist friends. How many times has one heard something like: "Judy Collins is an excellent singer, but we have no real need of her: we still have Joan Baez"? It is an ill-advised opinion, for it ignores the unceasingly evolving creativity of Judy Collins, as much as her eclecticism. Among the following few pages we will attempt to redress the balance somewhat. We cannot say that Judy Collins is "superior to" Joan Baez; her art is a fundamentally different one. And this point alone would justify our spending time with her.

Judy Collins was born in 1939 in Seattle, but she passed most of her youth in Boulder, Colorado. She studied at MacMurray College, Jacksonville, Illinois, and at the University of Colorado. Her father, Chuck Collins, despite being blind, was a musician of some local repute who, among other things, produced several radio programs on the West Coast. Plunged into music since infancy, Judy learned to play the piano at the age of six (she was to play it much later on many of her records and onstage). Though she suffered from polio-myelitis at the age of twelve, she nevertheless planned a career as a concert pianist. She can hardly have dreamed of folk music. . . .

But, having participated on numerous occasions in impromptu singing sessions with others, in the way that so many young Americans and even more young Britons do for pleasure, the light dawned on both her and her fellow students that she held strong potential. She began to play the guitar and to sing, and her friends encouraged her to perfect her instrumental and vocal techniques. She set to work on this with all the rigor and application which she had earlier applied to the piano. A summer at the village of Ferndale in the Rocky Mountains National Park was for her the source of numerous new songs, taught to her by a cosmopolitan collection of people she met, and it gave her the opportunity to experiment with leading the Spartan life suited for the flourishing of a practical interest in folk music.

At the age of nineteen, on leaving the univerity, she married a student, Peter Taylor. In order to help him through his studies, she began to sing in the clubs around Boulder. The following year they had a son, Clark, and when Peter Taylor obtained the post of teacher in English at the University of Connecticut, all three immigrated to the East Coast. Always wanting to learn about life and its natural product, folk music, and to discover herself (which is almost the same thing), Judy in her turn leaped into the New York adventure. She found new voice in the lively atmosphere of the Greenwich Village folk clubs: the Gaslight, the Bitter End, and the Village Gate taught her to follow in the footsteps of such masters as Fred Hellerman or Pete Seeger, at the same time giving her the chance to advance her professional career. She also met there some of the younger singers and songwriters: Mike Settle (who wrote the celebrated "Settle Down"), Bob Camp, and Bob Gibson.

The latter pair at the time formed a duo that was highly success-

ful around the clubs. Apart from his encouragement given to Phil
Ochs and his exposure of Joan Baez, already noted, one owes to Bob
Gibson several fine compositions that are now classics, such as "Well,
Well, Well."

And it was at Gerde's Folk City that Judy Collins first came across
the young Bob Dylan, who in the smoking kitchens sang to her
"Masters of War" for the first time. It was a memory that would
haunt her for long afterward.

Already noted as an up-and-coming young singer, in an era
where record manufacturers were assiduously hunting out new folk
talent, she signed a contract with Elektra, who released in 1961 her
first album, *A Maid of Constant Sorrow.*

It is worth noting at this moment yet again the large part played
by some of the record companies, then small and poor such as Elektra and Vanguard, in putting the new generation of musicians in
touch with a receptive public. As well as Judy Collins, we have already seen how Elektra launched, among others, Tom Paxton, Phil
Ochs, Fred Neil, and Mark Spoelstra. In *Actuel No I* [5] Jean-François
Bizot pointed out: "The small companies—Elektra, Dunhill, Island
in Britain—record the musicians that the larger ones aren't interested in. . . . Jac Holzman, who launched Elektra and originally
recorded folk music on an old-fashioned microphone in his sitting
room, admits that he is a poet: 'Poetry and music will change the
world,' he says."

This was at the end of the fifties, a time of dreams. . . .

Judy Collins was at the same time one of the creators and one of the
beneficiaries of that golden age, very much more authentic and creative than the commercial revival which had preceded it and which
was to continue parallel with it. In her first album as well as in her
second (*The Golden Apples of the Sun*), Judy chose—as did Joan Baez
around the same time—a program essentially drawn from traditional music, for the most part the products of Ireland, Scotland,
and the two Englands, the old and the new, of which she was particularly fond. Many of the ballads that we discussed in Part 1 are to
be found on these two albums. Take for example "Wars of Ger-
many," "John Riley," "The Rising of the Moon." Nevertheless, *The
Golden Apples of the Sun* represents a genuine musical evolution when

[5] New series, October 1970, p. 13.

compared with *A Maid of Constant Sorrow*. The difference lies far more in the intensity of the singing than in the songs that are sung. For Judy had hardly modified the spiritual embrace with which she had greeted folk music, any more than she had her repertoire, which we are shortly going to examine from the roots (if one excepts a borning taste for Jewish and Central European folk music: "Tell Me Who I'll Marry" is a Polish song adapted and translated into English). But in a year and a half she had above all reinforced her perception, deepened and pointed her sensibility beyond superficiality; she has preserved these with an admirable sense of discretion and nuance, and has displayed throughout a humanity and a communicable emotion which have become her permanent attributes. All qualitites which Joan Baez, except sporadically, lacks. Years later, *Golden Apples of the Sun* still displays a timeless freshness.

The album *Judy Collins No. 3*, released at the end of 1963, confirms the characteristics already discussed as an inseparable part of Judy Collins and heralds still another which we are coming to: eclecticism. For the moment, it is worth noting that with *No. 3* there is a very logical extension and evolution of repertoire, parallel to that of Joan Baez (this is one of their several points in common): Judy, in effect, under the pressure of events and guided by her meetings with others and the enlargement of her personal experience, from this time on devoted herself principally to the newborn "contemporary folk song" from the pens of authors like those who filled the pages of *Broadside*. She gives a definitive version of Bob Dylan's "Masters of War." She even sings the song of Shel Silverstein, known as the cartoonist in *Playboy* magazine as well as the author of several very fine, serious pop songs, such as the memorable "Hey Nellie Nellie" and the world-famous "Please Mrs. Avery." But by no means did she forget the works of people like Woody Guthrie, whose "Deportee" she revived; or of Pete Seeger, whose hymn for universal peace, "Turn! Turn! Turn!" and whose cowritten song about the impossibilities of life in the Welsh mining communities, "The Bells of Rhymney," she also recorded, nor did she forget the British tradition, on sea ("Bullgine Run") or on land ("Anathea") to which she owed so much.

This magnificent album, an essential part of the whole folk revival, was greeted with wild enthusiasm by the critics. To abstract Robert Shelton in *The New York Times* of December 15, 1963: by grace of a wise choice of songs as well as an intrepretation of them that is stunning in its depth and its maturity, *Judy Collins No. 3* was perhaps the album most representative of 1964. In it she takes her ravishing contralto voice toward zones of emotion and intellect that are new to the urban folk song.

In its issue of March 1964, *High Fidelity* echoed Shelton: here on a single record were all the great currents—political, social, moral— that had given form to the folk revival; and Miss Collins sang with exceptional beauty.

March 21, 1964, is a historic date in the career of Judy Collins who, on the occasion of her first full-scale concert at New York's Town Hall, was to make her mark as one of the finest white American female singers. Though deeply embedded in the roots of which she was a branch, she was also involved in more modern songs (two trends that have often been self-contradictory, but that in her case complemented each other); she was herself, she imitated nobody.

One can find evidence of all these qualities on her fourth album, *The Judy Collins Concert,* recorded live during this legendary performance. Vocally at the very height of her powers, Judy triumphed as she sang of the generosity, the love, the hope, and the beauty to be found in the American nightmare that surrounded her. She is helped by the songwriters whose works she had chosen, with her usual impeccable taste: traditional ("Bonnie Boy Is Young," "Wild Rippling Water," "Cruel Mother"); Tom Paxton ("Last Thing on My Mind," "Ramblin', Boy," "Bottle of Wine"); Fred Neil (in a raucous version of "Tear Down the Walls"); Dick Weissman ("Medgar Evers' Lullaby," hypothetically written for the child of Medgar Evers); Billy Edd Wheeler ("Winter Sky," "Red-Winged Blackbird," "Coal Tattoo," these two last describing the hunger and the poverty of the poor whites living in the mining regions); and of course Bob Dylan. On the evening in question she gave a rendition of "The Lonesome Death of Hattie Carroll," ranging from internal drama to sullen accusation that must have sent a shudder up the spine of more than one spectator. One notes (for the sake of jazz lovers) the magnificent part played by the cellist Chuck Israels on this recording.

Her fifth album, called *Fifth Album,* was released in 1965 and reveals to us further aspects of the personality and preoccupations of Judy Collins. To be sure, the traditional English repertoire ("So Early, Early in the Spring," "Lord Gregory") and contemporary songs on social or political themes ("The Coming of the Roads," "Carry It On," "In the Heat of the Summer," "It Isn't Nice") are still there; but now Judy has turned her interest (successfully) also to those contemporary songwriters who deal with more personal themes. In this respect, the remainder of the program on *Fifth Album* speaks for itself: from Bob Dylan she gives us "Tomorrow Is a Long Time" and "Daddy, You Been on My Mind," two songs never "officially" recorded by their author, both of which describe, one in melancholy and one in humorous terms, the ending of an affair: Judy Collins had divorced Peter Taylor. Side Two gives us a "Mr. Tambourine Man" that is if anything a more strident liberator of the conscience than Dylan's own version. One feels throughout the entire album that she is undertaking a quest for a new stability, resultant from a weariness of unending journeys which expresses itself by means of Gordon Lightfoot ("Early Morning Rain"), Eric Andersen (with the unforgettable assistance of John Sebastian's harmonica on "Thirsty Boots"), or even more her friend Richard Fariña, who accompanies Judy on dulcimer in Gil Turner's "Carry It On" and his own "Pack Up Your Sorrows," a song of consolation and friendship. No one could have summed up the magic of Judy Collins better than did Fariña in his eloquent poem on the back of the album sleeve.

For Judy Collins, just like Bob Dylan, feared possession by her public and being forced into the role of vanguard for a "cause." Little by little (unlike Dylan, where the rupture had been sudden and brutal) she disengaged herself from songs of protest. She explained her position very clearly to Irene Neves in an interview that appeared in *Life* (May 2, 1969): she was often asked why she no longer sang the protest songs that she had once, but she had come to the conclusion after a long period of reflection that she could make no effective political contribution with her music. It was nothing to do with her own personal feelings. But it did seem pointless to stand up and sing in front of an audience of people who did nothing more than agree with her. In practical life she was at present involved in two causes which she felt deserved all her efforts: conservation and the fighting of the draft. But singing these ideas at meetings, faced with an audience that she could recognize from the last meeting, became after a minute or two a distinctly unsatisfying experience.

Nobody could question the magnificence of her sixth album, *In My Life*. It is an album of memories and discoveries which marks the first step deliberately taken by her into the domain of pop music. Certainly one still finds traces of folk music proper ("Liverpool Lullaby"), but the whole album testifies to the will of an innovator, both superficially and in essence: the beginning of "Just Like Tom Thumb's Blues" seems like an approving wink at Dylan's approach to "Highway 61 Revisited"; "Hard Lovin' Loser," a homage to Richard Fariña, who by this time had died, is a half-spoken blues / rock number with humorous words and a reckless rhythm. Pop music is yet again the order of the day with the beautiful Beatles song that closes Side Two and gives its title to the album. But there are other tremendous discoveries to be made on the album, above all that of Leonard Cohen, with the ethereal poetry of "Suzanne" and the desperate irony of "Dress Rehearsal Rag" where Judy accompanies herself dazzlingly on the piano. The lyric of "Dress Rehearsal Rag," in extended sentences, is extremely complicated, the tune hard to sing: it was to be some while before the composer himself recorded this song on *Songs of Love and Hate*.

Judy Collins is also devoted to the theater of Bertolt Brecht and the music of Kurt Weill; she had even been seen in New York in the role of Polly Peachum in *The Threepenny Opera,* from which she gives here the famous song of Pirate Jenny. In *In My Life* she renders other homages: to Randy Newman ("I Think It's Going to Rain Today"), Donovan ("Sunny Goodge Street") and Jacques Brel. She sings Brel's "La Colombe" using the same adaptation by Alasdair Clayre as did Joan Baez on *Joan . . .* but with how much more success! Far from dominating Judy's voice, Joshua Rifkin's perfectly balanced orchestration assists both her and the song. Rarely has one heard such a fine combination of tenderness and drama except, perhaps, with Brel himself. Like Tom Paxton, Judy Collins has considerable love for Jacques Brel's songs.

It is with "Marat / Sade" (those who want a political song at any price will find it here) that we see one of the first symphonic songs in several orchestral movements. Even though it lasts less than six minutes, it nevertheless contains all the necessary ingredients and its impact is phenomenal.

Released at the end of 1967, *Wildflowers* is a little deceptive. More intimate than *In My Life,* it is also less strong in vocal terms and musically more variable. Several points are worth raising in connection with it: Judy Collins follows up her introduction to the work of

Leonard Cohen with splendid renditions of "Sisters of Mercy," "Priests," and "Hey, That's No Way to Say Goodbye." Also, from Canada she "discovered" Joni Mitchell, whose celebrated "Both Sides Now," released as a single, gave Judy her first appearance ever on the hit parade: the two female singers were to become great friends. Also in *Wildflowers* Judy takes her first tentative steps into songwriting ("Since You Asked," "Sky Fell," and "Albatross," arguably the best songs on the album). To conclude, she sings one track in Italian ("Lasso! di Donna" by the fourteenth-century Italian composer Francesco Landini) and one in French ("La Chanson des vieux Amants").

Who Knows Where the Time Goes?, released at the end of 1968, brings to mind a question apart from its title: is the singer trying to be trendy by using country and western arrangements (yes, she too) on several of the tracks? The effect is not really worthy of Ian Tyson's "Someday Soon," Dylan's "I Pity the Poor Immigrant," and Cohen's "Bird on the Wire." The rest is magnificent, however: the tumbling words of "First Boy I Loved" (alias Robin Williamson's "First Girl I Loved"; the contained emotion of "My Father" (Judy Collins' father died at the very moment she was writing this song); the allegorical Biblical drama, very somberly arranged, of Cohen's "Story of Isaac"; and Sandy Denny's fantastic song, "Who Knows Where the Time Goes?" And we rediscover Judy Collins' fire, perhaps lost for a moment in the reverie of *Wildflowers,* with "Hello, Hooray" and even more in "Pretty Polly." Departing from a traditional base, this last song is arranged to produce a sort of throbbing blues in which Steve Stills's guitar works wonders.

In general terms, *Who Knows Where the Time Goes?* is the portrait of a singer who has achieved an absolute mastery of her voice and her emotions, and who in practice excels in all the genres which she tackles. It was to set the scene for Judy Collins' future albums, though thankfully most elements of country and western were to disappear. To discuss them in detail would not be profitable—much better to listen to them!

part 3
Electric Children

americans

One of the most obvious effects that the work of Bob Dylan has had on American popular music has been to prove beyond all question that a song can be both an intelligent work of art and commercially successful. Let us be quite clear on this point: strangers to any kind of idealism, the directors of show biz (with a few dazzling exceptions, like Jac Holzman) think only in terms of sales, and the singer and the songwriter, whether or not he has talent, remains underground unless he is considered "commercial" by the record companies.

With the formidable blossoming forth of pop music that we can now look at objectively, it has become a catchphrase that the major record manufacturers sell the revolution at 45 rpm. During a congress of the record industry in London in 1968, the delegate from one of the most important American record companies declared that, as far as he was concerned, his firm would never finance the revolution in this way; a few months later, succumbing to the pressure of new ideas, of youth . . . and of the opposition, that very firm abandoned all its scruples.

To be sure, money is always a useful thing to have around, and even the most pessimistic realize that the pop phenomenon is in the process of revival—as was the case not long ago with folk music. This is, nevertheless, a truth that is a little theoretical: in the first place, a large number of the artists most cited and accused have never claimed to be revolutionaries and are not in fact political except in that they represent a certain section of the populace; in the second place, the true believers refuse to despair, even though it often seems that the genuinely revolutionary writers, if they exist, are lost from sight forever. Still, the other composers of the new style, even though totally lacking a political conscience, place themselves all the more directly in line with the day-to-day existence and emotions of the young people of the West in the sixties and early seventies. If it is unquestionable that some of them sometimes take refuge in dream or in psychological individual drama (one thinks here of Leonard Cohen, Donovan, or Paul Simon), this stresses the dejection and the insecurity at large in the world and thus in its way gives to their work a certain political sense. This trait distinguishes them completely from the harsh and heartless musical types that ruled the market toward the end of the fifties, even though these modern artists must needs express themselves through the medium of the conventional commercial structures—for want of any better way.

Surely variation is not yet dead, though its death often seems to be imminent; and it is clear today that the effect played by the folk revival has played a great part in keeping it alive: because of it, the notions of lyric, ideas, genuineness, and respect for the song have become of considerable importance. Between the revolution symbolized by the work of Dylan and the start of the galloping evolution of commercial music, there is a transitional period dominated by a style which, for want of a better term (and would there were one), we have to describe as "folkrock." We have preferred the expression, when dealing with the composers discussed in the following pages, that seems more apt: the electric children of Bob Dylan.

The genesis of folkrock came about through a very simple antinomy. There existed, in general terms, two sorts of living popular music in the States, if one discounts the omnipresent Muzak that still disfigures the land. On the one hand there was folk music and its direct derivatives, music that was in essence rural, not commercial, which had its basis in ideas, emotions, and opinions, individual or collective, and their honest expression. These songs were accompanied with traditional instruments, individually crafted and relatively rudimentary. But the songs, unfortunately, did not really relate to the lives and problems of a modern, urban, and not in the least folksy population. On the other hand, there was rock 'n' roll: dance music, with rhythms indirectly derived from the blues, commercial and city-oriented, with a far more elaborate instrumentation—drums, brass, amplification, and all that. Unfortunately, the lyrics and ideas of the rock 'n' roll current between 1955 and 1960 were nearly always conformist, mediocre, or even hypocritical, since they were motivated by the specter of financial gain on the part of the record company and, on the part of the singer, at best by a movement toward total rejection of the adult world in the great "conflict of the generations" which explained and resolved exactly nothing. The title of the film *Rebel Without a Cause* sums up exactly the sociological significance of rock 'n' roll. To these two types of music there were correspondingly two sorts of young people, quite distinct from each other: the devotee of folk ignored the devotee of rock 'n' roll, and vice versa.

The part played by the "inventors" of folkrock, even if unconsciously, was to unite, in the ideal case where the operation was a successful one, the two classes of young people under the banner of a new type of music (which the defeatists describe as a bastard child), that gave to each of the two basic forms the finest qualities of the other, in varying proportions: the moral, social, and lyrical aspects of folk, as well as some of its tunes; the finest correspondence of the instrumentation of rock 'n' roll to rhythm and the human voice toward expression of the anguish of modern urban life (one particular example that springs to mind is "Eve of Destruction"). And in the best cases there emerged a popular and very *adult* form of aesthetic expression—that at the same time spoke *our* language.

In Britain the case was a little different. It is an odd thing that, though it seems to be Britain that always leads the United States in originating new trends within the old frameworks (like the Liverpool Sound within the commercial pop framework), in terms of major developments and departures it is the United States that leads Britain. Hence folkrock is to Britain certainly a bastard child—in that it has no parentage.

This is not to say that Britain is without a folklore. Its folklore is, particularly in the Celtic countries—Scotland, Wales, and Ireland— far deeper, richer, and of longer tradition than that of the United States. But this tradition has had little or no effect on British folkrock, which conforms in almost all instances to the American version. And there is the strange situation that the British often produce better American folkrock than the Americans do.

There are a few examples of genuine British folkrock. Not long ago there was the release of *Henry the Human Fly,* an album by Richard Thompson, onetime member of Fairport Convention. This album, though not entirely successful, is interesting in that it is a brave attempt to sustain the adaptation of the British folk musical tradition to electric arrangement and contemporary lyrical themes.

Of course, Thompson had been doing this before in the songs that he recorded with Fairport Convention, but *Henry the Human Fly* is the first time he takes the full plunge—and to a great extent gets away with it. Two other examples spring to mind. Robin Williamson, a Scot, has been responsible for several songs that are firmly in the Scottish or Irish tradition, and Jonathan Kelly, an Irishman, has written several songs that are either based on genuine Irish mythology or, in the most interesting cases, are modern mythological stories: Kelly's music, however, is very much in the American folkrock vein. Both of these excellent songwriters will be discussed in due course.

Immediately behind Bob Dylan, without whom, one must yet again repeat, this evolution would have taken place years later if at all, Richard Fariña was one of the first to work in the direction of the unification of folk and rock. Poet, novelist, essayist, and even sometimes journalist, he had long been attached to the folk revival; we have already mentioned him while speaking of Judy Collins. He was married to Mimi Baez, sister of Joan and herself a singer, with whom he toured Europe in 1963 in the company of Eric von Schmidt. The poetic abilities of Richard Fariña, allied with his pronounced relish for traditional music (his dulcimer-playing was fantastic), naturally pushed him into becoming a songwriter.

Active in bringing other young artists (such as Mark Spoelstra) to the notice of the public while he was living in California, Richard Fariña did not forget to let his own light shine clear and in 1965 released an album, in company with his wife, that is absolutely packed with good things, under the symbolic title of *Celebrations for a Grey Day.* The other recordings and compositions that followed, such as *Reflections in a Crystal Wind* or "Hard Lovin' Loser," showed that Richard Fariña was assured of a great future as the creator of a form of pop music that was particularly original. Unfortunately, he never had time to be more than an illustrious pioneer: in the summer of 1966 he was killed in a motorcycle accident: exactly the death that he predicted, by a tragic irony, for his friend Bob Dylan. Albums by Richard and Mimi Fariña are almost impossible to obtain nowadays, which is one of the tragedies of folkrock.

One can hardly say the word folkrock without thinking immediately of Simon and Garfunkel. Both children of New York City's borough of Queens, Paul Simon and Art Garfunkel first met each other at school. Before they were thirteen years of age they had begun to sing together, rehearsing after classes. Secondary studies, however, separated them for the meantime, while Simon studied for a B.A. in English Literature at Queens College and Garfunkel studied for his doctorate in mathematics at Columbia University.

The two of them had already made several records together, and one Paul Simon song, "Hey Schoolgirl" had been a national hit. But these recordings were very much in the black-leather-jacket tradition of commercial pop music and are lyrically and musically a whit embarrassing.

In 1964 Paul Simon recorded for Columbia his first, impassioned, solo album, *The Paul Simon Songbook*. Two of the twelve songs on the album ("He Was My Brother" and "The Side of a Hill") were from the pen of his friend Paul Kane, while the ten others had been written by Paul Simon himself. These songs contained already the majority of the characteristic elements that would much later ensure the success of the duo and give it its personality: the sensitive voice of Paul Simon (which would soon be admirably juxtaposed with the fragility of Art Garfunkel's) and a straightforward and yet almost ethereal subtlety of guitar-playing (as on "Leaves That Are Green").

A little later than this the two of them made an album called *Wednesday Morning, 3 A.M.* in which they reinterpreted a number of traditional songs, from "Peggy-O" to "Go Tell It on the Mountain"; some by contemporary authors, like Bob Dylan's "The Times They are A-Changin' "; and a few by Simon himself, including "Sparrow," "The Sounds of Silence," the beautiful "Bleecker Street," and the title track, "Wednesday Morning, 3 A.M."

Paul Simon's lyrics are in general simple and direct, though one could hardly say they were simplistic. Unfortunately, the talent of Simon the writer is far from prolific. Always short of new compositions, he was to reuse many of the titles on these early albums— above all "The Sounds of Silence," but also "April Come She Will" and "Flowers Never Bend with the Rainfall"—in future recordings with Garfunkel.

Already one can see that one of the principal themes of his inspiration was the difficulty of communication between one individual and another:

> *and in the naked light I saw*
> *ten thousand people maybe more*
> *people talking without speaking*
> *people hearing without listening*
> *people writing songs that voices never shared*
> *no one dared*
> *disturb the sound of silence* *

And then there was loneliness, as in "A Most Peculiar Man," and in "Flowers Never Bend with the Rainfall," the people who are sure that tomorrow will always come:

> *so, I continue to continue*
> *to pretend*
> *my life will never end*
> *and flowers never bend*
> *with the rainfall* †

Alone of its type, one notes that there is on *The Paul Simon Songbook* a song preaching the liberation of blacks: "A Church Is Burning." All of these serious subjects do not stop Simon from showing another side of his nature, a withering sense of humor as in "A Simple Desultory Philippic," where outrageous plays upon words combine with evident pseudo-Dylanesque allusions.

In the months that followed the release of *The Paul Simon Songbook* he traveled to Europe, first of all to London, then to Paris. While singing in the evenings in a Paris nightclub, he suddenly found that the rock version of "The Sounds of Silence" that had been recorded with Art Garfunkel was now steadily climbing the *Cashbox* singles charts, and his return to New York was urgently required.

The origins of the rock version of "The Sounds of Silence" are interesting. Simon had recorded with Art Garfunkel an acoustic version of the song on *Wednesday Morning, 3 A.M.*, which was far from

---

* Paul Simon, "The Sounds of Silence." Copyright © 1964 by Paul Simon. Used by permission of Charing Cross Music, Inc. & Deshufflin, Inc., and Pattern Music, Ltd.
† Paul Simon, "Flowers Never Bend with the Rainfall." Copyright © 1965 by Paul Simon. Used by permission of Charing Cross Music, Inc. & Deshufflin, Inc., and Pattern Music, Ltd.

being the most successful of albums. While Simon was in Europe regretting his total lack of recording fame, the song was heard by a Columbia executive, who realized its hit potential—if it were electrified. Bass and electric guitar were promptly dubbed on, and the bastard product was released as a single to provide the first (and colossal) success of the duo, which re-formed in 1965 to begin a brilliant career.

The albums that followed (*Sounds of Silence* and *Parsley, Sage, Rosemary and Thyme*) show little in the way of influence from the folk tradition, unless it be in the theme of traveling ("Homeward Bound") or the arrangement of an old English song, "Scarborough Fair" to form "Scarborough Fair / Canticle." However, there is on *Sounds of Silence* a demonstration of Simon's mastery of the six-string guitar with a version of Davy Graham's classic "Angie." Opinions vary as to the worth of this version in comparison with those of Davy Graham and Bert Jansch, but a good number of people consider it the best (others think it's the worst).

Bookends, their fifth album, is the great triumph in the career of Simon and Garfunkel. The first side makes up a cohesive whole with the impersonal horror of "Save the Life of My Child" (which is yet sickly humorous), passing through the disillusion of "America," the souring of a relationship in "Overs," to reach eventually the pathos of "Old Friends," the old men who do nothing but sit in the park all day: the songs are embraced by the "Bookends Theme," where the old realize that all that's left are their memories, and enhanced by a short clip from recordings of old people speaking made by Art Garfunkel in various old people's homes around the United States. The second side is lit by the surrealistic humor of "Punky's Dilemma," the tender irony of "Mrs. Robinson," and the allegorical light-heartedness of "At the Zoo," as well as the superb "A Hazy Shade of Winter."

After their immense success, the music created by Simon and Garfunkel for the film, *The Graduate,* consecrated their reputation on an international scale. At the beginning of 1970 their album, *Bridge Over Troubled Water* (a mixture of some of the best and some of the worst of Simon's writing), achieved huge sales and remained at the top of the album charts, as had the title track in the singles charts, for months on end in several countries. The album shows a considerable enlargement of the duo's musical capabilities, not always for

the better, unfortunately. Of particular interest is the almost successful merging of an old South American tune and arrangement with
new lyrics by Paul Simon, "El Condor Pasa," and of course the brilliant "The Boxer."

Then they split up again. Garfunkel went off to act in films, with
a small part in *Catch 22* and the sole saving grace of *Carnal Knowledge*
with his admirable performance in one of the lead roles. Simon, on
the other hand, has since recorded two solo albums, *Paul Simon* and
Here Comes Rhymin' Simon, and has had several hit singles, notably
"Mother and Child Reunion" and "Me and Julio Down by the School
Yard." Simon's style has changed—as he puts it himself, it has become "funkier and simpler"—and he has absorbed new influences,
notably reggae music, the commercialized version of a West Indian
original that for a brief time dominated the singles charts. Garfunkel
has not been idle in musical terms, and released in late 1973 his own
album, *Angel Clare.*

If the success both in commercial and artistic terms (which comes
down, eventually, to the awakening maturity of the general public)
of Simon and Garfunkel is not considered by all critics as sufficiently
representative of the validity of folkrock (after all, their art is "fragile," their vision "superficial" and lacking in "virility"), then one must
turn for further examples to the various folkrock groups that have
achieved success. Primary among these is the virtual bomb that ex-
ploded in 1965 in the shape of the Byrds, one of the first, if not *the*
first, groups born out of the pop revolution of the West Coast. Their
two first albums on Columbia (*Mr. Tambourine Man* and *Turn! Turn!
Turn!*) show them emphatically to be the first electric children of
Dylan.

The treatment given to a song by the Byrds (in particular by
David Crosby and Roger McGuinn) was radically new: a melodic
beauty generated from a folk tradition that they knew well but with
rhythms often close to the very best of rock 'n' roll. From an instrumental and vocal point of view, they were perfectionists who had
learned from attentive listening to the Beatles, after the Everly
Brothers; their songs were either intelligently written or judiciously
chosen from the works of others. One gets the impression that the
Byrds attached great importance to lyrics, that they didn't see them
as just a useless appendage.

The Byrds were part of that generation of musicians who had accepted with open arms the doctrine of Dylan at that time. Their version of "Mr. Tambourine Man," which gave them their first breath of commercial success, was a logical part of that evolution and, though it may still continue to dazzle us, it is no longer a surprise that the Byrds should have produced it then. Even Pete Seeger, whose "The Bells of Rhymney" and "Turn! Turn! Turn!" they recorded, can hardly have found fault with their versions, rich and electric though they be. Indeed, though it is customary in general terms to see the lesser talents of the twentieth century as merely hiding behind a curtain of contemporary urban music and lush arrangements, the fact that the Byrds were five permitted them more variety (solo, chorus, complex harmony) than a duo like Simon and Garfunkel.

After their first two albums the group took an odd course: often dismantled altogether, sometimes diminished to only one or two members, re-formed with the addition of new blood, they returned to strength in 1969 with a magnificent contribution to the sound track of the film, *Easy Rider;* also, in some of their more recent recordings they show tendencies toward a form of country and western that is well structured and integrated by an eclectic and evolutionary process. Always led by Roger McGuinn, the Byrds usually consist of Clarence White (guitar), Gene Parsons (drums), and Skip Battin (bass), though they have often recorded in company with a man who has done much toward deciding the course their evolution should take: Al Kooper. However, as John Peel put it, every musician in the world has played in the Byrds at one time or another, and they still have the same sound.

One of the original members of the Byrds was David Crosby, who was later to be part of one of the first "supergroups," Crosby, Stills & Nash. Stephen Stills had at one time been a member of Buffalo Springfield, one of those groups that everybody started to appreciate after they had disbanded. Graham Nash had been the leader and guiding light of the Hollies, a commercial British soft rock group that in some ways seems never to have recovered from his departure. The first album that the trio made, entitled simply *Crosby, Stills & Nash,* was an impressively catholic selection of music. The range went from the deceptive simplicity of Crosby's "Guinevere" and

Nash's "Lady of the Island," both beautiful and principally acoustic tracks, to the fairly hard rock sound of "Long Time Gone," a Crosby track that foreshadowed much of his lyrical preoccupation in times to come.

Crosby, Stills & Nash played a large part in the film *Woodstock.* Apart from a filming of their performance of Stephen Stills's "Suite for Judy Blue Eyes," two of their songs were used as title music: Crosby's "Wooden Ships" and a rock version of Joni Mitchell's "Woodstock."

They were shortly joined by Neil Young, also a onetime member of Buffalo Springfield, and produced their second album, *Déjà Vu,* under the group name of Crosby, Stills, Nash & Young. Unfortunately, this album hardly bore out the promise of their first. Though a good enough collection of music in its way, one can't help but have the feeling that if you've listened to the first then you've really heard all there is to hear of the second. Their third album, a double called *Four Way Street,* consisted of live performances of music that had principally already been recorded on the earlier two.

Crosby, Stills, Nash & Young have for the most part gone their separate ways. Stills has formed a group called Manassas, with whom he has made several albums. Young has gone back to making his own solo albums, and has enjoyed considerable commercial success in so doing. Both Crosby and Nash have each made solo albums, and then joined forces to release one with them performing as a duo. It is certain that all four of them will keep popping up in the progress of rock music in times to come.

In many ways, the origins of the Band were not without resemblances to those of the Byrds. Originally, under the name of the Hawks, the group was under the leadership of Ronnie Hawkins (well known to rock 'n' rollers), and later accompanied Bob Dylan onstage during his tours of 1965–66, notably at the unique Olympia concert. All those who were lucky enough to see the combination of Dylan and the Hawks onstage remember the occasion with emotion and nostalgia. Hawkins departed and Dylan's tours a thing of the past, they installed themselves in a house known as "Big Pink" near Woodstock, and became the Band.

At Woodstock, during the year 1967, they continued to play with Dylan quite frequently, and the recordings that they made with him—"I Shall Be Released," "Tears of Rage," "This Wheel's on

Fire," "Please Mrs. Henry," "Open the Door, Richard (Homer)"— formed the basis for several Dylan bootleg albums, so much appreciated by the enthusiasts. In fact, Dylan and the five members of the Band (Jaime Robbie Robertson, Richard Manuel, Rick Danko, Levon Helm, and Garth Hudson) had decided unanimously not to make these recordings (known to the connoisseur as the Basement Tapes) public. On one hand, the music no longer corresponded with what Dylan wished to offer the public for his "revival"—*John Wesley Harding;* on the other, the time had now come for the Band to stand up as a group by themselves.[1]

Their first album, *Music from Big Pink,* was one of the sensations of summer 1968, in a comparable way to the Byrds' *Mr. Tambourine Man* three years earlier: they shared the characteristics of being able to compose songs at the same time topical and timeless ("The Weight") in a spirit drawn directly from the same line as that of Dylan's *Blonde on Blonde* or even *John Wesley Harding.* Like the Byrds, the members of the Band are almost maniacal perfectionists and one has to admire their acute sense of instrumental and vocal precision, all dressed up in a cloak of seeming informality, as well as their high technical standard. Again like the Byrds, while they are perfectly faithful to the *spirit* of folk music, they are able to inject old songs with refreshingly new treatments ("Long Black Veil") and can be classed as, among other things, the group that best interprets Dylan songs ("This Wheel's on Fire" and above all the timeless "Tears of Rage" and "I Shall Be Released" on *Music from Big Pink* and "When I Paint My Masterpiece" on *Cahoots,* their fourth album).

There are at least two characteristics that strongly differentiate the Band from the Byrds. First of all there is their complete lack of topical, political, and sociological references (the Byrds had dedicated "He Was a Friend of Mine" to the memory of John F. Kennedy and, on the album *Easy Rider,* devoted a track to the cosmonauts Armstrong, Aldrin, and Collins); like modern Dylan they take refuge in the creative powers of the individual. Secondly, there is their flavor of the countryside, the reflection of a long-dead America, of a world still innocent.

Their next album, *The Band,* was an even more impressive demonstration of creativity and skill, though following along the same

[1] *The Basement Tapes* has been released as a two-record set with Bob Dylan and the Band. Of the twenty-four songs on the discs, sixteen feature Dylan as lead vocal.

lines of development as their first. Though their third album, *Stage Fright,* was a little disappointing (one British musician said of it, that it amazed him how often the Band could do so little with so much), their fourth, *Cahoots,* showed them at their very finest. On it they interpret one Dylan song, "When I Paint My Masterpiece," in a way that must make Dylan envious, as well as ten Jaime Robbie Robertson songs, of which the most interesting is probably "The River Hymn," returning as it does very much to a land which, although not idealized in the Hollywood fashion, was certainly more innocent and genuine than the one that they inhabit now.

There are very few groups who can successfully combine genuine folk with genuine rock to produce that strange synthesis, folkrock. Customarily, "folkrock" groups are either direct descendants from Dylan or from Simon and Garfunkel. There are a few, however, most of whom are British and will be discussed later: this may suggest that the British folk tradition is easier to adapt to modern techniques.

But mention should be made here of four groups, though two are British, who fall well into the folkrock category: Magna Carta, Lazarus, Earth Opera, and Heron.

Magna Carta is well known for an ambitious project it undertook on record, their album *Seasons.* Of this album, one side is taken up with an at times excellent and always good sung and spoken account of the changing seasons of the year. The link figure is a pilgrim, a youth in spring and an old man in winter, who in that season passes on the burden of the year to the youth who will follow his road through the new year, and so forth. Both the songs and poetry that go to make up this epic effort are by Chris Simpson, who also writes all the rest of the group's material. Unfortunately, a lot of Magna Carta's music is rather too sugar-sweet, and the lyrics also often fall into this trap.

Lazarus is an American religious trio "discovered" by Peter Yarrow of Peter, Paul and Mary. Their music is gentle and unpretentious, frequently though not always with a strong religious flavor, and reminiscent of Crosby, Stills, Nash & Young, though if anything better. The harmonies are always precise and the instrumentation soothing perfect.

Earth Opera is a group that now seems to have disappeared.

Their guiding force was Peter Rowan, one of the best lyricists that the folkrock era ever produced. In particular, its first album, *Earth Opera,* shows Rowan at the absolute height of his songwriting power, and it is almost unbelievable that the group never made any commercial impact to speak of. A song like "Death by Fire" demonstrates the surrealistic power of his lyrics, backed ably by a strange conglomeration of musical instruments, predominantly the electric mandolin. Their second album, *The Great American Eagle Tragedy,* falls far short of the standard of the first, though there is an enlargement of their musical range with the incorporation of saxophones, flutes, and a battery of session musicians.

Heron is a British group who make the same mistake as so many of their compatriots, such as Magna Carta: their music has a strong tendency to be too slight and oversweet. On the other hand, their instrumental abilities cannot be denied, and their albums are never unpleasant to hear. Their first, *Heron,* boasted loudly on the cover that it had been recorded live in a field, and the quality is such that it might tempt other musicians to question whether recording studios are in fact necessary. Their second, a double album called *Twice as Nice and Half the Price,* shows an extension of the musical idioms to which they have become familiar: judging by the occasional note of birdsong that creeps in, it too was recorded in a field.

Oddly enough, seldom if ever have groups added much of an impetus to the development of contemporary folk. Whether it is that the work of the individual songwriter is lost in the trappings of the group, or merely that the very finest of songwriters in general prefer to work on their own or merely with session musicians, it is hard to tell. Groups such as Peter, Paul and Mary have of course in their time "spread the good word," but for some reason no group has actually taken the lead in terms of determining a style.

In taking his first steps into the world of contemporary American folk, already rich in strong personalities, Arlo Guthrie (born in Coney Island in 1947) was possessed of a celebrated surname. It was up to him to make his own given name as illustrious: this was not as easy as one might imagine. The first trap to avoid was that of imitating his father, to produce a new copy of Woody, in short to be musically a "father's boy." He preferred, and for good reason, to play the good son in extending his father's work to subjects that were close to him, to translate what he saw into the language of modern America, far removed from that of the 1930s. A road that Woody himself, without doubt, would have taken had it not been for the illness that prematurely silenced him. Arlo was therefore first to receive notice via the celebrated and genial spoken blues, "Alice's Restaurant," which occupies the whole of Side One of the album of the same name.

"Alice's Restaurant" is the droll and lively story of the arrest of Arlo Guthrie and one of his friends, following the heinous crime of dropping litter in a prohibited area, prior to Arlo's receiving his draft notice. The satire of the police and army is at times ferocious: to the officer who reads in his dossier that he has already been in prison, Arlo replies that surely just because he dropped litter doesn't mean that he isn't moral enough to kill women and children. "Alice's Restaurant," which occupies the whole of Side One of the album of became almost the official song of the festival.

The success of the song brought in its wake a number of cover versions, a cookbook (*The Alice's Restaurant Cookbook*), and above all, thanks to the genuine talents of Arlo as a comedian and to the understanding of Arthur Penn, a marvelous film which to some extent has become something of a cult item.

The second trap Arlo had to avoid was of settling back comfortably in the success he had so easily achieved with "Alice's Restaurant" and of serving the same thing again in various different guises. But he didn't fall into it: we can recall in this respect his extremely significant action at the Newport festival the year after his "discovery." During the final concert when everybody was hypnotized by his presence and shouting for him to play "Alice's Restaurant" with the sort of insistence one can imagine, Arlo refused to perform it and, in its place, improvised in homage to his father a new version, equally hilarious, of "Motorcycle Song" from his second album.

His third album, *Running Down the Road,* signified a genuine evolution. The first four pieces, following the current tendency, make use of a Nashville accompaniment. And the result is charming, the atmosphere intimate and friendly without any trace of that affectation which has so often spoiled experiments of this type. It's too much to say that Arlo "reinvented" country and western, despite what others (and some surprisingly well known others) have said of him, but he has certainly incorporated it in the most natural fashion.

Never leaning on the instrumentation, on the contrary he dominates it with his own strong voice (he has warned people who want to listen to him that he sings "just as bad as Woody") and his perfect guitar playing. "Oh! In the Morning," which closes Side One, is in quite a different style: a slow melody sung in a melancholy tone accompanied by a solo piano . . . and a triumph of originality. Side Two is more varied: "Coming into Los Angeles," which opens the side, is a mixture of modern pop and country and western with a lyric full of irony (about the customs, this time), and was one of the successes of the film *Woodstock;* the well-known traditional number, "Stealin'," is treated in turn to a Nashville accompaniment, but without ever becoming hackneyed, perhaps due to a comfortable and amusing use of female back-up singers. "My Front Pages" seems to be a reaction to Dylan's "My Back Pages" (the inevitable comparison) but is far less serious in tone. A Pete Seeger instrumental, the delicate "Living in the Country," allows the listener to catch breath before "Running Down the Road," the key track of the album and the one that gave it its title.

The track is a veritable apotheosis, the only resolutely pop piece on the album, by virtue of its impressionistic and quasi-spatial instrumentation (this may sound confusing and pretentious, but is valid here). Arlo, in his turn inspired by the theme of the open highway and the interminable journey (symbolized by the splendid motorcycle photograph on the cover), narrates to us his impressions and reflections about the land that he has traveled through and, even more important, the people he has encountered en route. And, as with his father before him, he loves them.

The road he is traveling continues through *Washington County,* his fourth album, and looks as if it's going to be the one he follows for quite some time to come. The political vision of life that ran like a spine through his father's work is missing from Arlo's, and even less are his observations linked to sociological conditions. In fact, a valid criticism of his music could be that it has a certain anachronistic flavor: and yet, its sincerity requires no defense.

We discover in the person of Richie Havens a black artist, certainly originally inspired by the blues, but who in his approach has taken advantage of the techniques and styles of a pop music that is dominated by whites, whether they be artists or audience. This point

alone confers upon Richie Havens a unique importance as a representative of the fallout of the folk revival in modern pop music.

Richie Havens was born in 1941 in the Bedford-Stuyvesant section of Brooklyn which has today become a black ghetto but which
was at that time populated by a mixture of Italians, blacks, Puerto
Ricans, and Jews. He was the eldest son of a family of nine children
whose father played the piano but worked for his living as an elec-
troplater. Richie swiftly learned to sing, without training, and at the
age of fourteen formed with some of the boys of his neighborhood a
group called the McCrea Gospel Singers, which could be heard in
the streets of Brooklyn. None of them had at that time any thought
of going professional: Havens himself planned to be a surgeon. But,
though he was a conscientious student, he left school—and then his
family—at the age of seventeen, not as a demonstration of revolt but
because he thought the time had come to try to discover another way
of life.

The other way of life, of course, was to be found in Greenwich
Village. But before he came around to music as a way of earning his
living, he sold tourists portraits which he painted in the streets. And
one day he bought himself a guitar. It was then that he discovered
by accident, for nobody gave him any sort of teaching, his own personal way of open-tuning the guitar, and the origin of the sonorous
tone which would make his playing recognizable among thousands
of others. During the next three or four years, while working successively in a string of restaurants, then in a doll factory, he spent his
evenings playing for free in the Greenwich Village cafés.

Two albums (*Electric Richie Havens* and *Richie Havens Record*)
launched him into professional status, but he really took off with the
signing of a contract with Verve-Forecast in 1966, consummated by
the magnificent albums: *Mixed Bag, Something Else Again, Richard P.
Havens, 1983,* and *Stonehenge.*

In perfect spiritual communion with his musicians (Paul Williams, second guitar; Joe Price, African drums; Eric Oxendine [a
Cherokee], bass), Havens insists that they play as a group and refuses to give himself pride of place. He does not dispute, however,
that his powerful voice and its curious timbre stand out markedly,
whether he likes it or not, in the overall musical effect. An inheri-
tance from the blues, his voice has the same spontaneity, suspense,

the ability to bind the listener, humor perhaps, and the same raw-ness: as Havens explains, a good part of what we say is conveyed to the listener less through the meaning of the words, more through the actual sounds (as most poets would agree), and that the com-munication is received not simply by the ears but through the skin, under the skin. The euphoric impression created by listening to this group, reinforced by the visual excitement that communicates itself when one is lucky enough to see them live (they had been a prized attraction at large festivals like those at Newport, Woodstock, and the Isle of Wight), backs up Richie Havens' statement.

However, this originality of Richie Havens, great though it be, is not his only distinguishing feature. For his lyrics, by a sort of verbal magic, also play a role, whether in those songs that he writes himself or those that he chooses to reinterpret. For Havens is very much a poet as well as a musician, as is plain by the liner notes he writes for his albums and by his own impressive songs: "The Klan," for ex-ample, which re-creates in the first person the interior and exterior cry of suffering of a man lynched by members of the Ku Klux Klan. But the lyric, leaving behind the problem in particular terms, ex-pands to regard it more in universal terms.

This constant call for the liberation of each and every person perhaps allows us to understand better the connection between Ha-vens' music and that of Bob Dylan, and the way in which the former serves intelligently the latter. This characteristic culminates in "Maggie's Farm."

While preoccupied with the sorrows of his age (racism, as we have seen, and also war: "Handsome Johnny," heard in the film *Woodstock* and on the album *Mixed Bag*), the world inside Richie Havens' mind is peopled by fascinating images: as, for example, his interest in stories of vampires, reincarnation, the fantastic in general, and in Oriental systems of meditation. Unconscious contradictions or, on the other hand, a way of resolving disparate things? It doesn't matter . . . even less so for us, in the presence of an extremely at-tractive and perhaps even indispensable personality: for proof, his recent idea of creating a company whereby the musical control is by the musicians themselves, without the constraints of commercialism and the risks of bureaucratic exploitation of the artists, and the put-ting into practice of the idea in the form of his own record label,

Stormy Forest. A remarkable innovation this, the sun in that world of show-biz grayness in America. . . . "Here Comes the Sun."

With Tim Hardin we come to one of the most original singer-songwriters engendered by the folk revival. Situated right on the frontiers of modern sung poetry, he is nevertheless incontestably inspired by the mainstream of traditional folklore.

Tim Hardin was born some thirty years ago at Eugene, Oregon, to a family that already had its fair share of musicians: his mother was a concert violinist and his father a jazz player. As a student he found himself more and more oriented toward folk music and, after serving in the Marines for two years (in Laos and Cambodia), he began to play in the clubs in Boston and Cambridge, Massachusetts, and to record. He very rapidly and skillfully assimilated the traditional music of the South, both white (a repertoire of Cajun songs and songs by Hank Williams) and black (Mississippi blues).

In his early albums—particularly *This Is Tim Hardin!*—he is distinguished by an extremely personal and inspired guitar style and a vocal performance astounding in its exactitude and its fire, as on pieces like "Working on the Railroad" or "The House of the Rising Sun." The spirit of Tim Hardin is not without similarities to that of the Dylan of 1961–62.

Like Dylan, Hardin had within him the ingredients for a great creator and, after his promising beginnings as an interpreter of traditional material, he became a songwriter in his own right. On his albums as a songwriter (on Verve-Forecast) one can easily follow the musical transformation that he underwent: the tone has become more intimate, the voice perhaps more delicate. From the blues he has inherited the ability to express pain, the suffering of a man who wishes to live with the maximum intensity and express through his art moments of sadness as much as moments of joy. Lovingly, he dedicates to his wife an autobiographical song, "The Lady Came from Baltimore," but realistically also asserts, "Don't Make Promises."

In time, Tim Hardin achieved a well-deserved measure of fame and success, but this was through the activities of other artists. If his own recordings were bought by only a restricted audience of devotees, his songs were recorded by a variety of well-known artists: such as the Nice who recorded "Hang on to a Dream," or, in the case of

"If I Were a Carpenter," Joan Baez, Johnny Cash, Bobby Darin, The Four Tops, and, in a French translation, Johnny Hallyday (whose French translation of the title incorrectly ran "*Si j'étais une charpentier*").

All the same, it was with a work that no one except the author has recorded—or *could* record—that the qualities of Tim Hardin as poet and musician really came to the fore in 1969: reminiscent perhaps of the emergence of Leonard Cohen. The wonderful album *Tim Hardin Suite for Susan Moore and Damion—We're—One, One, All in One*, which he dedicated to his wife and son, is in fact a single piece of work from beginning to end, in a much more structured and definite way than was, say, Dylan's *Blonde on Blonde*. An extraordinarily comfortable and sensitive combination of music, song, and spoken poetry, with an incredible emotional strength, this suite constitutes a decisive step toward an enlarged perception in directions and zones of feeling that Dylan has never explored and which owe nothing to the emotional safaris of Cohen. As one critic put it, *Suite for Susan Moore and Damion* marks a revolution in folk music comparable to that caused in pop music proper by the Beatles' *Sergeant Pepper's Lonely Hearts Club Band*.

More recently, he recorded *Bird on the Wire*, an album of sad songs—as is the title track, which is a Leonard Cohen song. Because he showed on this album as elsewhere his preference for concentrating on the unhappy as well as the happy aspects of life, Hardin earned, in Britain at least, a rather bad reputation among the never very sensitive columnists of the commerical pop music press. It appears that Tim Hardin, like all men of right mind, has ignored their carping.

Whatever one's feelings in the matter, no one can deny the beauty and the complete originality of Tim Hardin's work.

The first thing that struck one about Janis Ian was her youth and the precocity of her talent. Some dates will attest to her amazingly early maturity: born on April 7, 1951, in a New York middle-class family to broad-minded, well-educated, and music-loving parents, she wrote her first song at the age of twelve and a half, entitled "Hair of Spun Gold." *Broadside*, interested in the talent of Janis Ian, published the song in 1964.

It was in 1966, after her dramatic first appearances at Greenwich

Village's Village Gate, that Janis made her first album for Verve-Forecast. Immediately the record earned the admiration of the educated public, but also the disapproval [2] of the Establishment. This was due to the most noticed song on the album, "Society's Child," which tackled the problem of racial discrimination in a new fashion and without mincing words: for a schoolgirl of fifteen, not a bad start.

Why so much hassle over a song? Making use of an episode in the life of one of society's children (one would like to think that it is Janis Ian herself, but she has definitely stated that it is not), she attacks, all at the same time, racial discrimination, familial authority, the reactionary antiquity of the educational system, the contempt for love, the alienation which is its result, through the fact that at least temporarily a young white girl resigns herself to accepting what she is told, to stop meeting the young black whom she loves. Lyrically and musically, the "schoolgirl" doesn't miss a trick.

Certainly, her education in song is established on a base that she herself has defined as "Baezo-Seegerian" and, as she has often said, since she grew up with folk music, all her songs are capable of being sung to the sole accompaniment of the acoustic guitar. And this is what she does, and brilliantly so, when singing in public. But for her records she makes use of guitarists, bassists, organists, and drummers (she herself plays guitar and piano) of the first quality: on her third album, *The Secret Life of J. Eddy Fink,* Richie Havens is one of the drummers.

From *Janis Ian,* her first album, to *Stars,* her fifth, by way of *For All the Seasons of Your Mind, The Secret Life of J. Eddy Fink,* and *Who Really Cares?* there is no doubt that there has grown up a "Janis Ian sound": the way of combining the voice and the instruments, done with a great delicacy and possibly also a certain detachment, are extremely individualistic: as far as we know no well-known artist has attempted to record cover versions of her songs.

Looked at purely musically, Janis Ian's recordings have always been extremely well arranged. Unfortunately, in *Who Really Cares?*

---

[2] "Disapproval" is perhaps rather a mild word when speaking of the Establishment's reaction to "Society's Child." At least one disc jockey was beaten up for playing the song on his program, and it was well known that several of the radio stations practiced a form of unofficial censorship in regard to it: whether this censorship was imposed from within or without is not known.

the themes of the songs are not in the most distinguished or individ-ualistic vein. One hunts for the masterpiece but, unlike her earlier records, the hunt is in vain.

As far as we can see, the problem for her at the time of *Who Really Cares?* is very clear: the early works of Janis Ian were signified by her extreme precocity. Her preoccupations (racism, interracial love, education, the dilemmas of the young in the world of the old) tes-tified to her rare maturity. Now that she has achieved physical matu-rity, it seems that she has difficulty in reaching her second wind; the songs on *Who Really Cares?* are attempts to find it. On two or three of the tracks there are moments of great beauty: in "Galveston," the very jazzy "Orphan of the Wind," and above all in "Month of May." But taken all together, *Who Really Cares?* hasn't the same cohesion as an album like *The Secret Life of J. Eddy Fink.*

Nevertheless it seems that the future holds great promise for Janis Ian as songwriter. After *Who Really Cares?* we waited for her next album . . . and the wait was for some years. Then in 1974 her fifth album, *Stars,* was released. It is an album with occasional mo-ments of brilliance—"Stars" and "Dance with Me"—but is of an overall standard far below that of her earlier work. Her first four albums are now hard to get, though they can occasionally be found in secondhand record shops: they have long ago been deleted. But with behind her the power of these years, she can hardly fail to make a lasting impact on the world of folkrock in particular and the world of pop music in general. Her more recent releases, especially *Between the Lines,* offer strong evidence of her increasingly mature and developing talent.

Melanie Safka was born in Astoria, New York, and taught herself music througout her schooldays, happily skipping her textbooks in favor of her six-string guitar. At the end of 1968 she recorded for the newish label Buddah her first album, one of obvious freshness and originality, *Born to Be* (rereleased as *My First Album*).

On first listening, the voice seems quite bizarre: very piercing, quavering, and even a little savage. The intonations are sometimes childish, perhaps not without affectation . . . but the ear becomes accustomed to it eventually. From time to time while listening one thinks of Buffy Sainte-Marie, or Janis Ian, or Edith Piaf, or even Janis Joplin. In the first place, Melanie's voice recalls that attacking power of Joplin's; in the second, there is a trace of cynicism and self-assuredness; in the third place, occasionally, there is a sort of "bub-blegum" feeling about her singing.

These traces of outside influence are of secondary importance only, for Melanie brings to song elements that have not been obvious before her: above all, a very fresh and pristine sense of humor ("Bobo's Party" certainly, but also "Animal Crackers"). Also there are examples of simultaneous irony and tenderness: the tenderness of a justification for promiscuity in "I Really Loved Harold," or vicious irony as in "I'm Back in Town," the gentleness of her rendition of "Christopher Robin" contrasting with the irony of the disillusioned innocent in "Merry Christmas." The range of feeling which she asks us to share is immense, but above all Melanie has the ability to communicate directly with each listener. She appears literally to be the eternal seeker, the eternal experiencer (unlike Janis Ian, who perhaps has a fault in that she inspires in the listener a sense of detachment). Her version of "Mr. Tambourine Man" is so personal that anyone who'd never heard of Dylan would be unable to believe that it wasn't the product of Melanie's own writings.

After this first triumph, Melanie participated in the 1969 Woodstock Festival to universal approval and went on to record her second album. Many are the songwriters who, after the shouting about their first record has died down, seem unable to stretch to producing a second that is both as good and yet not merely a repeat performance of the first.

Not so Melanie. Her second album, *Melanie No. 2,* without reducing the merits of *Born to Be,* testifies nevertheless that she is far from resting on her laurels. She has become the perfect mistress of her voice. While still able to express tearing sadness or volcanic power, her inflections are now impeccably controlled. This point is particularly in evidence in "Tuning My Guitar," and even more so in "Johnny Boy," with its gradually increasing quasi-Brelian escalade of volume: she reaches out to seize her listeners, who have no choice but to allow themselves to be swept into the song, unable to move in case they spoil its beauty. And the rhythm is stronger: in this respect, the possibilities glimpsed in "Bobo's Party" and "Animal Crackers" are realized in "Soul Sister Annie," "Uptown Down," and "Baby Guitar." The piano, incidentally, is put to marvelous use on this album, as is the countering of the violence of the percussion with the softness of the guitar and cello on "For My Father."

In her third album she began an association (that still continues) by incorporating the voices of the Edwin Hawkins Singers, acclaimed at the Isle of Wight Festival in 1970. *Candles in the Rain* is rather a mixed bag of an album, going from the impressive simplistic beauty of the title track to such banalities as the world-famous, "What Have They Done to My Song, Ma?" via a rather good but not outstanding version of the Jagger / Richard composition, "Ruby Tuesday." But the best track of all on the album is unquestionably "Leftover Wine," where Melanie skillfully employs the full range of her voice to produce impressions of loneliness and desertion.

And then the albums came so thick and fast that it is hard to tell them apart. There was *The Good Book, Four Sides of Melanie* (as one might guess from the title, a double album), *Garden in the City,* and so forth. In a way this is a pity, since it detracts from the status of Melanie as singer-songwriter that there is so much of her recorded work around, not all of which is up to the very highest standards. Nevertheless, she still stands as one of the finest living examples of modern American female folksingers.

Two American songwriters who have recently sprung to prominence must be mentioned, each of whom have in their own way contributed to a new trend in modern folkrock: David Ackles and Don McLean.

David Ackles has in fact been around for quite a while, even though his name has hardly become a famous one. Possessed of a deep, emotionally rich, and moody voice, he is a pianist par excellence and a songwriter of unbelievable emotional depth. Elton John in several interviews has proclaimed himself to be one of David Ackles' greatest fans.

His first album, *David Ackles* (sometimes to be found under the title *The Road to Cairo*), achieved recognition among a small circle as one of the best rock albums of 1968. Apart from "The Road to Cairo," a version of which by Julie Driscoll was a hit of sorts, there are several first-rate songs on the album. "Down River" tells in the first person the story of a man who has spent some years in prison and who returns to find that the woman he loved has married one of his school friends: not the most original of plots, perhaps, but dealt with in an unusual fashion; the ex-convict doesn't react with hate or violence, as one might expect if the song were written by anyone else except Ackles, but puts a brave face over his pain as he passively watches the world he'd planned falling to pieces in front of his eyes. And the listener is pulled into the song to identify strongly with the prisoner, so that he becomes less of a listener and much more of a participant.

In "His Name Is Andrew," Ackles tells, again in the first person, of a man who is the epitome of Colin Wilson's "Outsider," and who reacts in the negative fashion by totally rejecting the world about him. He tries to find some sort of comfort from God, the God that he was taught about as a child, but he finds it impossible to penetrate the clergy and the God that is hidden behind them. The last few lines of the song are:

> *my name is Andrew*
> *I work in a canning factory*
> *I do not have a friend*
> *I choose to wait alone*
> *for this life to end . . . .**

Also of considerable note on the album are "Blue Ribbons," the tale of a girl left pregnant by the man she thought loved her and whom she trusted (yet again told in the first person); "Be My Friend" which, without ever becoming corny, puts across the thesis that life can only be made better by individuals attempting to make the lives of other individuals more rewarding, that unless there is friendship then no political system can lead humanity toward Utopia; "Sonny Come Home," about a man who tries to return to the home of his boyhood only to find that what he has remembered is distorted and that this is a home he will never be able to return to; and a beautiful love song called "When Love Is Gone." *David Ackles* is a musical feast indeed.

His second album, *Subway to the Country,* is by contrast disappointing. The mellowness of the first album is largely missing, and in most cases Ackles is unable to involve the listener in his songs in the

* David Ackles, "His Name Is Andrew." Copyright © 1968 by Warner-Tamerlane Publishing Corp. All rights reserved. Used by permission of Warner Bros. Music and B. Feldman & Co., Ltd.

way that he did throughout *David Ackles*. Three songs stand out, however. "Main Line Saloon" paints a horrific surrealistic portrait of modern America, where people are reduced to the level of animals seeking what they need and ignoring the consequences to themselves and others. "Subway to the Country" is a very mature song, the song of an impoverished father to his two children: one day he will find a subway to the country, taking them out from the city to find a place where there is grass and frogs and stones you keep . . . And "Out on the Road" is a song of pain, in some ways a reiteration of "Be My Friend" and yet a recognition of the fact that, however hard one might attempt to realize one's ideals, one is almost certain to fail. All in all, *Subway to the Country* is a very good album, but in comparison with *David Ackles* . . .

Up to this point, Ackles' recorded work testified to a highly skilled and original songwriting talent coupled with a performing ability that achieved new boundaries of emotional range. No one could have predicted the effect of his third album, *American Gothic*, which was to become a best seller in America, though hardly so elsewhere. In *American Gothic* Ackles has extended the range of the popular song far beyond any barriers that had previously been accepted. In some of the songs he produces music that owes any influence it shows to Bartók; in others he achieves the culmination of the mellow emotion he had shown in his earlier albums.

The title song, "American Gothic," tells of a husband and wife trapped in a situation that they no longer even attempt to escape from. He is a farmer who spends most of his profits on liquor and pornography, she whores to earn enough for new clothes and trinkets. Both know what is going on, neither will admit it to the other, both are killing themselves internally. A pathetic situation and yet, as Ackles sums it up, the ones who suffer least are the ones who suffer by their own choosing. The melody is at first hearing harsh and unaccommodating and apparently heavy-handed: it is only after listening to it a few times that one realizes the subtlety of both melody and arrangement and hence of the entire song.

"One Night Stand" is also a subtle song, this time almost a love song. The narrator is getting dressed in the morning, having spent the night with a girl he has met, and suddenly he realizes that she means much more to him than just another one-night stand. He daydreams aloud about the things they could do, spend a few days together, get to know each other better, and then realizes that they both have commitments and other lives to lead and that it can never be anything more than just a fleeting relationship.

The two finest—and most unusual—songs on the album are "Midnight Carousel" and "Montana Song." The former tells of a girl who breaks free from the restraints of her family and the society around her to answer the call of the wildness within herself. She is drawn to the carnival where she meets and makes frenzied love to a "man in red." Through what society might call her atavistic responses, she has achieved a greater expansion of herself as a human being. What makes the song so unusual is the music, which is strongly reminiscent in several ways of the Bartók school. Where the verse is essentially discordant (or, at least, far from melodic in the customary sense), the refrain is set to a gypsy violin tune, with a far more rapid tempo than the rest of the song. And then there is a repetition of a most peculiar rising progression to the words that she speaks—not in justification, for she has no need or desire to justify herself—but in explanation that she is flame, lightning, and the stars.

"Montana Song" is long and symphonic in scope. The narrator makes a quest to find the farmhouse where his ancestors originated, where they fought the hostile environment to try to carve out a living from the land, only to find that their offspring preferred to throw their parents' efforts away and go to live the easy life of the city. The narrator has with him the family Bible, from which he reads snatches that lightly depict the difficult pioneer life that the old people lived. Once again the music extends its range far beyond what one would expect from the average pop album, into ragtime, into modern atonal orchestral music, and so forth.

David Ackles, as I have said, is not a well-known name, and perhaps he never will be. His work is not always easily apprehended immediately, his melodies, though beautiful, are not catchy in the customary sense: he is not a writer of commercial singles but a mature songwriter who is probably doing more than anyone else— including Dylan, Cohen, or anyone you care to name—to explore the possibilities of complicated expression within the limits of word-combined-with-music. Perhaps he is a songwriter's songwriter; perhaps his work would be more appreciated by those whose tastes do not generally extend to pop music. It's hard to say. Certainly he has succeeded far more than any in providing a lasting picture of an age, a culture, and an observant man caught up in the middle of it all.

By contrast, Don McLean, who has emerged on the scene far more recently, is well-known internationally through his immense hit single, "American Pie," which is a sort of surreal musical history of pop music.

His first album, *Tapestry,* went largely unnoticed, which is a pity. McLean is a direct musical descendant of Pete Seeger (of whom he is a friend): his songs principally consist of voice plus guitar and very little else. Both his voice and his guitar can stand up to this exposure: unfortunately, in many cases, his songs cannot. Where Ackles with a few words can vastly extend the range of the listener's conception, McLean in general uses rather a lot of words to point out something patently obvious. Nevertheless, it would be wrong to dismiss him as a songwriter totally without talent—he is far from that.

On his first album, the most notable song is the title track, "Tapestry," which tackles the subject of pollution head on and yet manages not to repeat too much of what everybody else has already said before. One skillful technique is his use of scientific descriptive imagery without appearing to be pretentious—the sun is "like the yolk of an egg in albumen," for example.

His second album, *American Pie,* is the home of two singles: "American Pie" itself, which sold three and a half million copies in the three months after its release and which is genuinely an excellent piece of work; and "Vincent," an embarrassing homage to Vincent van Gogh which succeeds only in ensuring that any listener who might have been interested in Van Gogh's paintings would no longer be so. "Vincent," though its sales do not compare with those of "American Pie," was a number one hit in several countries. The other songs on the album tend to point up McLean's weakness, the fact that he often steers very close to the borderline between poetry and kitsch, sometimes too close.

His third album, *Don McLean,* was received more or less in silence but did show what a talented songwriter McLean has the potential to be. Whether he will realize this potential, and become one of the primary songwriters of the next few years, or whether he will sink into undeserved obscurity like so many others before him, is something that only time will tell.

Leaving the United States, and before beginning our discussion of the folk "Renaissance" in Great Britain, it is only natural to turn first to the situation in Canada. Canada hasn't entered our discussion in this chapter to any great extent as yet since, for reasons that are obvious (historic, geographic, linguistic, and economic . . . and hence political), Canada has been in the best position for reaping the benefit of developments from the joint American folk tradition, though without modifying or enriching these developments in any noticeable fashion. So we have chosen, and the motives for so choosing will be explained below, to treat separately the two personalities who between them constitute all that is currently understood by Canadian contemporary folk, Joni Mitchell and Leonard Cohen.

The common ground between Canadian and United States folk is fairly self-evident: the importance as a basis of the British or pseudo-British ballad, the role played by the sea, but also the wide open spaces, in the themes of their songs, the exploitation of the forests (the lumberjacks), an Indian presence repressed in an almost identical way by a white population drawn from various of the countries of Europe (Greece and Italy in particular). Unfortunately the influence of the folklore of these latter has had an almost negligible effect, partly because they have tended to become lost among the far greater numbers of the English-speaking colonists, and partly because they didn't usually stay very long (two generations at most) before making the trek toward the United States.

It is more worthwhile for the observer to try to find those few differences that do exist between the two lines of tradition. One outstanding difference is the almost total absence of a black population in Canada; as one might expect, this shows up in the fact that the blues are quite missing from Canadian folk, and, coupled with the repression of the Indians, has led to the white preponderance in the nation's culture. This explains why every visitor to Canada can hardly help but notice the immense popularity there of country and western; the radio programs and record sales testify to this. One notes in this respect the artistic and commercial success of Gordon Lightfoot whose "Early Morning Rain" is a "standard" that has been sung by Judy Collins, Peter, Paul and Mary, and even Bob Dylan.

Richard and Mimi Fariña, the brilliant duet that was broken up by Richard's untimely death in a motorcycle accident.

Paul Simon and Art Garfunkel, one of the most successful acts on the international scene (CBS RECORDS)

Arlo Guthrie, son of Woody and star of the film *Alice's Restaurant*, sings and plays with Pete Seeger. (DIANA DAVIES / INSIGHT)

Tim Hardin, composer of
"If I Were a Carpenter,"
"Lady Came from Baltimore,"
and the epic *Suite
for Susan Moore and Damion*
(GM RECORDS)

Melanie, whose individual and passionate voice has been as much
responsible as her undoubted songwriting talents for her gathering an
impressive number of devotees (PETER SCHEKERYK / NEIGHBORHOOD RECORDS)

Donovan and Richie Havens (DIANA DAVIES / INSIGHT)

Poet, novelist, and songwriter, Leonard Cohen brought a new breadth of imagery to the contemporary music scene.

John Renbourn, one of the founder members of Pentangle

Sandy Denny, who was for a long time the guiding light of Fairport Convention, formed the short-lived band Fotheringay, and nowadays sings alone. (GERED MANKOWITZ / ISLAND RECORDS)

Fairport Convention in 1974. From left to right: Dave Pegg, Dave Swarbrick, Dave Mattacks, Jerry Donahue, and Trevor Lucas (BRIAN COOKE / ISLAND RECORDS)

Al Stewart has recently turned his attention to historical songs with his brilliant album, *Past, Present and Future* (MICHAEL ALLARD)

Jonathan Kelly, one of the more recent arrivals on the British folk scene (GAFF MANAGEMENT LTD.)

James Taylor,
composer of "Fire and
Rain" and "Sweet Baby James"
and, in the background,
Joni Mitchell
(DIANA DAVIES / INSIGHT)

Joni Mitchell, the poet
turned reluctant superstar
(DIANA DAVIES / INSIGHT)

On his own records, Lightfoot frequently makes use of accompaniments typical of the Nashville studios, where he usually records. Among other things, Johnny Cash is held in very high esteem by the Canadian public.

One could here object that, if the ethnic minorities have been either swallowed or expelled by the English-speaking majority, what about the French-speaking Quebeçois: they at least can speak for themselves. And it is true that, to the extent that the Quebeçois are the "niggers of Canada," the vivacity of their songs is hardly surprising. Their traditional folklore, the heritage for the most part of French mainstream folklore, gives them a solid basis. And, unlike the French themselves, they have had the sense not to kill their folk tradition, the desire to affirm their independence ensuring that if anything they consciously cultivate it.

The extraordinary explosion of the movement of Quebec *chansonniers,* led by Félix Leclerc, followed by Gilles Vigneault, Raymond Levesque, Claude Léveillée, Robert Charlebois, and several others, is nothing but a necessary and logical product of this preservation and cultivation of French folklore and culture so dearly and justifiably undertaken.

All these factors prompted Gilles Vigneault to declare: "It is false to say that there is such a thing as Canadian song: there is North American song and Quebecan song. Leonard Cohen and Joni Mitchell have tremendous talent, but they could have been born in New York or, more likely, in California, without it making any detectable difference to the character of their work, which is *not* Canadian. Canada, in fact, is a country that doesn't exist; it has political parties, cities, everything . . . it misses nothing except a population, a little detail which no one notices!" [3]

Joni Mitchell is considered by many critics of the folk movement as the finest female lyricist / composer / performer that the English-speaking world has produced in recent years. Though perhaps a little sweeping, this statement at least justifies close examination of her work, which is attractive and outstandingly original.

At first, Joni Mitchell's ambition was not to be a singer. Born in 1943 at McLeod in the province of Alberta, she dreamed over all of

[3] Interview with Gilles Vigneault by François Ayral in *Pop-Music,* no. 3, April 16, 1970 (translated).

becoming a painter, with the hope of being able to earn her living by selling her canvases (it is worth noting in passing that she designed the covers of her first three and her sixth albums, decorating them with excellent paintings). For this reason she enrolled for a course at the Alberta College of Art in Calgary. During her leisure hours, she learned to play the ukelele. And soon, as chance would have it, she found herself engaged to sing for an evening in a sort of local folk club. To begin with, Joni Mitchell contented herself with reinterpreting traditional ballads, but she very soon passed this stage and began to write her own songs. This new art banished painting into the background, and she has been quoted as reflecting that she has never had occasion to regret the choice she made. We neither. . . .

For Joni brought to song uncounted enrichments. Certainly, the first time one hears her, either onstage or on record, one cannot put out of one's mind a certain trace of the influence of Judy Collins: indeed, Joni is the first to admit this, adding also that Judy Collins is one of her best friends. One recognizes in the inflections of her voice the same fire, the same passionate ardor, even though modified by an admirable reserve. But one mustn't attempt to take the parallel too far in case one finds oneself doing an injustice to both artists. Certainly it would be arrant nonsense to subscribe to the at one time frequent allegation that Joni Mitchell was just another Judy Collins.

On the contrary, the great merit of this Canadian émigrée to California (Laurel Canyon, immortalized by John Mayall's album, *Blues from Laurel Canyon*) is that she has permitted herself a certain degree of imitation (not plagiarism—even imitation is too strong a word) of an archetype of the genre in order to point up her own talents. If you're looking for an overt difference, it is that Joni Mitchell is a more personal and intimate performer than Judy Collins.

One of the sources of Joni's inspiration is the argument within herself between the choices of going back to nature and the peace of the countryside and even more the storm of the sea, or maintaining contact with reality, typified by modern urban life. This contradiction is made obvious on her first album, *Joni Mitchell,* where Side One is titled "I Came to the City" and Side Two "Out of the City and Down to the Seaside." One recognizes here a contradiction that runs throughout the history of North American folklore.

On the other hand, Joni's style of writing is not without occasional parallel, though perhaps it is more direct, to that of Leonard Cohen. One can find an example of this in "Michael from Mountains," a sort of second cousin to "Suzanne." The protagonist plays the role of a guide who takes you by the hand and shows you that the world, even with its uglinesses, can still reveal beauty and mystery.

Other themes are memories of friendships and loves ("I Had a King"), the way that a chance unusual meeting can be lifted above its own banality ("Nathan La Franeer," is a taxi driver). And then there is inexplicable drama, murder by an unknown hand against a backdrop of sea, related back to the murder of emotion, as in "Pirate of Penance," recorded with a double-tracked vocal to produce an extremely poignant effect.

In her second album, Joni Mitchell starts to lean toward certain contemporary problems, such as the inhumanity of the United States, which contrasts tragically with the plethora of American wealth: she expresses it in terms of the utmost delicacy in "The Fiddle and the Drum," sung unaccompanied. Throughout the album *Clouds* (which contains the song made famous by Judy Collins and Mary Hopkin among others, "Both Sides Now"), her voice is fresh, pure, and almost naïve, certainly moving, with very little in the way of instrumentation beyond her six-string acoustic guitar. A trace of organ is present in one of the songs, "Roses Blue," in the same way that there was a trace of trumpet on "Nathan La Franeer" on the first album. Musically the result is successful—commercially also, as the sales of the album in the United States and Canada testify.

If there is a fault in *Clouds* it is its lack of cohesion, and this fault is totally lacking in her third album, *Ladies of the Canyon*. Here the instrumentation is a little more wide ranging: apart from the fact that on several tracks Joni herself plays piano, there is the addition in places of instruments such as clarinet, saxophone, and so forth. And the album in total is a far more mature expression than the two which went before it. "For Free" is a very subtly constructed song, based on the reflection of Joni Mitchell the successful star that she would like to join the street player on the corner and give people pleasure "for free," yet all the time knowing that she can't. Also on the album is a quiet version of her song "Woodstock," accompanied solely by electric piano, which can be compared only favorably to the version performed by Crosby, Stills, Nash & Young for the film of the same name. "Willy," by the way, one of the love songs on the album, is reputedly dedicated to Graham Nash, known by the nickname of Willy. Once again she deals delicately with social problems in the title track, "Ladies of the Canyon," which portrays the quiet decay of the dilettante upper middle classes.

With her fourth album, *Blue,* Joni Mitchell's international commercial success finally granted her "star" status. *Blue* is a strange album, substantially more personal than those that preceded it, and, as the title might suggest, a very depressing and depressed collection of songs. It shows Joni Mitchell kicking back against the corruption of the rich superstar world that she has penetrated into, the corrupted values and the smell of too much wine and the fishnet stockings. The most powerful track of all is "The Last Time I Saw Richard," which tells of a friend of hers who set out to be a bohemian and ended up married with a color TV and all the trappings of modern middle-class middle age. As the song proceeds, the revelation is gently made that Joni Mitchell is on the same road, knows that she is on the same road, and can think of no way of turning aside. The intensity of the song is devastating.

Her fifth album, *For the Roses,* delves further into the same preoccupations, and is perhaps the more affecting for the apparently superficial way in which they are stated. The title track, "For the Roses" (reminiscent of Janis Ian's "42nd Street Psycho Blues" on *The Secret Life of J. Eddy Fink*), is Joni speaking to the young and newly discovered writer of song, with stars in his eyes heading up the ladder of success, warning him to be careful of what the businessmen of the music industry will try to turn him into. "Let the Wind Carry Me" tells of the split within a family as the daughter grows up and goes her own way; Mother is shocked but Father tells her to leave the girl alone. Throughout the album the instrumentation is delicate, though perhaps fuller than in her earlier albums; but nevertheless the basis is firmly provided by Joni Mitchell's guitar or piano.

This is something that distinguishes Joni from practically every other songwriter of the last few years. Where others have bolstered their music by the importation for recording sessions of hordes of electric guitarists, drummers, bassists, and so forth, not to mention full-scale string orchestras and / or mellotrons and moogs, Joni has constantly kept her feet very much on the path of the folk tradition that gave her birth. Where electric instruments are employed, their use is subtle and unobtrusive; they are embellishments rather than props. And she is wise, for her voice, her songs, her playing of the guitar and piano need no ancillary aids. They are complete in themselves.

One cannot think of a rise to commercial success to compare with that of Leonard Cohen, poet, songwriter, and novelist. And this rise is all the more remarkable when one realizes that Cohen is not a writer of catchy hit tunes and banal lyrics, but a poet who weaves complex tapestries of words around the strange and surreal world he depicts. Even Dylan was well installed before he began to employ the rich imagery and complex system of allusion that typified his *Blonde on Blonde* period. But Cohen, who was already well known in Canada and the United States as a poet and novelist, somehow contrived from the date of release of his first album (*Songs of Leonard Cohen*) to make a whole generation of listeners look for something more in songs than a statement of feeling or the simple telling of a story.

It was Judy Collins who first "discovered" Leonard Cohen, recording several of his songs long before he himself began to record. But even so, the world hardly waited with bated breath for the release of *Songs of Leonard Cohen,* which arrived more or less unheralded in the record shops and promptly began to sell consistently at a rate that was just not quite sufficient for it to appear in the charts. But people began to sing "Suzanne," "Hey, That's No Way to Say Goodbye," and "So Long, Marianne" in folk clubs, people began to play the album to their friends, who went out and bought it . . . and before long Cohen had built up a vast number of followers, quite without the normal publicity machine and the customary series of plugs on radio.

It was thus to nobody's surprise (except for the very people who hadn't been playing his music on radio) when his second album, *Songs from a Room,* became instantly a best seller (repeating the pattern followed by the Incredible String Band some years before). Oddly enough, *Songs from a Room* is nowhere near as good an album as was *Songs of Leonard Cohen.* There are several fine tracks on it—one thinks of "Bird on the Wire" instantly—but it far from achieves the same consistency of excellence as the earlier album. The hypnotic power of Cohen's word-weaving, the strength of imagery and mysterious, mystical allusion are missing; the album is patchy rather than coherent.

Cohen's live performances have always been few and far between and have tended to give the false impression that he is a folksinger pure and simple, which he is not. The reasons for this misapprehension are obvious: firstly, he accompanies himself on a gentle acoustic guitar, and his songs (or sung poems) are performed in a way that ensures above all that every word can be heard; secondly, he was brought to public notice by Judy Collins, who most certainly *is* a folksinger, and she it was who persuaded him to record the songs himself and to perform at the Newport Folk Festival of 1967; thirdly, his albums are produced by Bob Johnston, who also produces various other luminaries of the folk or country and western world such as Bob Dylan, Johnny Cash, Marty Robbins, and Simon and Garfunkel; finally, and more generally, Cohen is acknowledged in folk circles as being very much "part of the family."

So much for the origins of the misapprehension. For Cohen in fact has never really fitted well into the bracket of "folksinger" (still less the sometimes applied label of "revolutionary"). Technically, his music has no relation whatsoever to any of the Anglo-American folk music traditions. Though he played in a country and western group when he was around fifteen or sixteen years old, and though a song like "The Butcher" might be said musically to owe something to the blues (it is the only example, and it takes a stretch of the imagination), these points can be considered negligible in light of the extremely sophisticated aspect of his melodies and accompaniments (subtle, unobtrusive, and excellent) which owe nothing at all to traditional folk music. As for his lyrics, the same qualifications apply: the words are meticulously chosen, the imagery and symbolism quite unusual, the constant opposition and comparison of materialism with mysticism . . . in brief, the panoply of the intellectual poet, not of the folksinger.

In his third, and artistically most successful, album he does indeed include one track that falls squarely into the stream of country and western, "Diamonds in the Mine," which provides necessary light relief from the gloomy yet beautiful ambience of the rest of the album. Indeed *Songs of Love and Hate* is a veritable treasury of good things, penetrating to deeper levels than Cohen has ever achieved before. Most of the songs speak of pain of some kind or another, from the anguish of "Dress Rehearsal Rag" to the resigned acceptance of the exquisite "Famous Blue Raincoat" or the detached objectivity of "Joan of Arc."

His fourth album, *Live Songs,* is exactly what the title might suggest: a collection of live performances of songs that are mostly available already on his earlier albums. As such, it is no more than an interesting appendix to the sum of his earlier work—and this is the attitude that shows in the sales of the album. His fifth album, announced as his last (he is returning to novels and poetry), *New Skin for the Old Ceremony,* shows a substantial falling-off in his powers.

And so the world of music appears to have lost one of its most original and important creative artists. Whether one can call him a folksinger or not, Cohen has had more of an effect on the mainstream of contemporary folk songwriting than many an artist who has built firmly upon traditional soil. His is a harsh loss in that one always felt that there was so much more that he could have given us. More recently, Leonard Cohen has begun making a few personal appearances to perform his songs, including some new ones which he may yet decide to record.

british

One of the primary characteristics of the people of the British Isles is the way in which they cling to their tradition, and folklore is by no means an exception to this well-known rule.

Among the traditional singers active during the 1950s one could do no better than cite the example of Shirley Collins, whose role in England is comparable to that of Jean Ritchie in the United States. One notes among other things that Shirley Collins, at the instigation of Pete Seeger, has several times gone on tour in the United States; she was with Alan Lomax in 1959 when he discovered the bluesman Fred McDowell.

She is still one of the most active participants on the English folk scene, is still to be seen on many occasions giving concerts, still releases excellent albums fairly frequently.

Also worthy of note is a young English trio, unfortunately now dissolved like so many groups, The Young Tradition, who were particularly to the fore during the years 1968–69. Made up of two men, Peter Bellamy and Royston Wood, and a woman, Heather Wood (no relation to Royston), The Young Tradition was one of the finest traditional folk groups it was our pleasure to hear. Although all three came from city backgrounds and had passed through the urbanizing hands of the university, they succeeded remarkably in capturing the essence of English rural folk. Their talent was justly recognized in the United States, where in particular they achieved considerable success at the Newport and Philadelphia festivals of 1968 and 1969. Before their dissolution at the end of 1969, the three singers had the time to leave a concrete memorial in the form of two albums on the Vanguard label.

The other countries of the United Kingdom have also not been without their traditional singers and/or groups. Scotland has (on one level) Callum Kennedy, Kenneth MacKellar, and Robert Wilson, and (on another level) Robin Hall & Jimmie MacGregor, Alex Campbell and Hamish Imlach. Ireland has (on one level) Dana and (on the other) the Dubliners.

Robin Hall & Jimmie MacGregor, who for a large part of their career sang with Shirley Bland and Leon Rosselson as the Galliards, are in many ways the perfect example of a folk group. Their repertoire, which is mainly though by no means entirely Scottish, consists of traditional songs sung in a traditional manner but with a high degree of professionalism which ensures that their audience is not solely composed of die-hard "folksies." Without the assistance of electric instrumentation or orchestral backing, using only voices, acoustic guitars, and occasionally banjoes, double basses, and so forth, they nevertheless succeed in producing remarkably clean, uncluttered, and yet complex renditions. In this respect they resemble a rather similar Scottish folk group that has come to the fore in more recent years, the Corries, now composed of two men but originally also including a girl and known as the Corrie Folk Trio.

Alex Campbell is the grand old man of Scottish folk music. Well known for his capacity to down enormous quantities of beer and / or whiskey before going onstage, Alex has in his deep, grave voice performed all over the continent of Europe with considerable success, particularly in Scandinavia. He could hardly be further from Robin Hall & Jimmie MacGregor; where their special appeal is the professionalism with which they perform, Alex Campbell's is the exceptionally attractive blend of gutsy sloppiness with which he sings and plays. Here he is like Hamish Imlach (who similarly has a huge capacity for alcohol before or during his performances) who has, however, as yet still to make much of an impact outside his home country.

The Dubliners are an Irish group who, like Alex Campbell, concentrate on producing a professional sound. Five men strong, they have produced a number of albums and are rare among traditional folk practitioners in that in recent years they have had a chart-busting single, "Seven Drunken Nights," one of the most unusual hits on the British commercial scene for some time. Of course, to be a commercial success, the old Irish song had to be heavily censored, but so it goes. . . .

The appearance throughout the British Isles during the 1960s of

a proliferation of folk clubs has been attributed to a general flourishing of music and social clubs of all sorts during that period: to us this
explanation, however plausible it may appear to be, is insufficient.
One must remember the British love of communal singing. The
"propagandizing" work of several other singers has served effectively to keep the flame alight. At the first stage there was the work
of Ewan MacColl, particularly in his collaboration with Peggy
Seeger, that we have already noted. The songs of Matt McGinn and
Bob Davenport, as well as part of the repertoire of Alex Campbell,
are a part of the same line: writing and performing modern songs
using traditional bases.

The following stage in the evolution of the (this time urban) folk
movement in Britain came around the year 1960 with the appearance of three immensely talented performers, all known principally
for their skills with the guitar: Davy Graham (composer of "Angie,"
the instrumental that has now become a classic), Bert Jansch, and
John Renbourn. The two latter, oriented as they are primarily toward blues but also strongly toward traditional British music, have
followed an extremely interesting recording career with numerous
albums, sometimes together and sometimes separately, on the
Transatlantic label. More recently they have been the keystones of
the formation of a group poised midway between traditional folk
and modern electric rock: Pentangle.

Perhaps better than in any other case, the "phenomenon of Donovan" (as he is somewhat nauseatingly described on his live album)
allows one to understand to what extent the lesson of Dylan is or has
been transferable from the United States to the musical world of
Great Britain. One must realize that, despite the frequently stressed,
genuine similarities between the two men, to see Donovan as nothing
more than the "Scottish Dylan" is to recognize only a part of his talents. In fact, Donovan's art has never given the chaotic impression,
the living Rimbaudian atmosphere, of that of the composer of *Highway 61 Revisited*. And if the wind blows more often in Donovan's
songs than in those of Bob Dylan, it isn't the cold and clammy gust
that swirls down Desolation Row but the harsh wind off the sea that
tosses its way across Scotland.

Donovan Leitch was born in 1946, to a working-class family in
Glasgow (also the hometown of Bert Jansch). His childhood passed

in the suburbs of this Northern capital disrupted only by an attack of polio, which fortunately cleared up, at the age of three. Later, he and his parents went to live on the outskirts of London. At school his teachers found him a little strange because of his predilection toward horror stories, which he wrote and illustrated himself. Feeling himself naturally disposed toward design, he signed up at a fine arts college. However, he stayed there for only a year. As he laughingly recalled, he had to stay on for another year to get a grant, and he had to have a grant to stay on for another year. For Donovan, that was the end of formal education.

It was thus equipped that he, like so many others before him, took to the road. Accompanied by a friend, Donovan traveled for several months around the British Isles. Speaking little, listening to others, and walking, the two boys had many strange encounters. Carrying his guitar, Donovan learned from all the sorts of music that he came across, including jazz, and wrote his earliest songs. Returning to London at the age of eighteen, he made his first demo tape in a recording studio. Even before Pye released his first album, *Catch the Wind,* Donovan was not unknown to the British public, having made an appearance on the television program "Ready, Steady, Go."

The album *Catch the Wind* already offers an almost complete panorama of the musical and lyrical options open to Donovan in the future. Though there is from time to time the definite influence of blues, it is in the British-type songs that Donovan seems most at ease, partly because of his origins and partly due to the nature of his voice, which is delicate, tremulous, and sometimes almost hesitant. One can see quite obviously on Donovan's second album for Pye, *Fairytale,* a tendency to abandon the blues in favor of the British ballad-style song and also toward a rather plastic but nevertheless very fine form of reverie, as in "Colours." But this is compensated for by the more and more tenacious references toward a jazz style (as in the accompaniment of "Sunny Goodge Street") and the protest song, typified by his recording as a single of Buffy Sainte-Marie's "Universal Soldier."

After a period of about a year when Donovan, fleeing from the clinging arms of show biz and refusing to be burdened with his title of the "Scottish Dylan," took refuge in a Scottish castle, he reappeared at the 1966 Newport Folk Festival and sang in company with Joan Baez. His song "Sunshine Superman" firmly traveling up the hit parades finally meant that Donovan was a figure to be reckoned with in the United States.

His first album with Epic (though still released in Britain by Pye) took up the baton from his fellow British musicians in conquering the United States, following the example of the Beatles and the Rolling Stones. The album, *Sunshine Superman,* is one of Donovan's most varied: apart from an allusion to his friend, the Scottish guitar master Bert Jansch, "Bert's Blues," the ballad remains dominant, though not in a strictly folklorish fashion but oriented more toward the theme of "stories for grown-up children," as in the beautiful "Legend of a Girl Child Linda." There is also a song about drug experiences, "The Trip," the occasional use of the sitar, and, in the title track and "Season of the Witch," a more elaborate and resolutely rock arrangement.

The influence of *Sunshine Superman* since its release cannot be overstated. Although in Great Britain it did not immediately make a huge impact, it has become one of those albums that practically everyone interested in pop music owns. Certainly it has now become recognized as the absolute acme of Donovan's writing career, in comparison with which all his later work, however excellent it may be from time to time, pales.

Some months later, the release of the single "Mellow Yellow," in the same vein as "Sunshine Superman," confirmed Donovan's status as one of the most important singer-songwriters of the epoch, at least commercially, though one might well question the validity of the song's aesthetic status.

If the album *Wear Your Love Like Heaven,*[1] which followed shortly afterward, gave Donovan a new commercial success, it was deplored by the purists on account of its lesser originality and inspiration as well as for a certain cloying slickness in the arrangements which in themselves betrayed, quite in opposition to what was happening with Dylan, a genuine retrogression rather than a further advance . . . which was to come later.

After this diversion, through which Donovan risked charges of

[1] *Wear Your Love Like Heaven* and *For Little Ones* were released together as a boxed and rather strangely coupled double album in Britain entitled *A Gift from a Flower to a Garden* and bearing a picture of Donovan with the Maharishi. But then, after the Beatles, everybody was having his or her picture taken with the Maharishi those days. . . .

succumbing to show biz, there came the release of *For Little Ones,* which was almost entirely comprised of children's songs accompanied solely by the acoustic guitar.

While he for a time approached the level of releasing two new albums a year—*Greatest Hits, Hurdy Gurdy Man* (United States only), *Donovan in Concert* and *Barabajagal* (United States only)—Donovan nevertheless prefers the peaceful retreat of his Scottish home to making too many tours or too many public appearances—lapsing into idleness, some say; and often his friend Derroll Adams avers that he is the only one who can tear Donovan away from his dreams. All the same, Donovan sang for free, although he was not officially on the program, during the huge concert in Hyde Park in June 1969 that was organized as a memorial to Brian Jones. Unfortunately, he spoiled it a little by preaching the virtues of getting back to the simple things of life and being happy with nothing but the gifts of the land before climbing into a chauffeur-driven Rolls-Royce.

The year 1970 marked for Donovan a musical advance that even his most ardent admirers had hardly hoped for any longer: accompanied by a new backup group at the Bath Festival, then at the Isle of Wight Festival, he gave most impressive performances. The album *Open Road,* released immediately after the latter festival, seemed to show that he was progressing toward regaining his second wind, the second wind which had been so long awaited, through his new experiences working with other musicians.

But after that, it seemed that down was the only way for him to go. Not long after the release of *Open Road* he dissolved his backup group and released a double album of songs for children, *H.M.S. Donovan.* Where his earlier attempt in this direction, *For Little Ones,* had had a simplicity that ensured it stayed well clear of syrupy self-indulgence, *H.M.S. Donovan* was not so fortunate. As one critic remarked, one couldn't blame Donovan for going in his own direction, it was just that you wished he would come in *your* direction sometimes.

After this there was a long gap before *Cosmic Wheels* was released in 1973. An album that received a mixed reception from the critics, with opinions varying from brilliant to drivel, it received an almost unanimous reception from the public at large: drivel. The greatest depth to which it plunged was "The Intergalactic Laxative," which was considerably worse than its title might suggest. The one or two really fine performances on the record are lost completely in the rather self-indulgent and tasteless remainder.

Where will Donovan go from here? It's hard to guess, since his evolution has never followed anything like a clearly defined path. One can only hope that he will reinstate in his songs that immediacy and lyricism that distinguished his earlier work and, in particular, those songs written around the time of *Sunshine Superman.*

One of the most interesting tendencies in British groups and singers is the way in which, in a few cases, they are able to make use of the rich folk music tradition of their country as a scaffolding on which to build a kind of music that is quite dissimilar from the original and in many cases quite new.

Prime among all the groups in this category is incontestably The Incredible String Band. Originally formed in 1965 by Clive Palmer with Robin Williamson, and then with the addition of Mike Heron, they shortly afterward became a duo with the departure of Clive Palmer (who was years later to form COB). Apart from their frequent references to old ballads, they were distinguished in their early recordings by their intelligent and marvelously harmonic use of various non-English musical instruments, such as the sitar, tabla, shanai, gimbri, soondri, and so forth—in fact, Robin Williamson is reputed to play more than forty musical instruments!

Their first album, *The Incredible String Band,* recorded while Clive Palmer was still with them, is of interest primarily because of the promise that it shows; but their second, *The 5000 Spirits or the Layers of the Onion,* demonstrated that there was a significant new force on the British scene. As it still is today, it was difficult then to classify The Incredible String Band's music. Is it folk? Or pop? Or . . . And it was hard at first for the British public to accept a form of music that was so different from anything that had been heard before. Nevertheless, songs like Mike Heron's "Hedgehog Song" or "Painting Box" or Robin Williamson's "First Girl I Loved" were soon to be heard occasionally on the radio or whistled through the corridors of British universities.

There was a reasonable delay before the release of their third album, but when it appeared it immediately became number four in the British album charts, something most unusual for what had been up to then classed as "minority" music. And *The Hangman's Beautiful Daughter* remains to this day one of the finest examples of what modern song can be at its very best. It would be hard to discriminate by picking out any tracks for special mention, but it is worth noting Mike Heron's "A Very Cellular Song."

Wee Tam and The Big Huge, their next release, was a double album that developed the various lines that had been started in *The Hangman's Beautiful Daughter*. The entire double album possesses a lyric sensitivity that has yet to be found on any other modern music album—at least in English—and adds weight to the assertion that the best modern poetry is being written in the form of song. Of particular note is Robin Williamson's "Maya" which develops a mystic, almost surrealistic vision couched in an imagery that has all the strength and beauty of the best of Dylan Thomas.

After some time, this was followed by *Changing Horses* and *I Looked Up,* both of which are albums that find the String Band in a dilemma. By this time, the group had been officially increased to four in strength with the addition of Rose Henderson and Licorice McKechnie, though both girls had added vocal assistance on earlier albums.

Changing Horses is rather self-indulgent, though it contains some first-rate music. It is centered around two extremely long songs, Mike Heron's "White Bird" and Robin Williamson's "Creation," neither of which, though both possess moments of dazzling lyricism, can be counted as a total success.

This, too, is the fault at the heart of *I Looked Up,* where two long Robin Williamson songs, "Pictures in a Mirror" and "When You Find Out Who You Are," tend despite everything to inspire tedium. The latter album, however, contains several of Mike Heron's best and most popular songs: "Black Jack Davy," "The Letter," and especially "This Moment."

The Incredible String Band then staged in London and elsewhere a theatrical show (described as a "surreal parable") called *U*. It was greeted with critical contempt by the mass media, though in fact those of the general public who went to see *U* came away with usually strongly favorable impressions. The String Band was joined for this venture by the dancing troupe Stone Monkey, led by Janet Shankman who was later to become Robin Williamson's wife, and the results were released as a double album. *U* is perhaps the most difficult to approach of all String Band albums, but one that contains any amount of excellent music. One song that is of particular interest is Robin Williamson's "Queen of Love" which, for the first time on an Incredible String Band album, has an orchestral arrangement.

The film about the band, *Be Glad for the Song Has No Ending,* originally made for the BBC's "Omnibus" series, was in fact never televised. It was, however, shown at various movie houses and in particular at the ICA in London. An album of the music from the film was released, the first that the group recorded for the Island label, the high point of which is an extremely long instrumental track (just over twenty-seven minutes) that occupies the whole of the second side. Here the String Band allowed itself the full scope of all the instruments that the four members could play, and the result is an ever-changing but always highly musical sequence of tonal images.

Just before the release of this album, Island also released a solo album by Mike Heron, *Smiling Men with Bad Reputations.* At the time this was a strange departure for a member of the String Band, since the album is resolutely rock-oriented: on one track Mike Heron is backed by most of The Who. And, unfortunately, the experiment is not really a successful one: in too many cases the arrangements, rather than supporting the songs which are in any case weaker than is customary for Mike Heron, destroy them. But, while one has reservations about the status of the album in itself, the lesson of it was not to be forgotten by the String Band as a whole, whose music from this point on becomes more and more turned toward electric amplification.

Liquid Acrobat as Regards the Air showed The Incredible String Band back at the top of its powers once more: the album even received an almost rave review in the *Manchester Guardian!* But by the time the album was made, Rose Henderson had left the group to be replaced by Malcolm Le Maistre, onetime member of Stone Monkey. This album signifies a considerable tightening up of the group's musical endeavors: most of the songs are very short and concise, though perhaps the album's finest track is the exception, Robin Williamson's eleven-minute "Darling Belle." On only one track does this tightening up bear anything but sweet fruit: "Painted Chariot," a

Mike Heron song that was originally of a fair length but is here kept so concise that it loses most of the power that it once had.

It is on *Liquid Acrobat* that electric instruments begin to play a major part in the group's music. "Dear Old Battlefield," a Robin Williamson song, and "Painted Chariot" are both more to be classed as rock songs than in any way as folk songs, while electric instruments appear on most of the other tracks in one form or another.

With *Earthspan*, released late in 1972, The Incredible String Band reached its second peak. Here the musicians brought electric instrumentation fully under their control which, coupled with superb orchestrations scored by Mike Heron, allowed them a far wider canvas than ever before. And also of significance is the emergence on this album of Malcolm Le Maistre as songwriter, with his wry surrealism and acute powers of observation. *Earthspan* is a superb album from any point of view, mixing elements of rock with those of jazz, traditional folk, and classical music to give a result that is as impressive for its variety as for its originality.

Very soon afterward Licorice McKechnie left and, for their next album, *No Ruinous Feud,* the String Band was joined by Gerard Dott, a wind instrument player of considerable accomplishment. *No Ruinous Feud,* released fairly early in 1973, is an odd album, developing the lines suggested by *Earthspan* but somehow unable to match up to the earlier album. Although it is distinguished by two of the finest songs the group has ever recorded, "Down Before Cathay" by Malcolm Le Maistre and "Little Girl" by Mike Heron, it is unfortunately also distinguished by some of the worst, especially "Circus Girl" by Robin Williamson and an instrumental called "Second Fiddle" that was borrowed from someone else's reggae album!

In fact, the general deterioration of the Robin Williamson songs recorded by the group over the last two or three years is highly disappointing, particularly in light of his earlier work with "Maya," "Witches Hat," or "Darling Belle," but even more so when listening to his solo album, *Myrrh,* released some while before *Earthspan*. On this album Williamson's writing is at its full power, conjuring images from Celtic folklore ("The Dancing of the Lord of Weir") and adding new dimensions to the commercial rock song ("Sandy Land"). Exactly what has happened since is anybody's guess.

Recent Incredible String Band concerts give the impression that the trend of *Earthspan* and *No Ruinous Feud* will continue, with electric instrumentation and Mike Heron's superb orchestration becoming more and more predominant, despite further personnel changes: the group is now six strong after the departure of Gerard Dott.

But, as has often been pointed out by critics and others, every Incredible String Band album is different from the one before it, and no one can predict with certainty just which direction it is going to take next. Whatever it is, almost certainly it will be a direction worth following.

Other British "folkrock" groups, despite the fact that their members share a common folk heritage with Robin Williamson and Mike Heron, associate themselves to a greater degree with pop music in a more modern (and also more conventional) sense of the term.

Nevertheless, as has been mentioned earlier, on the initiative of the guitarists Bert Jansch and John Renbourn, there was formed, at the end of 1968, the quintet known as Pentangle. Joined by a bassist, Danny Thompson, and a drummer, Terry Cox, they found a female singer, Jacqui McShee, with whom they developed a repertoire composed partly of British ballads and partly from the jazz knowledge of the bassist and drummer and the blues orientation of the two guitarists. This has resulted in a music that is described as varied by those in favor, as chaotic by those who decry, but which is certainly pleasant to listen to, even though it lacks a certain amount of soul and even vigor.

Of their several albums, perhaps the best known (though they are one of those groups where it is hard to pick out the best known) are *Basket of Light* and *Cruel Sister*. Though on the former album there is a statement of their traditionalist view in that it is written on the jacket that every instrument played on it is without the benefit of amplification, on the latter electrical instruments play their part. And this is perhaps some indication of their indecision.

Pentangle enjoyed a brief period in vogue, but a series of unfavorable concerts and poor-selling albums seems to have spelled out their dissolution. Certainly both Jansch and Renbourn are now performing and recording singly and together without the group and, despite their successful American tour of 1969, it seems that the

Pentangle will not be heard of much more. In some ways it seems a pity that the initial promise of the unique combination of talents was never fully realized.

Fairport Convention was a group originally formed in November 1967 consisting of Judy Dyble (vocals, Autoharp, piano, and recorder), Ashley Hutchings (vocals, bass), Richard Thompson (vocals, guitar), Simon Nicol (vocals, guitar), Martin Lamble (drums), and Ian Matthews (vocals). In May 1968 Judy Dyble left the band, eventually to form Trader Horne, and was replaced by Sandy Denny. From that point on the membership of the band reads like a section of the Biblical "begat" chapters. By 1972 they comprised Dave Swarbrick (violin, vocals), Dave Pegg (bass, mandolin, vocals), Trevor Lucas (guitar, vocals), Jerry Donahue (guitar, vocals), and Tom Farnell (drums). But it was in the era when Sandy Denny was with them that Fairport was at the height of its artistic and commercial success.

Sandy Denny is a superb singer and songwriter, as well as a highly professional guitarist and pianist. Her songs with Fairport include the immortal "Who Knows Where the Time Goes?" and "Fotheringay," the former recorded with great success by Judy Collins and the latter to lend its name to the group Sandy Denny formed after her departure from Fairport Convention in December 1969.

Around the time that she was with Fairport, the group was essentially interpreting songs in an American "folkrock" way, though performing material that was fairly well based in British traditional music. When Sandy Denny left to form the short-lived Fotheringay and then go it on her own as a solo artist, the focus of the group swung immediately toward a more British traditional approach. This was considerably due to the arrival of Dave Swarbrick, Britain's finest folk violinist (with the possible exception of Robin Williamson).

Their more recent performances, with the influx of Trevor Lucas and Jerry Donahue, are tending to return to the original image of Fairport, though certainly they have not forgotten any of the lessons learned over the years of constant changes of lineup and direction.

Sandy Denny called her group Fotheringay as a reflection of her interest in the life and character of Mary, Queen of Scots. Although the group lasted only from March 1970 to January 1971 and made just one album, it set in a very short period of time a new high of perfection for other groups to strive toward: in fact, it was possibly too perfect. Sandy's principal colleague in the venture was Trevor Lucas, onetime member of Georg Hultgreen's Eclection,[2] and other members of the group were Gerry Conway, Pat Donaldson, and Jerry Donahue. Most of the songs on their only album, *Fotheringay*, are by Sandy herself, the standout track among them being "The Sea," which is strongly reminiscent of "Who Knows Where the Time Goes?" Among the others is a Trevor Lucas composition, "The Ballad of Ned Kelly," one of the few songs from Britain's Worship-Ned-Kelly era that rose above the level of the bandwagon. Although their blend of folk and rock was too bland for many tastes, their excellent matching of Denny's voice against the mellow instrumental accompaniment rendered Fotheringay something special among groups, and one that would almost certainly have changed the course of future British folk . . . if only the group had lasted longer.

The group that probably most deserves the label "folkrock" is one called Trees, whose members are Celia Humphris (vocals), Barry Clarke (lead guitar, dulcimer), David Costa (electric twelve-string, acoustic guitar, mandolin), Bias Boshell (bass guitar, vocals, piano, acoustic twelve-string), and Unwin Brown (percussion, vocals). As one commentator put it, it's amazing that five musicians of such outstanding quality should exist for so long unknown, and even more amazing that fate should decree they play together.

For the most part, Trees has taken well-worn folk themes and infused into them an electric arrangement of such far-ranging imagi-

[2] Eclection deserve at least a footnote in any book about "folkrock." It originally comprised Georg Hultgreen (who wrote most of the group's songs), Trevor Lucas, Michael Rosen, Gerry Conway, and an Australian with one of the finest, richest, and strongest female voices ever recorded, Kerrilee Male. Their only album (*Eclection*, 1967) predated the type of music that was later to receive more popular attention through Fotheringay and others. Against a backdrop of exquisite orchestral arrangement, their excellent mix of retiring instrumental skill and smooth harmony made for a tight "folkrock" sound that should have survived. Georg Hultgreen's songs displayed a rare sensitivity, despite their occasionally being marred by glaringly bad lines, that was far in advance of its time.

More recently the group has had a new lease on life in the guise of Dorris Henderson's Eclection. However, though the name is there, none of the original members is, and the music, excellent, tight, heavy rock though it be, bears no resemblance to the original.

nation that the listener no longer recognizes the song as a hackneyed one. The prime example of this process is on their second album, *On the Shore,* in the form of an eleven-minute version of "Sally Free and Easy." To a song that has been sung by the unaccompanied solo voice in folk clubs since time immemorial, they attach the most beautiful classically influenced piano overture and an arrangement that is elaborate without ever being in danger of seeming pretentious. This, together with the incredibly tender, delicate sensitivity of Celia Humphris' vocals, ensures that the version is a definitive one.

Julie Felix must be acknowledged as, at least in the eyes of the general public, one of the leading figures in the original British folk revival. Although an American, a native of California, she was part of the British folk scene, probably rebelling against the exclusive hold on the public attention that Judy Collins and Joan Baez had in her own country and hence preferring to make her home in London, which she did in 1964.

She rapidly came to the fore, and concerts at the Royal Festival Hall on London's South Bank and appearances on several BBC television programs ensured that she became accepted as one of the rising luminaries of Britain's popular music scene. Like her two compatriots, Julie Felix is not essentially a songwriter: she is "merely" an interpreter, but quite often one of the first order. It is not so much that she is incapable of writing her own material but more that she finds her talents have total satisfaction in performing the works of others. Her repertoire is always chosen with great taste, discrimination, and originality. If her favorite composers are well known, she often manages to select for her own records their forgotten or less well-known songs, such as Dylan's "Chimes of Freedom," Woody Guthrie's "Deportee," Phil Ochs's "Bracero" and "The Flower Lady" (which latter song was, it must be confessed, a disaster when performed by Julie Felix) or Tom Paxton's "This World Goes Round and Round," all of them titles much neglected by many of her colleagues.

Simple, direct, and natural, Julie Felix, sort of a star despite herself, has lost none of her original qualities. If there existed a kind of ethical code of the urban folksinger, she, along with Pete Seeger and far too few others, could be cited as exemplary.

It will already have been noted that there is a predominance of Scots in modern British "folkrock" (Bert Jansch, Donovan, Robin Williamson, Mike Heron), and the man who deserves to be placed in the 1970s as Britain's leading solo songwriter is no exception.

Al Stewart was born in Glasgow in 1945, but shortly afterward his family moved to the south of England. Leaving school at the age of seventeen, he played for a couple of years with local pop groups and then as a backup musician for such diverse artists as the Rolling Stones and Tony Blackburn before he eventually turned his efforts toward making it as a solo artist. At one point along the road he shared an apartment with Paul Simon and Art Garfunkel, and this had an influence on the clean, uncluttered feeling that his music has always had.

Extraordinarily skilled as a practitioner of the acoustic six-string guitar, he drew from one London critic the comment that his was the first genuinely individualistic technique to appear on the West End scene since the departure of Bert Jansch and John Renbourn for the Albert Hall. Mind you, it wasn't to be long before Al filled the Festival Hall and, awhile later, the Rainbow.

His first album, *Bedsitter Images,* is distinguished by the high quality of the songwriting and Al Stewart's singing and playing, but also by the crushing insensitivity of the orchestral arrangements. Apart from the title track, "Bedsitter Images," which as one might guess conjures up the dreary desolation well known to anyone who has ever lived for long in a bedsitter, there are "Beleeka Doodle Day," named by one critic from the music papers as track of the week— and deservedly so—"Swiss Cottage Manoeuvres," which is particularly wrecked by the orchestra with ludicrous trumpet fanfares at beginning and end, "Samuel, Oh How You've Changed," "Scandinavian Girl," and two brilliant but quite dissimilar instrumentals, "Denise at Sixteen" and "Ivich." *Bedsitter Images* was reissued much later as *The First Album,* with the notable omission of "Scandinavian Girl" and the inclusion of two other songs of no particular distinction.

Love Chronicles, his second album, came as a shock in several different ways. On the musical level, gone are the soupy morasses of orchestration and in their place is an exquisitely tight rock accompaniment, including among the distinguished session musicians Jimmy Page, who was later to form Led Zeppelin. The songs are generally longer and more maturely developed, and Al Stewart's vocal and instrumental technique much advanced. But it was on the lyrical level that the greatest shock came.

On *Bedsitter Images* there had been several songs that made reference to modern sexual mores—notably "Swiss Cottage Manoeuvres" and "Pretty Golden Hair," a song that dealt with the homosexual exploitation of a pretty young man—but *Love Chronicles* dealt almost to exclusion with the subject. But, and this is important, it does so in a valid way. It is not an album of musical titillation but a fairly serious analysis of the various complications and gratifications of emotional and physical relationships in modern Britain.

The album opens with "In Brooklyn," one of Al Stewart's most popular songs, which is a lighthearted rendition of a brief affair in the United States. This is followed by "Old Compton Street Blues," which tells the story of how a girl started out wanting to be a movie star and ended up being a Soho pavement prostitute. The pathos inherent in the situation is treated with enough sensibility to ensure that it never lapses into pathos. And throughout there is genuine sympathy (sympathy, not pity) for the unfortunate woman trapped within her course, never a breath of condemnation—much later Mike d'Abo was to do the same sort of thing, with perhaps the same success, in his "Little Miss Understood."

The third track, "The Ballad of Mary Foster," is in two parts. The first describes a typical bourgeois family, with a right-wing reactionary father, a son who is following in Daddy's footsteps, and a rather fading mother. In the second part, which is quite different in tune and rhythm, the mother speaks, and tells how her son was born through her living with a jazz musician who left her pregnant, and the way that she met David Foster, who married her and gave her child a father. Now she lives a barren life, thinking of the gaiety of the past and looking forward only to the desolation of the future. As an in-depth examination of the sadness behind the glossy facade of so many middle-class families, "The Ballad of Mary Foster" has no peer in popular song.

The fourth track, and the last on the first side, has as title a phrase of Bob Dylan's, "Life and Life Only." It deals with the encroachment of middle age, through the characters of a bachelor schoolmaster, a wife whose husband is being unfaithful, and a clerk whose main hobby is watching the birds. On the beach at Bournemouth sits the narrator, looking at them as they disport themselves in their various ways and wondering which one of them he will turn out to be.

Side Two opens in lighthearted vein with "You Should Have Listened to Al," which is then followed by the magnum opus of the album, "Love Chronicles." This is a sixteen-minute track that deals with the evolution of Al Stewart's attitude toward sexual relationships, from the earliest days of kissing when the teacher wasn't looking, through a long period of indiscriminate fucking to arrive eventually at lovemaking. While decried by the prudes (who are nearly always the prurient) as an exercise in sentimental, self-indulgent titillation, "Love Chronicles" is in fact an incredible advance in popular song, lending to the whole medium a maturity that it could never previously have claimed.

But of course it was the prudes who ruled (and still rule) the mass communications media, and the album was banned from BBC radio (theoretically only the album, but in practice for a long while Al Stewart himself). Despite this, it still managed to win the award from *Melody Maker,* the largest British pop music magazine, of Folk Album of the Year.

Al Stewart's next album, *Zero She Flies,* came as a disappointment—as in many ways it was bound to do. Essentially, though the arrangements are equally fine and Al Stewart's voice has if anything yet again improved, the songs are nowhere near as strong. True, there are occasional high points—very high points—in the form of "Gethsemane Again," "Electric Los Angeles Sunset," "Manuscript," and "Zero She Flies," not to mention "A Small Fruit Song" which has an inexplicable charm all of its own. But all in all the album lacks the coherence and lucidity, the vigor and drive, that enhanced *Love Chronicles.*

It was to be some time before a new Al Stewart album came along, but eventually it did, in the shape of *Orange.* This contains some of his finest writing, songs like "Night of the Fourth of May" and "Songs Out of Clay," perhaps surpassing anything that he had written before, and one instrumental, "Once an Orange, Always an Orange," certainly exceeding in scope and technical pyrotechnics any of its predecessors. But, though it is a fine album, it still cannot measure up to the standard set by *Love Chronicles.*

But, with his 1973 release, *Past, Present and Future,* Al Stewart at last firmly advanced beyond anything that he had previously done. The songs are no longer oriented toward modern mores or problems at all, but deal almost exclusively with the past. Opening with "Old Admirals," which is a song about Admiral Lord Fisher, it continues with "Warren Gamaliel Harding," about the President of the same name. "Soho (needless to say)" is set in the late sixties, and paints a picture of the colorful cosmopolitanism that infused the Soho of the era. "The Last Day of June 1934" is about Hitler's extermination on that day of Ernst Roehm and his followers, who represented the only real threat within the Nazi hierarchy to the former's total dictatorship. At the time no one thought too much about the elimination, but if it hadn't been for it there might never have been a Second World War. . . . The side is closed by "Post World War Two Blues," which is the only unsuccessful track on the album, and even then only partially so. Its theme is essentially a bundle of things that happened after the end of the Second World War.

Side Two opens with a masterly piece of work, "Roads to Moscow," which Al Stewart dedicates to Alexander Solzhenitsyn. During the Second World War, when the Germans invaded Russia, the Russian Army was forced to fight all the way in retreat to the gates of Moscow, then all the way back again to the gates of Berlin. As a reward, uncountable numbers of them were imprisoned in labor camps by Stalin. The song tells, with an amazing immediacy considering that it was written by a man who was born at the end of the war, the story of one of these soldiers.

"Terminal Eyes," which follows "Road to Moscow," is a late 1960s-style psychedelic pop song, confessedly influenced almost to exclusion by the Beatles' "I Am the Walrus." And the third and last track on the side is yet another masterpiece, "Nostradamus." Based on the prophecies of Nostradamus himself, it incorporates within its framework an extensive and brilliant section of solo acoustic guitar work, signifying the passage of the prophecies from what is our past to what is yet to come. Both this song and "Roads to Moscow" were quite extensively played on radio and television around the end of 1973 and the beginning of 1974, something most unusual for a medium mainly tied to the three-minute bubblegum single, since the two songs are just under nine minutes and just under ten minutes long respectively.

With *Past, Present and Future* Al Stewart reestablished himself firmly as the doyen of all British singer-songwriters, and the album has attracted to him a lot of attention that he has hitherto, for some unknown reason, been without. It is only to be hoped that this process will continue.

In terms of album and single sales, Al Stewart is outclassed completely by a songwriter called Cat Stevens.

Stevens originally started as a writer of commercial singles that enjoyed a brief vogue around the Carnaby Street era, "Matthew and Son" being perhaps the best known. After that he disappeared for some time, during which he went through a period of serious illness, before returning with the album *Mona Bone Jakon.*

His return was heralded enthusiastically by the media, who plugged his singles dutifully. And to a certain extent it was well-deserved enthusiasm. During his period of absence he had learned a lot, and his style had mellowed and matured (interesting to compare with Dylan's similar period of disappearance).

Mona Bone Jakon was followed by *Tea for the Tillerman,* which is an extremely fine album. The instrumentation is particularly magnificent, delicate acoustic guitar work admirably blending with Stevens' unusual vibrato voice. The songs themselves are excellent combinations of folk and pop, using the best of both genres, as in "Wide World" particularly.

The year 1971 saw the release of *Teaser and the Firecat,* which repeats the formula of *Tea for the Tillerman* but without the same degree of success. The terseness, almost curtness, which gave the songs on the earlier album much of their appeal, is no longer so operative, and in contrast most of the songs on *Teaser and the Firecat* are rather flaccid and lyrically weak. The one glorious exception is a rendition of Eleanor Farjeon's hymn, "Morning Has Broken," where Stevens' voice, coupled with a gently intricate piano part, captures a mood of naïve wonder. A pity that the remainder of the album contains songs like "Tuesday's Dead" and the unfortunate "Moonshadow."

But mention must be made of the cover of *Teaser and the Firecat.* As with *Tea for the Tillerman,* it consists of a cartoon by Cat Stevens himself. Stevens has often said that one of his aims in life is to be a professional cartoonist: certainly, judging by the jacket of *Teaser and the Firecat,* he could make a brilliant career in that field.

Catch Bull at Four, which followed in 1972, is a much more interesting album. Musically there is not obviously a great deal of change, though it is notable that Stevens has become rather more ambitious in his musical tackling of various subjects. "Angelsea" is perhaps the best example of this. But lyrically there has been a great development: the weak lyricism of *Teaser and the Firecat* is replaced by a more powerful imagery and a more reflective, if occasionally rather bitter, mood. "18th Avenue (Kansas City Nightmare)" is as good an example as any. Reminiscent of Elton John's and Bernie Taupin's "Holiday Inn" (on the Elton John album *Madman Across the Water*), which has a rather similar theme, it is perhaps the more successful of the two songs, though superficially lyrically simpler. The whole is enhanced by the interpolation of an elegant orchestra middle section.

"The Boy with the Moon & Star on His Head" on the same album is another example of Stevens' fine imagery. It tells of a man on his way to his wedding who is waylaid by a gardener's daughter: they make love and, while she is sleeping, he continues on his way to be married. The months pass and one morning he finds on his doorstep a boy with the moon and a star on his head. The boy grows and preaches that love is all.

By comparison the single taken from the album, "Can't Keep It In," is extremely disappointing, and falls into the trap that Stevens has always had to be wary of: that of using a lot of words to say nothing.

Foreigner, which was released in 1973, continued the same trend as *Catch Bull at Four,* though once again there is a certain looseness that renders the album strangely unsatisfying. If Stevens can control this in the future, then he should become one of the most interesting songwriters on the current British scene.

Probably the most neglected British songwriter of all is Beau. Born C. J. T. Midgley in Leeds in 1946, Beau spent a year preparing his first album, *Beau,* released by Dandelion in December 1969. It contains thirteen songs, the last of which is a reprise of the first, that are beautiful and elaborate, studiously written, and yet not without a considerable amount of freshness.

Although having experimented by playing music in groups and

being able himself to play guitar (six-string, twelve-string, and bass), banjo, piano, organ, accordion, and percussion, Beau preferred to concentrate on the development of an extremely personal technique of playing the acoustic twelve-string guitar so that, in his own words, it "stands on its own, and not just as a six-string technique with six additional strings to play with." The result militates strongly in favor of a reassessment of the rich harmonic and melodic (and to a lesser extent, rhythmic) possibilities of an instrument about which one might have thought that everything had been said.

The themes of his songs, written in a classical but never banal style, deal with his dreams of nature and the elements, such as the sun ("Morning Sun," "Sundancer"), the rain ("Rain"), the sea ("Fishing Song") or the seasons ("The Summer Has Gone," "The Ways of Winter"); with friendship and camaraderie ("Welcome"), past history ("1917 Revolution," "The Painted Vase"), or the present ("A Nation's Pride," strongly reminiscent of Phil Ochs's "One More Parade," and particularly the magnificent "Pillar of Economy"). On the sleeve of the album Beau cites Ochs as one of his influences as well as Leadbelly, Woody Guthrie, Josh White, Tom Paxton, and the Beatles.

Although the sole accompaniment on *Beau* was his own twelve-string guitar, on his second album, *Creation,* there are the elements of a rock band. And the experiment is not wholly successful. Although the electric instruments can in cases add an extra dimension, as in "Ferris Street," they are in general merely distracting, and the songs on the album where Beau sings with only the twelve-string guitar stand out as landmarks of simplicity. Moreover, the songs on *Creation* haven't the same quiet strength as on the earlier album: in particular, the title track, which is a whispered poem to the strains of electronic creation-of-the-earth effects, is pretentious nonsense.

The two most interesting songs are "There Once Was a Time," which is a painfully accurate portrayal of a decaying beauty queen, and "Silence Returns," with its odd syncopation and its dramatic use of electric instrumentation.

Although *Creation* was released in 1971, and appears to have been the last album by Beau, it is to be hoped that he will return in the future to the recording scene. Even if one overlooks his generally excellent songs, his technique of twelve-string guitar playing has a lot to teach the average guitarist, and the gentleness of his music and the emotions that it portrays would be a breath of fresh air in a music world dominated by electric violence.

Perhaps the most recent British songwriter of note to emerge is Jonathan Kelly, an Irishman whose style is similar to that of Al Stewart, though debatably with a wider range of subject matter. Kelly has been the object of much enthusiasm in the music media, though this has not apparently been reflected in record sales.

His first album, *Jonathan Kelly*, shows great promise, promise that was to be realized with his second album, *Twice Around the Houses*, which is a magnificent collection of songs. We mentioned earlier that Scottish songwriters have the advantage of being able to draw on the amazing Celtic mythology that is their heritage: the Irish Jonathan Kelly is also able to exploit this, and does so in one or perhaps two of the songs on this album. The first is "The Ballad of Cursed Anna," a straight product of Irish (and, oddly enough, other) folklore. The powerful tale of Cursed Anna, who steals through a kiss the youth of young men so that she herself may remain forever young, is captured splendidly by Kelly in what appears at first sight to be an almost naïve style.

It is with "Hyde Park Angels" that Kelly steps beyond his tradition, to create the elements of a new mythology, in much the same way, though using a totally different method, as Dylan did before him. The story tells of a young man, new to London, who, while wandering in Hyde Park, meets an angel who plays to him on her lyre. When he awakens in the cold she is gone, but she can never be gone from his memory: he spends the rest of his life searching for her.

There is an amusing story about the song's chorus that Kelly quite happily tells. Wanting to call upon a saint of some kind for assistance (in the song), he discovered that he didn't know which saint would be suitable on such an occasion. So he picked up the telephone and got in touch with a branch of the Roman Catholic Church: which saint should he pray to at a time like this? The woman at the other end of the line spent a few minutes looking up references and told him that he would be best served by praying to either Saint Bruno or Saint Dionysius. Saint Bruno was unsuitable, it being the name of a popular brand of pipe tobacco, so Saint Dionysius it had to be . . . and Saint Dionysius it is in the song.

Perhaps the most notable of the songs on *Twice Around the Houses* are the love songs: these comprise the famous "Madeleine" as well as "Leave Them Go," "I Used to Know You," and "Rock You to Sleep." Kelly manages on all of them to steer a tricky course right on the verge of schmaltz, lifting into the higher world of aesthetics emotions that could be mundane in less skilled hands.

His third album, released in 1973, *Wait Till They Change the Backdrop,* is so different from *Twice Around the Houses* that it is difficult to believe that it is by the same artist. Although Kelly's range of musical styles has vastly increased, probably due to the influence of his friend Peter Wood, it is questionable whether this development is a good thing. Where before both lyrics and melody were tightly constructed into a cohesive, compact whole, now the lyrics have become rather loose and the music occasionally simply boring.

Nevertheless it is not an album without fine moments. "Wait Till They Change the Backdrop" and "Turn Your Eye on Me" are splendid songs, and "Godas," "Down on Me," and "Chains" are enjoyable (though the latter two show almost a paranoia that is quite opposed to the emotions expressed in several of the songs on *Twice Around the Houses*). But others of the songs ("I Wish I Could" and "Beautiful Eyes," for example) are so far below the standard of Kelly's earlier work that one wonders why on earth they were included.

Which way will Kelly turn? Toward the lyrical tightness and musical compactness of his earlier work, or toward the lyrical and musical laxity of some of his more recent? There is simply no way to predict, but one can only hope it will be the former. In that case Kelly could well become the most influential songwriter of his generation . . . but one has no way of knowing if that will happen. . . .

future connections

Before the end of our voyage through the centuries of folk music—though one must hope that the end of the voyage will signal the departure point for a new journey—we will spend a few pages on the more recent evolution of the folk movement in the United States.

Above all, the author is conscious of certain inevitable omissions, which doubtless each reader will regard as unpardonable lacunae. The reasons are easy to understand: they are principally the plethoric production of the American record firms, the more and more frequent discoveries of genuinely original talents, and the unceasing and extremely rapid evolution of each of these new songwriters. All of these are factors that one is quite happy about, since they are revealing of the extreme vitality of young America, but they make impossible the construction of an exhaustive tableau—something that we cannot pretend to have done. And all these factors, coupled with the difficulties undergone by a foreign observer in attempting to obtain information, however careful and attentive he is, explain why we have had to be selective, accepting the risk of occasional arbitrariness. All the same, the reader is asked to judge our efforts in light of the fact that it is not feasible, and is even undesirable, to deal scientifically with a phenomenon tied up with artistic self-expression, with all its subjectivities and irrationalities.

We could extend the book by recounting the activities, all worthwhile and backed up by plenty of recordings, of a Laura Nyro or a David Blue; of the brilliant Ralph McTell; or even more of a Tim Buckley, that little-known innovator; of Steeleye Span, that excellent traditional folk group; of an Elton John or even a Gilbert O'Sullivan; of Van Morrison, that exiled Irishman who, like so many of his ancestors, has sought a new home in the United States (*Astral Weeks, Moondance,* and so forth, are recommended); of Country Joe & the Fish, the California group who has allied the militant spirit of folk music to avant-garde pop; or, more recently, of a Loudon Wainwright III, a name well worth remembering; or then there is . . .[1]

What one can do, on the contrary, is to attempt to delineate several general tendencies in the musical and thematic evolution of the folk movement in the last year or two, tendencies that seem to us to have consequences beyond merely the artistic plane. The first phenomenon, we're pleased to say, is the decline of the "star" system. The vast number of excellent new singers, such as those we have just mentioned, are a symptom of this. Even in a country as vast and highly populated as the United States there simply isn't the room for fifty or so superstars of the order of Bob Dylan. In fact, the singers themselves do not seem to be careerists of the old type (wasn't it Dylan himself who was the first in recent years to break away from the bonds of show biz?), and instead aim toward intense communication with their audiences, to be understood by them, to understand them, and hence to help them understand themselves. It is a lesson already learned by folk musicians, and applicable (if God is on our side . . .) elsewhere—until finally the only "star" worthy of the name will be all of us.

The second immediately discernible phenomenon in the new songs which are being written is the abandonment of the traditional protest song in the folk movement. There again, it was Bob Dylan (and with what clarity!) who sounded the alarm. Since 1965, this genre of song has dramatically lost popularity and, and this is important, most of all in the most militant radical circles. As Irwin Silber has justly pointed out, the protest song helps our conscience, but the fact of listening, all approving, to the protests of other people does little more than stifle our own potential for protest and action. Without going so far as to decry the protest song as an extension of petit-bourgeois ideology (we have already given many examples of its powerful progressive influence on twentieth-century American history), we must recognize that, at least today, it can be no more than at best reformist, even if it has implicitly the same revolutionary values as it did in the time of Woody Guthrie. The reality of the 1970s

[1] The reader is invited to add his own list after this point.

is a far cry from that of the 1930s. There is no doubt that, were Woody still alive, his writing would be very different.

And does this crisis of conscience (hard for some, but necessary) signify the pure and simple condemnation of the political song? On the contrary: it has done nothing more than allow those who sing and write to explore new methods, new forms of creation. This has caused a certain amount of confusion: some, like Dylan and Judy Collins, have eradicated all trace of politics from their repertoire; others have hesitated between withdrawing into themselves and radical action, even subversive: we can take in this respect the example of Phil Ochs in that he typifies the malaise of thousands of young Americans; yet others, like Joan Baez, have taken refuge in passive civil disobedience; and some, finally, have sought new vocations: attacking the forces of evil on the level of their exterior manifestations (Phil Ochs again, but also Janis Ian) or developed group music, amplified, so that it can be heard vibrating through the streets, at demonstrations and at meetings: this is part of the aim of, not only Country Joe & the Fish, but also the Village Fugs and the Grateful Dead on the West Coast. In New York, David Peel and The Lower East Side has revived this—the group is to music as the Bread and Puppet Theater is to theater. The group's first album, *Have a Marijuana*, was recorded for Elektra in the open air in the Manhattan streets, with crowd participation. To take an example from the record: "Here Comes a Cop," designed to assist preparations to resist arrest, was born at the moment that a policeman approached to disperse the group. At this level, of course, the first stutterings of a new form of political musical expression, critical tolerance is necessary: more decisive results will come along sooner or later.

These results will go in parallel with the political evolution of young America—of which, at the final count, music is a revealing pointer (the form of self-expression preceding the audience), far more accurate than haircuts or the judges of popular opinion. We will give here only a single example, but a significant one: the appearance of a new movement to aid the "Poor Red" was soon followed by the creation of the first all-Indian rock group which, what is more, makes a boast of the fact: Redbone. Their music doesn't at all follow the road taken since FAIR but in itself forms a decisive step. And naturally the same is going on for blacks.

And whites? There, despite the examples earlier studied, one finds not without surprise that since 1968 there has been a return in force of country and western, which has in various ways infiltrated the repertoires of many artists who are far from being involved in matters rural. Without doubt Bob Dylan (decidedly the perennial inspiring dynamic!) with his *Nashville Skyline* has inspired emulators. The aesthetic renaissance of country and western having been realized, it remains only to renew its poetic and ideological content. One has seen that Dylan himself has *not* done this: by conscious choice, one supposes, and not because it would be impossible. However, an extremely interesting album was released in the autumn of 1968 (about six months before *Nashville Skyline*), *Mr. Bojangles,* which gave an affirmative answer to the question of whether the style of country and western was capable of being the vehicle of sincere, genuine, and communicable thought. The artist whose album it is, Jerry Jeff Walker, well deserves to be mentioned. Since then, the year 1969 onward has seen other happy attempts at adapting this despised style to the genuine problems of humanity. It is thus that the failure of Joan Baez on the level of interpretations is counterbalanced by the success of Tom Rush and, on the level of songwriting, by those of James Taylor (*Sweet Baby James, One Dog Man*), Paul Siebel (*Woodsmoke and Oranges*) and of course the extremely popular and prolific Kris Kristofferson.

As far as groups are concerned, we've already mentioned the adoption of certain country and western techniques by the Byrds and the Band. One could also mention in this connection the Grateful Dead and Crosby, Stills, Nash & Young. But though their music is excellent, it owes its character to elements other than country and western, whose contemporary value (despite the several brilliant individuals we have just mentioned) has yet to be proved.

And so: a montage of ideas, races, and musical genres that were until recently separated—who could complain?

Yet for how long will America continue to oppress her children, so that they have to sing so often—and so well?

selected bibliography

Baez, Joan. *The Joan Baez Songbook*. New York: Ryerson Music Publishers, 1964. Sixty-six songs from Joan Baez' repertoire.

Carawan, Guy, and Carawan, Candie. *Freedom Is a Constant Struggle*. New York: Oak Publications, 1968.

————. *We Shall Overcome! Songs of the Southern Freedom Movement*. New York: Oak Publications, 1963.

Carter, June. "I Remember the Carter Family." *Sing Out!* June/July 1967.

Charters, Samuel B. *The Poetry of the Blues*. New York: Oak Publications, 1963.

Civil War Songs. New York: Oak Publications, 1967. Fifty Civil War songs, from both Confederates and Unionists.

The Clancy Brothers and Tommy Makem Songbook. New York: Tiparm Music Publishers, 1964; New York: Macmillan, 1969, and Collier Books, 1971.

Cohen, Leonard. *Songs of Leonard Cohen*. New York: Amsco Music, 1969.

Collins, Judy. *The Judy Collins Songbook*. New York: Grosset & Dunlap, 1969. Fifty-six songs from Judy Collins' repertoire, with photographs and autobiographical fragment.

Coulonges, Georges. *La Chanson et son Temps, de Béranger au Juke-box*. Paris: Éditions Français Réunis, 1969.

Dunson, Josh. "Folk-Rock: Thunder Without Rain." In *The American Folk Scene* by Peter Lyon. New York: Dell, 1967.

————, and Asch, Moses. "Is Cash Killing Folk Music?" In *The American Folk Scene* by Peter Lyon. New York: Dell, 1967.

Elliott, Jack. "Ramblin' with Jack Elliott." *Sing Out!* March/April 1970.

Goldstein, Richard. *Goldstein's Greatest Hits: A Book Mostly About Rock 'n' Roll*. Englewood Cliffs, N.J.: Prentice-Hall, 1970.

————. *The Poetry of Rock*. New York: Bantam Books, 1969.

Guthrie, Arlo. *This Is the Arlo Guthrie Songbook*. New York: Collier Books, 1969.

Guthrie, Woody. *American Folksong*. Disc Company of America, c. 1947; New York: Oak Publications, 1961. A collection of autobiographical writings, extracts from songs, and illustrations by Guthrie.

————. *Born to Win*. New York: Macmillan, 1965. Edited by Robert Shelton. About seventy extracts and letters by Woody Guthrie.

————. *Bound for Glory.* New York: E. P. Dutton, 1943, 1968; New York: New American Library, 1970. Autobiography illustrated by the author.

————. *California to the New York Island.* New York: Oak Publications, 1968. A collection of songs interspersed by Guthrie's writings. Preface by Pete Seeger.

Hill (Hillstrom), Joe. *The Letters of Joe Hill.* Edited and compiled by Dr. Philip S. Foner. New York: Oak Hill Publications, 1965. Forty-five letters and twelve songs.

————. *Songs of Joe Hill.* Edited, illustrated, and compiled by Barrie Stavis and Frank Harmon. New York: Quick Fox, 1960. Twenty-three songs.

Houston, Cisco. *900 Miles.* Edited by Moses Asch and Irwin Silber. New York: Oak Publications, 1965. Seventy extracts from Cisco Houston's repertoire, with musical transcriptions by Jerry Silverman.

Irish Songs of Resistance. New York: Oak Publications, 1967. Fifty songs from the struggle for the freedom and independence of Ireland.

Jackson, Mahalia. *Movin' Up.* New York: Hawthorn, 1966. Autobiography.

Jones, LeRoi. *Blues People.* New York: Morrow (Apollo Books), 1963.

Keil, Charles. *Urban Blues.* Chicago and London: The University of Chicago Press, 1966.

Larkin, Margaret. *Singing Cowboy.* New York: Knopf, 1931. Republished: New York: Oak Publications, 1963.

Ledbetter, Huddie (Leadbelly). *The Leadbelly Songbook.* Edited by Moses Asch and Alan Lomax. New York: Oak Publications, 1963.

Lester, Julius. "Mirror of Evil." *Sing Out!* October/November 1967. A penetrating sociopolitical study of young America in context of the urban folk revival, written by one of the young musicians who was involved in it.

Lyon, Peter. *The American Folk Scene.* New York: Dell, 1967.

MacColl, Ewan. *Folksongs and Ballads of Scotland.* New York: Oak Publications, 1965. Seventy traditional Scottish songs.

————, and Seeger, Peggy. *The Ewan MacColl–Peggy Seeger Songbook.* With a Foreword by Irwin Silber.

Monroe, Bill. Interview in *Sing Out!* July/August 1969.

The New Lost City Ramblers Songbook. New York: Oak Publications, 1964. Contains 125 songs from the repertoire of one of the finest American white traditional folk groups.

Ochs, Phil. *Songs of Phil Ochs.* New York: Appleseed Music, 1964.

————. *The War Is Over.* New York: Barricade Music, 1968. Complete songs from the albums, *Phil Ochs in Concert, Pleasures of the Harbor,* and *Tape from California;* articles and poems by Phil Ochs; interview with Phil Ochs by Gordon Friesen and Sis Cunningham.

Oliver, Paul. *Blues Fell This Morning: The Meaning of the Blues.* New York: Horizon, 1961.

————. *The Story of the Blues.* Philadelphia: Chilton, 1969.

Paxton, Tom. *Ramblin' Boy and Other Songs.* New York: Oak Publications, 1964.

Pennebaker, Donn Alan. *Don't Look Back.* New York: Ballantine Books, 1968. Complete script and prolific photographs from Pennebaker's film.

Peter, Paul and Mary on Tour. London: Blossom Music. Fifteen songs from their repertoire.

Radosh, Ron. "Commercialism and the Folksong Revival." In *The American Folk Scene* by Paul Lyon. New York: Dell, 1967.

Reuss, Richard A. *A Woody Guthrie Bibliography.* New York: The Guthrie Children's Trust Fund, 1968. A complete annotated bibliography of books, articles, poems, and essays by or about Woody Guthrie.

Reynolds, Malvina. *Little Boxes and Other Handmade Songs.* New York: Oak Publications, 1964. Fifty-three songs.

Ribakove, Sy, and Ribakove, Barbara. *Folk-Rock—the Bob Dylan Story.* New York: Dell, 1966.

Ritchie, Jean. *Singing Family of the Cumberlands.* New York: Oak Publications, 1963. The story in forty-two songs of a traditional American family.

Russell, Tony. *Blacks, Whites and Blues.* New York: Stein & Day, 1970.

Scaduto, Anthony. *Bob Dylan.* New York: Grosset & Dunlap, 1972; New York: New American Library, 1973.

Seeger, Pete. *American Favorite Ballads.* New York: Oak Publications, 1961. Eighty-four Anglo-American ballads from Pete Seeger's repertoire.

———. *The Bells of Rhymney.* New York: Oak Publications, 1964. Eighty songs from Pete Seeger's contemporary repertoire.

———. *How to Play the Five-String Banjo.* Beacon, N.Y.: Published by the author, 1961.

———, and Silverman, Jerry. *The Folksinger's Guitar Guide.* New York: Oak Publications, 1962.

Silber, Irwin. "Folk Music and the Success Syndrome." In *The American Folk Scene* by Peter Lyon. New York: Dell, 1967.

Sing Out! December 1967/January 1968 (vol. 17, no. 6). Special tribute issue for Woody Guthrie.

Yaryan, Bill. "Derroll Adams." *Sing Out!* January 1967.

discography

Ackles, David
  David Ackles (or *The Road to Cairo*)
  Subway to the Country
  American Gothic
Adams, Derroll
  Portland Town
  (with Jack Elliott) *Roll on Buddy*
Allwright, Graeme
  Le Trimardeur
  Joue, Joue, Joue
  Le Jour de Clarté
  A Long Distant Present from Thee
  . . . Becoming
  Recollections
Andersen, Eric
  Today Is the Highway
  'Bout Changes 'n' Things
  Avalanche
Anthology of American Folk Music, Vol.
  I: Ballads

Baez, Joan
  Volume 1
  Volume 2
  In Concert
  In Concert, Part 2
  There But for Fortune
  Farewell Angelina
  Noël
  Joan
  Baptism—A Journey Through Our
    Time

  Any Day Now
  David's Album
  One Day at a Time
Band, The
  Music from Big Pink
  The Band
  Stage Fright
  Cahoots
  Moondog Matinee
Beau
  Beau
  Creation
Blue, David
  David Blue
  Those 23 Days in September
Blues Project, The (with Dave Ray,
    Eric von Schmidt, John Koer-
    ner, Geoff Muldaur, Dave
    Van Ronk, Ian Buchanan,
    Danny Kalb, Mark Spoelstra)
Blues Roll On, The
Broadside, Volume 1
Broadside Singers, The
Broonzy, Big Bill
  Big Bill's Blues
Brothers Four, The
  Song Book
  Greatest Hits
  Sing of Our Times
Buckley, Tim
  Tim Buckley
  Happy Sad
  Lorca

Byrds, The
  Mr. Tambourine Man
  Turn! Turn! Turn!
  Notorious Byrd Brothers
  Sweetheart of the Rodeo
  Ballad of Easy Rider
  Byrdmaniax

Canned Heat
  Boogie with Canned Heat
Carr, Leroy with Scrapper Blackwell
    and Josh White
  Blues Before Sunrise
Cash, Johnny
  Orange Blossom Special
  At Folsom Prison
  At San Quentin
  Hello, I'm Johnny Cash
Chicago: The Blues Today, Vols. 1, 2,
  and 3
Cohen, Leonard
  Songs of Leonard Cohen
  Songs from a Room
  Songs of Love and Hate
  New Skin for the Old Ceremony
Collins, Judy
  A Maid of Constant Sorrow
  The Golden Apples of the Sun
  No. 3
  The Judy Collins Concert
  Fifth Album
  In My Life
  Wildwood Flowers
  Who Knows Where the Time Goes?
  Whales and Nightingales
Collins, Shirley
  The Sweet Primroses
Country Blues, Vols. 1 and 2
Country Joe & the Fish
  Greatest Hits
Crawford, Pink
  Western and Folksongs
Crosby, Stills & Nash
  Crosby, Stills & Nash
Crosby, Stills, Nash & Young
  Déjà Vu

Donovan
  Catch the Wind
  Fairytale
  Sunshine Superman
  Mellow Yellow
  Hurdy Gurdy Man
  Barabajagal
  A Gift from a Flower to a Garden
  Open Road
  H.M.S. Donovan
  Cosmic Wheels
Dylan, Bob
  Bob Dylan
  The Freewheelin' Bob Dylan
  The Times They Are A-Changin'
  Another Side of Bob Dylan
  Bringing It All Back
  Highway 61 Revisited
  Blonde on Blonde
  John Wesley Harding
  Nashville Skyline
  Self Portrait
  New Morning
  More Bob Dylan's Greatest Hits
  Pat Garrett and Bill the Kid (sound
    track)
  Dylan
  Planet Waves

Eclection
  Eclection
Elliott, Jack
  Jack Elliott
  Talking Woody Guthrie
English, Logan
  Songs of the Gold Rush

Fairport Convention
  What We Did on Our Holidays
  Unhalfbricking
  Liege and Lief
  Full House
  Angel Delight
  Babbacombe Lee

Jack Orion
Birthday Blues
It Don't Bother Me
Nicola
(with John Renbourn) Bert and
John
Jefferson, Blind Lemon
The Immortal Blind Lemon Jefferson
Jefferson, Blind Willie
His Story and Recordings
Johnson, Robert
Robert Johnson, King of the Delta
Blues Singers

Kelly, Jonathan
Jonathan Kelly
Twice Around the Houses
Wait Till They Change the Backdrop
King, B. B.
Completely Well
Koerner, Ray and Glover
Blues, Rags and Hollers

La Farge, Peter
As Long as Grass Shall Grow
Lazarus
Lazarus
Leadbelly
Library of Congress Recordings
Leadbelly Sings Folksongs (with
Woody Guthrie, Cisco Hous-
ton, Sonny Terry, and
Brownie McGhee)
The Midnight Special
Lester, Julius
Departures

McAdoo, Bill
Bill McAdoo
MacColl, Ewan and Peggy Seeger
The New Briton Gazette, Volume 1
The Amorous Muse
McDonald, Country Joe
Thinking of Woody Guthrie
McDowell, Fred
Long Way from Home

Magna Carta
Magna Carta
March on Washington (with Joan
Baez, John F. Kennedy, Mar-
tin Luther King, Jr., Marian
Anderson, Odetta, Rabbi Joa-
chim Prinz, Bob Dylan, Whit-
ney M. Young, Jr., John
Lewis, Roy Wilkins, Walter
Reuther, Peter, Paul and
Mary, Bayard Rustin, A.
Philip Randolph)
Mayall, John
Bluesbreakers
Blues from Laurel Canyon
Médini, Lise
Song, Protest Song
Melanie
Born to Be
Melanie No. 2
Candles in the Rain
Melanie in Concert
The Good Book
Garden in the City
Memphis Quartet
Spirit of Memphis Quartet
Memphis Slim
Memphis Slim
Mills, Alan
O Canada
Chants et Danses du Québec
Mitchell, Joni
Joni Mitchell
Clouds
Ladies of the Canyon
Blue
For the Roses
Court and Spark
Morrison, Van
Astral Weeks
Moondance

Negro Prison Camp Worksongs (notes
and commentary by Pete
Seeger)

Neil, Fred
Tear Down the Walls
Bleecker and MacDougal
New Lost City Ramblers
Songs of the Great Depression
Newport Folk Festivals
Numerous titles on Vanguard
Nightingales, The
The Sensational Nightingales
Norman Luboff Choir
Songs of the West
Nyro, Laura
New York Tendaberry

Ochs, Phil
All the News That's Fit to Sing
I Ain't Marching Anymore
Phil Ochs in Concert
Pleasures of the Harbor
Tape from California
Rehearsals for Retirement
Phil Ochs' Greatest Hits
Odetta
Odetta at the Gate of Horn
One Grain of Sand
Odetta Sings Dylan

Paul Butterfield Blues Band
East-West
Paxton, Tom
Ramblin' Boy
Ain't That News!
Outward Bound
Morning Again
The Things I Notice Now
Tom Paxton 6
How Come the Sun
Peace Will Come
The Compleat Tom Paxton
Peel, David, and the Lower East Side
Have a Marijuana
Pentangle, The
The Pentangle
Sweet Child
Basket of Light
Cruel Sister

Peter, Paul and Mary
In the Wind
In Concert
A Song Will Rise
See What Tomorrow Brings
Album
Album 1700
Late Again
Peter, Paul and Mommy
Redbone
Redbone
Reed, Jerry
Nashville Sound
Reed, Jimmy
Jimmy Reed
Reynolds, Malvina
Malvina Reynolds
Ritchie, Jean
British Traditional Ballads
Robbins, Marty
The Drifter
Rush, Tom
Got a Mind to Ramble
Long John . . .
Take a Little Walk with Me
Driving Wheel
Sainte-Marie, Buffy
It's My Way
Many a Mile
Little Wheel, Spin and Spin
Fire and Fleet and Candlelight
I'm Gonna Be a Country Girl Again
She Used to Wanna Be a Ballerina
Illuminations
Best of Buffy Sainte-Marie
St. John, Bridget
Songs for the Gentle Man
Seeger, Pete
American Favorite Ballads
Western Story—Frontier Ballads
Les Chansons de Pete Seeger à Paris
Hootenanny with Pete Seeger
I Can See a New Day
God Bless the Grass
We Shall Overcome!

index

(*Song titles are in quotation marks; album titles are in italic type.*)